The Future of American Politics

The Future of
American Politics

by Samuel Lubell

HARPER & BROTHERS, NEW YORK

Library of Congress catalog card number: 52-5462

*To the memory of my mother, who pioneered
on the urban frontier*

Contents

The Future of American Politics

1

The Shape of Things to Come

Late last November I was invited to talk politics with a group of political writers from sixteen states. The informal discussion was part of a seminar for state-house reporters arranged by the American Press Institute of Columbia University. On two points all the persons present were agreed—that the 1952 Presidential election would be one of the most important in American history, and yet rarely has it been more difficult to grasp what is stirring behind the puzzling behavior of the voting public.

This book is an attempt to take the mystery out of present-day American politics. That a new, baffling set of political forces is reshaping our political life was demonstrated dramatically four years ago by President Harry S. Truman's astonishing victory. Since then other election upsets have confirmed the disappearance of much of what has come to be accepted as the "traditional" pattern of American politics.

There are two basic reasons, I believe, why the American voter has become such an enigma to even the experts and the professional politicians. First, we are moving into a new political era in which the old rules and axioms no longer apply. Second, we are in a period of party realignment, with millions of voters being tugged in conflicting directions at the same time.

Of the many trends remaking the politics of our time, eight prime forces stand out:

1. The simultaneous "coming of age" of the various urban

"minorities," which has transformed the nature of machine politics and thrust the old-time political boss on the defensive in a desperate struggle for political survival.

2. The rise of a new middle class, conservative in the manner of all middle classes, yet with its political attitudes rooted in memories of discrimination, poverty and the Great Depression.

3. The Negro in restless migration and the conflict of tension versus tolerance which he touches off wherever he appears.

4. The quickening economic revolution in the South, which has altered the dynamics of Southern sectionalism to where it has become a pressure for political unification with the rest of the nation.

5. The abrupt upheaval in world strategy, with the collapse of German and Japanese power, and which has eliminated the old basis of American isolationism and yet, paradoxically, has strengthened it as a vengeful memory.

6. The quiet, yet fundamental, change that has taken place in the farmer's relationship to the town, which bars any return to the farm politics of the 1920's.

7. The growth of organized labor to unprecedented financial and membership strength and yet, with it, ironically, has come an ebbing of labor's political vitality.

8. The impact of the cold war upon the so-called Welfare State, which has veered the conflict over the role of government into new, still dimly perceived channels.

Whoever is the victor in November—whether it be Truman again, General Dwight Eisenhower, Robert Taft, Paul Hoffman, Justice Fred Vinson—no matter who is elected president, he will find his administration engaged in a ceaseless struggle to bring these forces into political balance.

Each of these eight waves of the present could be termed a small revolution in itself. Collectively they are parts of a larger political revolution—namely, the transformation of the

United States from a nation with a traditional Republican majority to one with a normal Democratic majority.

That does not mean that the Republicans cannot win the Presidency. Currently, at least, their chances are bright indeed. The significance of the Democratic rise to majority standing lies in the fact that with it has come a wholly new orbit of political conflict—an orbit as controlling upon the Republicans as upon the Democrats, and one which is likely to govern the course of American politics as long as the animosities and loyalties of the New Deal remain in the memories of the bulk of voters.

Some historians have pictured the New Deal as the latest round in what Vernon L. Parrington termed the "ceaseless conflict between man and the dollar." But the distinctive feature of the political revolution which Franklin D. Roosevelt began and Truman inherited lies not in its resemblance to the political wars of Andrew Jackson or Thomas Jefferson, but in its abrupt break with the continuity of the past. If, as Charles A. Beard contended, the Civil War was the "Second American Revolution," then the toppling of the dominance held by the Republicans for nearly three fourths of a century can be considered as the Third American Revolution.

One reason why the emerging pattern of American politics has gone unrecognized for so long is the failure to grasp this hidden revolution which accompanied the rise of the new Democratic majority. When we examine this new orbit of political strife, we shall find a clear, if surprising, answer to the mystery of Truman's sensational 1948 triumph. Here, also will be found the explanation of the puzzling paradoxes which have characterized Truman's Presidency; also of Henry Wallace's utter failure to win the former supporters of the La Follette Progressive movement; also of the inability thus far of the Republicans to resolve their own curious contradictions.

Much else that has been taken for granted about American

politics must be re-evaluated. For example, the widely held belief that isolationism was the product of the peculiar geographical insularity of the Midwest fades into myth when examined in the light of this hidden revolution. Nor is it entirely accurate to describe today's Republican-Democratic contest as a conservative-liberal tussle. One major handicap the Republicans have been laboring under is that many voters think of them as the unsound, speculative party of our time. The mistake is being made to assume that the labels of one political age are applicable to a quite different political era.

My own study of why the politics of our day differ so fundamentally from those of the past has led to the development of a new theory of the nature of American political parties. If this theory is valid, a good many textbooks on American politics will have to be rewritten.

Usually books on politics and political history are written around the principal politicians strutting across the stage in Washington or at the national conventions. One chapter in this study does explore why the bitter feud between Congress and the President which began in 1937 has raged so long and seems less reconcilable today than when it began. For the rest of my story though, I have deliberately swung the spotlight away from Washington out into the country. It is there, among the people themselves, that the real drama of political realignment is being acted out.

The frame of this narrative is provided in the main by the major voting elements which Roosevelt brought together into victorious coalition. Republican Presidential hopes hinge, of course, on being able to win over some of the twenty-odd millions who voted for Roosevelt for four successive terms. By following the *changing* dynamics of the Democratic coalition, we will be able to determine how much of the Roosevelt Revolution still survives. The inner conflicts and reconciliations of the Roosevelt coalition also provide the key to such questions as:

What holds the discordant Democratic elements together, even after Roosevelt's passing? What is splitting them apart? When the deadlock, which currently grips this Democratic majority, breaks—as it must—what new political realignment will emerge?

When the break does come it will mark one of the decisive turning points in American and world history. The political crisis which wracks the United States today is largely a reflection of the fact that the nation no longer has an effective majority. So furiously divided is the Democratic coalition that it has lost all capacity for decisive political action. What is fundamentally at issue in 1952 is whether a new majority, capable of decision, can be formed, or whether today's stalemate is to drag on.

In the chapter which follows we will see how almost every aspect of American life has been drawn into this deadlock—our hopes for peace and fears of war, the value of what we earn and of what we save, the very structure of government and of the society in which we live. We will also see how strangely these many forces in deadlock have swirled together into the person of President Truman.

Before turning to look at Truman in this new light, it might be well to describe briefly how this study was conducted. The inspiration for this book traces back to a post-mortem of Roosevelt's third term victory which I did for the *Saturday Evening Post*. That survey left me with the conviction—as stated then, in January, 1941—that the people who had elected Roosevelt would vote for him "for a fourth and a fifth term as readily as for a third"; also that "once Roosevelt is out of the picture this vote will not slip back automatically into its former slots."

After Truman's victory the *Post* had me do a second post-election analysis, which took me back to many of the same areas and families I visited in 1940. Both these surveys were necessarily hurried ones. With the help of a fellowship from the John Simon Guggenheim Foundation I have spent most of the last two years in an exhaustive and, I believe, definitive study, not only of the Roosevelt-Truman elections but of Presidential voting since the Populist offensive of 1892.

My first step was to analyze the election returns for each of the more than 3,000 counties in the United States and for our major cities, ward by ward, and, in some areas, getting down to precincts. Few of these statistics appear in this text. I have used the election returns as tracer material, akin to radioactive isotopes, through which the major voting streams and trends in the country could be isolated and followed in all their fluctuations from election to election.

Having sorted out the streams of voters who tend to shift together, I then did two other things. I pored through all the available library material, from census data to local histories, piecing together the distinctive economic, religious, cultural and political characteristics of these major voting elements. Finally, I spent many months traveling through the country, visiting strategic voting areas and talking firsthand to voters in every walk of life.

Studied in this fashion, election returns become strangely exciting. For every Presidential election really is a self-portrait of America, a self-portrait with each ballot serving as another brush stroke and through which all the emotions of the American people find expression. Into that portrait go all their inherited traditions; the clashings of different economic, social and sectional interests; the tensions of race, religion and color, as well as the strivings toward tolerance and Americanization; the transitions of aging and rising generations, the tenacious grip of memories of the past; the ferments of hopes for the future.

Every election, of course, brings its own distinctive issues. But the manner in which the voting of varied groups has shifted in the past makes it clear that every voter's mind really operates at two levels, one conscious, the other subconscious.

Often the campaign oratory is but the small talk which conceals the almost instinctive predispositions which all of us carry in the backs of our minds. Certainly no basic reshuffling of party alignments is possible unless the subconscious, emotional loyalties of the voters are reshuffled. It is these subconscious, emotional political currents which I have sought mainly to chart and fathom.

What has emerged is not a history in any formal, academic sense. Nor is it a reporter's impressions of the "political pulse of the nation." Rather I have tried to combine the crafts of both historian and reporter in the belief that this is the only effective way of writing about a political revolution which still is going on and whose course shifts as we ourselves change.

2

The Man Who Bought Time

1. The Truman Riddle

When the Seventy-fifth Congress reconvened in January, 1938, most of the Senators were dismayed to find that the first order of business before them was the antilynching bill. Particularly among those Senators whose constituencies straddled Northern and Southern prejudices the prospect of having to vote on the proposal stirred much anguish. As one of these Senators explained to a leader of the Southern opposition, "You know I'm against this bill, but if it comes to a vote I'll have to be for it."

This Senator went on to recall how a favorite uncle had served in the Confederate Army and how his mother still associated all Republicans with the "redleg" abolitionists who had helped make the Kansas-Missouri border a guerrilla battlefield during the Civil War period. "All my sympathies are with you," the Senator fervently declared, "but the Negro vote in Kansas City and St. Louis is too important."

Turning to go, Senator Harry S. Truman added almost wistfully, "Maybe the thing for me to be doing is to be playing poker this afternoon. Perhaps you fellows can call a no quorum."

This episode is related here for the first time in print not to raise doubts about President Truman's sincerity in the matter of civil rights—of that more later—but because it brings into focus so clearly the essential political qualities which made Truman President and which have remained the key to his whole administration. Few Presidents have seemed more erratic and puzzling to their contemporaries; yet few occupants of the White House have run more consistently true to form.

Truman is commonly pictured as "a little man" hopelessly miscast for the "biggest job in the world." Yet how many of our Presidents have given the historians more to write about? Almost any one of a number of his actions would make his Presidency memorable—the dropping of the first atomic bomb, the Truman Doctrine of resistance to communism, the Marshall Plan, the Berlin Airlift, his spectacular election triumph in 1948, his abandonment of the tradition of "no entangling alliances" with the signing of the North Atlantic Defense Treaty, our armed intervention in Korea, the firing of General Douglas MacArthur.

The strange thing about these precedent-shattering actions is how basically unchanged things have been left. After seven years of Truman's hectic, even furious, activity the nation seems to be about on the same general spot as when he first came to office.

Consider the three principal conflicts which have dominated the Truman years and whose interweavings form the fabric of our times:

Domestically, our economy still trembles with the alternating fevers and chills of threatened inflation and threatened depression, even as it did when the war ended. The cold war with Russia continues to pursue its malarial course, now and then sinking into endemic concealment, only to flare up in blood-letting recurrence, with no end in sight. Although both the Wallaceites and Dixiecrats have been discredited, the civil war inside the Democratic party rages as relentlessly as ever.

Nowhere in the whole Truman record can one point to a single, decisive break-through. All his more important policies reduce themselves to one thing—to buying time for the future. Far from seeking decision, he has sought to put off any possible showdown, to perpetuate rather than break the prevailing stalemate.

The mystery of where Truman has been heading can be answered simply. All his skills and energies—and he has been among our hardest-working Presidents—have been directed to standing still.

This persistent irresolution can hardly be blamed on a lack of personal courage. A less courageous—or less stubborn—man, in fact, would not be so resolutely indecisive. It took courage to order American troops into Korea. It also took courage to dismiss General MacArthur at a time when the Republicans were howling so furiously for Secretary of State Dean Acheson's English mustache. Characteristically, both these moves, each so bold in itself, neatly neutralized themselves into a policy of limited action.

This faculty for turning two bold steps into a halfway measure—no mean trick—is Truman's political hallmark. If it applied solely to our relations with the Soviets one might conclude that it was the only shrewd course left between an inability to make peace and an unwillingness to go to war. But the same middle touch can be seen in Truman's handling of domestic political and economic problems. When he takes vigorous action in one direction it is axiomatic that he will contrive soon afterward to move in the conflicting direction. In the end he manages to work himself back close to the center spot of indecision from which he started.

In the fight against inflation, for example, Truman has warned again and again of the calamitous consequences of uncontrolled price rises and, just as repeatedly, he has followed these warnings with actions which aggravated the dangers of inflation. When the last war ended, he eloquently called for holding the line against inflation to avoid another boom and collapse such as followed World War One. Still,

despite the enormous backlog of spending power left over
from wartime savings and profits, Truman supported repeal of
the excess profits tax, wage increases and liberal credit policies,
all of which pumped still more money into the economy.

Again, when Truman called a special session to enact the
Marshall Plan, he demanded legislation to control prices.
When the Korean War broke out, however, he pointedly
refrained from requesting price control powers, even while
asking for the broadest authority to mobilize the economy.
Why did he seek price control in 1948 but not in 1950?
Could it have been that in 1948 he requested legislation which
he knew would not be enacted so he could blame the Republican-controlled Congress for whatever happened, while in
1950 he feared that price powers *would* be given him, leaving
him no alibi for failing to check the rise in living costs?

Even after Congress forced price control powers on him,
Truman delayed acting for several months, while wholesale
prices leaped 14 per cent and the real value of every defense
dollar was cut by one fifth. By the spring of 1951, with the
renewal of price control at issue, Truman had once again
donned the armor of the champion of the voting consumer.

There is a good deal more behind this curious jerkiness
which characterizes Truman's administration than the politician's common desire to face both ways at the same time.
Partly it can be attributed to Truman's personality. Where
Franklin Roosevelt radiated serene self-confidence, Truman
seems afflicted by an inner sense of inferiority. It may be an
outgrowth of the shyness forced on him as a child because of
nearsightedness, or of the financial failures of his father who
lost the family farm speculating on the grain market and was
reduced to the job of night watchman, or of Truman's own
business reverses and his lateness in getting into politics.
Thirty-eight years old when he ran for his first political office,
he was fifty when he won his seat in the U. S. Senate. On

reaching Washington he felt his inadequacy so keenly that he announced he intended to go to law school at night.

Whatever the psychological reason, Truman's personality does seem to demand that he alternate between crafty caution and asserting himself boldly, even brashly, as if proving something to himself. His usual instinct appears to be to play things close to his vest, but periodically he has to unbutton his vest and thump his chest.

Many of his explosive flare-ups probably are forced by his irresolution in allowing situations to build up until drastic action becomes unavoidable. With the RFC and Internal Revenue Bureau frauds for example, he let matters drift for months until it became clear that a major scandal was in the offing and only then instituted his own "shake-up."

The real key to Truman's determined indecision, however, is the fact that he is the product of political deadlock. It was because stalemate fitted his nature so snugly that he became President. Truman can be considered a "political accident" in the sense that Roosevelt's death brought him to the White House. But there was nothing accidental about his being in the line of succession. Only a man exactly like Truman politically, with both his limitations and strong points, could have been the Democratic choice for Roosevelt's successor.

2. How Presidents Are Made

The ruthless, Darwinian process of natural selection which Truman had to undergo to reach the White House was provided by the fierce struggle between the President and Congress which burst into the open early in 1937 with Roosevelt's proposal to pack the Supreme Court and which has continued to the present.

Roosevelt's winning a third and fourth term has obscured the fact that the last major measure of a New Deal nature which he was able to get through Congress was the Wages and Hours Law in mid-1938. With the failure of the attempted purge of the more conservative Democratic Senators and the Republican gains in the 1938 Congressional election, the anti-New Deal coalition came into undisputed control on Capitol Hill. After that Roosevelt never could work his will with Congress. Through the power of veto, he usually could hold the rebellious Congress in check. Congress, for its part, was able to block any Roosevelt proposal it disliked.

That this President-Congress deadlock did not paralyze the effective functioning of the government can be credited largely to the development of a new profession in Washington—that of the so-called "border-state" politician, who undertook to act as political brokers between the White House and Capitol Hill.

Although many members of this bloc actually came from the border states, the label really represented a state of mind. In favor of Roosevelt's foreign policy, the border Democrats were middle of the roaders on domestic issues. They leaned more toward the farmer than toward labor, but still were not antilabor. In fact, they consciously made a point of remaining acceptable to both the liberals and conservatives, to both the isolationists and interventionists.

Theirs was the balance of compromise, which they employed to mediate between the Democratic extremes, being careful never to throw their influence finally on one side or the other. Probably the most effective single member of the group, until his elevation to the Supreme Court, was South Carolina's Jimmy Byrnes, whose talents were admirably suited to cloakroom negotiation.

In many ways this border-state bloc, which included Senators like Dick Russell of Georgia and Carl Hatch of New Mexico, constituted the real locus of political power in Washington. Roosevelt soon learned what Truman has discovered that to get any proposal through Congress required the approval of these middle-of-the-road Democrats. Even today, whenever the border-state Democrats swing their influence against the Administration it gets beaten.

By political geography and personal temperament, Truman was a typical border-state Senator. Campaign biographies usually describe him as having been one of Roosevelt's most faithful supporters and in his first year in the Senate Truman did go down the line for every New Deal measure. But in the struggle within the Democratic party, which developed during Roosevelt's second term, Truman had a way of straying in and out of both camps.

He backed the resolution introduced early in 1937 by Byrnes condemning sit-down strikes. Although supporting Roosevelt on packing the Supreme Court, Truman voted for Pat Harrison of Mississippi for Senate majority leader against Alben Barkley, the White House choice. A regular member of John Garner's convivial "Board of Education," Truman supported the Vice-President's efforts to block a third term.

Garner had calculated that a majority of the 1936 convention delegates consisted of postmasters, marshals, internal revenue collectors, and other federal officeholders, plus their relatives. Hoping to deprive Roosevelt of this support, Garner contrived the Hatch Act, which barred federal officeholders from political activity. Truman supported the Hatch Act. Early in 1940 he issued a statement, "I am not for anyone for a third term."

Nor was Roosevelt especially friendly toward Truman. Several times Truman complained to James A. Farley, then Democratic National Chairman, of being treated unfairly on patronage matters. Roosevelt preferred to consult with Missouri's Governor Lloyd Stark, who was planning to oppose Truman for the Senate. Late in 1939 Roosevelt tried to get Truman to withdraw in Stark's favor by offering him a $10,000-a-year appointment to the Interstate Commerce Commission.

Truman has described the 1940 Democratic primary as

the crucial battle of his entire political career. With Boss Pendergast in jail, the Kansas City organization could not be counted upon for its usual ingenious vote. Truman had no funds of his own for campaign purposes—he couldn't even prevent the family farm from being foreclosed.

One noon at lunch in the office of Edward Halsey, then secretary of the Senate, Truman complained of his difficulties in raising funds for radio talks and political advertising. Byrnes was at the same table. In 1938 Byrnes had taken the lead in opposing Roosevelt's efforts to purge some of the more conservative Senators like Walter George, Bennett Clark, Millard Tydings, Pat McCarran and Guy Gillette. Although Truman was not being openly purged by Roosevelt, Byrnes still felt that no President should interfere in Democratic primary contests. Byrnes sought out Bernard M. Baruch, who had helped finance the fight against the purge, and interested him in Truman's behalf.

Up to this time, Bennett Clark, then senior Senator from Missouri and now a federal judge, had been on the fence taking no active part in the campaign. When Clark decided to support Truman, he also went to Baruch for campaign funds. Again, Baruch contributed generously.

Truman's biographers have made much of his loyalty to those who stuck with him in 1940, like Harry Vaughan and Secretary of the Treasury John Snyder. Yet, during the 1948 campaign, when Baruch refused to join a Democratic fund-raising committee, explaining that he never had accepted such a post before, Truman upbraided Baruch with the taunt that politics was not a one-way street. That action hardly jibes with the legend of Truman's code of unswerving loyalty to his political friends.

It was Baruch, moreover, who sparked the idea which inspired Truman's successful 1948 campaign strategy. Shortly after the Republican Convention, Baruch suggested to Truman that he call the Republican-controlled Congress back into special session, thus providing an arena in which the Republican performance could be matched against the newly drafted Republican platform. Truman was so enthusiastic over this suggestion that he sent Clark Clifford to New York City to discuss the idea more fully with Baruch on the eve of the latter's departure for Europe.

That Baruch should have been interested in Truman by Byrnes, who has become a leader of the anti-Truman opposition within the Democratic party, must surely rate as one of the more ironic footnotes in American political history. The irony deepens in view of how the famous Truman Defense Investigating Committee came to be set up.

Early in 1941 Representative Eugene Cox of Georgia, an uncompromising Roosevelt foe, began demanding an investigation of defense spending. The prospect of an inquiry headed by Cox, a zealot by nature, sent shivers through the heads of the defense agencies. One day Roosevelt explained the concern of the Army and Navy to Byrnes, without referring to Cox by name. "I can fix that by putting the investigation into friendly hands," Byrnes assured the President. Under its rules, Byrnes explained, the House could not authorize an investigation for a week but the Senate could act in a few hours.

Some weeks earlier Truman had introduced a resolution for an investigation, which had been referred to the Committee on Audit and Control which Byrnes headed. Calling Truman to his office, Byrnes asked him why had he introduced the resolution? Truman explained that some Missouri contractors were complaining that the big companies were getting all the defense construction contracts. A little pressure on the War Department, he felt, would be a good thing.

"What would you do if the resolution were reported out?" Byrnes asked.

THE MAN WHO BOUGHT TIME 17

"I know there isn't a chance in the world of your reporting it out," Truman replied. "But if you did I wouldn't conduct the investigation in a way that would hurt defense. You could count on me for that."

Shortly afterward the resolution was reported out and, although no one dreamed it, a new President was in the making.

Truman's able management of the Defense Investigating Committee transformed him into a figure of national importance, earning him a reputation for honesty and fearlessness. What was not widely appreciated was how adroitly Truman appealed to both Democratic factions. Since his Committee's reports were sharply critical of the defense agencies the conservative Democrats were pleased, as were the Republicans. Since the "military" was a favorite committee target the New Dealers also were gratified. An informal understanding existed between the Truman Committee staff and Donald Nelson, the chairman of the War Production Board. Whenever Nelson ran into particular difficulty with the War or Navy departments, he would "leak" his troubles to the Truman Committee, which would then bring pressure on the military.

While the Truman Committee was conducting its able investigations, the attrition of the wartime "Battle of Washington" was steadily shifting the political balance against Roosevelt in favor of Congress. A variety of factors entered into this—the off-year Republican gains in 1942; the vengeful fury of the isolationists who, although supporting the war, drummed constantly with criticism of home front bungling; the failure to bring prices and wages under control; the feuding and squabbling among the government administrators; also the rising resistance in various quarters to wartime restrictions.

In the case of the rubber crisis, the rumbling resentment on

Capitol Hill broke through with the passage of a bill which would have disrupted the whole mobilization machinery by setting up a separate rubber administrator independent of Donald Nelson. Roosevelt vetoed the measure. But, confronted with the likelihood that his veto would be overridden, he called upon Baruch, Harvard president James B. Conant, and Karl Compton, then president of the Massachusetts Institute of Technology, to investigate the situation. Their report, unsparing in criticizing the administrative irresponsibility, saved Roosevelt's veto.

The following month Roosevelt pulled Byrnes off the Supreme Court and made him "assistant president" with an office in the White House. The political significance of this action was largely overlooked. It meant that Congress had gained the ascendancy in Washington. After that, the overhanging political question facing the administration became how to come to terms with the dominant coalition in Congress.

Significantly, all of the new administrators Byrnes brought in either had served in Congress or were acceptable on the Hill. Scrappy Leon Henderson gave way as price administrator to Prentiss Brown, a former Senator. Marvin Jones, a former Congressman, was appointed Food Administrator, Fred Vinson, now Chief Justice of the Supreme Court, was brought off the Court of Appeals and named Director of Economic Stabilization.

It was hoped that Vinson, who had been a highly popular member of the House Ways and Means Committee, would be able to charm Congress into accepting a stiff tax bill. When Vinson appeared to request $10,500,000,000 in additional taxes, his former colleagues listened to him with obvious good humor. They laughed at his jokes and chuckled when, in his colloquial way, he took out his lead pencil to do some figuring. But when it came time to write the tax bill they ignored everything Vinson had said.

Only about two billion dollars in new taxes were voted. When Roosevelt vetoed the bill, condemning it a bit too pungently perhaps, the Senate rose in front page revolt. Barkley resigned as majority leader, rebuking the President who made hasty amends. Ironically, few of Roosevelt's actions were more conservative in the true meaning of the term or more justified in the national interest than this veto of so obviously inadequate a tax bill. The Senate, though, was less concerned with the merits of its tax position than with showing Roosevelt who was boss.

Further weakening Roosevelt's influence with Congress were the victories of American arms abroad. That may sound like a paradox. But since a two-thirds vote of the Senate would be needed to approve any peace treaty, Roosevelt had to edge closer to the views of Senator George and Senator Arthur Vandenberg, the Republican leader, who headed the conservative coalition in the Senate. Also, with the war's end in prospect, the struggle over who was to control the political destinies of postwar America broke forth in savage earnestness.

To make sure that the future of America would be shaped without benefit of New Deal planning, the Senate killed the National Resources Planning Board. Instead it created its own Postwar Planning Committee, vigilantly headed by George and Vandenberg, which was determined to stamp "conservative" on every postwar policy.

But the problems of war and peace could not be separated so cleanly. Since war contracts were already being canceled, reconversion policies had to be laid down while the war was still on. The Senate, though, bristled jealously at any suggestion of Administration action. Searching for some means of bridging the paralyzing deadlock of suspicion, Roosevelt asked Baruch to prepare a report on reconversion policies. In formulating some of the policies, as in the contract termination law, what Baruch and his associate, John M. Hancock, really did was to negotiate a treaty of peace between Congress and the Executive, as if they were foreign powers.

By the time the 1944 Democratic convention opened in Chicago, the balance of Washington power had shifted so strongly that Roosevelt's running mate had to be acceptable to the conservative Democrats in the Senate. Henry Wallace, on whom Roosevelt had soured before the end of the 1940 campaign, was never really in the running. He served as a stalking-horse behind whom labor and the big city delegates could hold their votes and bargaining power. The logistics of the Battle of Washington required that the Vice-Presidency go to one of the border-state Democrats who had made a veritable profession of reconciling the warring Democratic wings. The real choice lay between Byrnes and Truman, who had gone to Chicago to nominate Byrnes.

Three principal objections were raised to Byrnes. Negro leaders opposed him as a Southerner. Ed Flynn, the Democratic boss closest to Roosevelt, argued that Byrnes would "hurt the ticket" since he had been converted from Catholicism. Then, as "assistant president," Byrnes had been too forceful for the liking of some labor leaders.

Truman's record, by contrast, could hardly have been more shrewdly tailored to the needs of a compromise candidate. Usually a safe administration vote, he enjoyed the asset of having been opposed for re-election by Roosevelt, which reassured the more conservative Democrats. He had supported Roosevelt in the World Court and neutrality battles, yet two of the Senate's leading isolationists, Burton Wheeler and Bennett Clark, were the men Truman usually looked to for political guidance. Although acceptable to labor, Truman had opposed the sitdown strikes and had voted for the Smith-Connally antistrike act, but not to override Roosevelt's veto of it.

Truman had voted for price control but against the wartime limitation of $25,000 a year on salaries. He had favored all

relief appropriations but had helped kill the WPA theater
project.

In nominating Truman the embattled Democrats actually
were voting to keep the line of succession to the Presidency
from passing to either the Northern or Southern Democrats.
The 1948 convention found the deadlocked Democrats in the
same plight—with the same result. When the Philadelphia
convention opened, the clamor to ditch Truman was joined
in by such factional rivals as Dixiecrat Southerners and the
Americans for Democratic Action, by James Roosevelt and
big city bosses like Jacob Arvey of Chicago and Frank Hague
of Jersey City. Their unanimity in desiring to get rid of
Truman was surpassed only by their inability to agree on anyone to take his place.

This same necessity to preserve the precarious balance
within the party dictated the nomination of Barkley, another
border-state Senator, as Vice-President.

If the 1952 convention is not to blow up, the Democratic
nomination almost certainly will again have to go to some
member of what might be termed the border-state dynasty,
which has held the balance of political power in Washington
since 1938. To shift the line of Democratic succession to
either the North or South would split the party. That, of
course, is the distinctive political strength of Chief Justice
Vinson, whom Truman is reported to favor in case he decides
not to run again. Like Truman, Vinson has been tested so
thoroughly in Washington warfare that each hostile Democratic wing feels it knows how far he will go and—what is
equally important—not go.

3. The Red Queen

Compromise made Truman President and—despite the con-
troversies he has stirred, the officials he has fired and the
terrible-tempered letters he has written—compromise has
remained the unswerving objective of his Presidency. If this

has been obscured it is because of a failure to appreciate that the only form of compromise currently possible is stalemate.

Broadly speaking, any middle-of-the-road politician faces one of two prospects. He can allow himself to be torn in two by the forces he is attempting to conciliate. Or he can draw strength from both irreconcilable extremes by playing one off against the other. In view of Truman's Senate record it is no surprise to find that he has followed the latter course.

His role has been to raise all issues but to settle none. He has repeatedly pressed vigorous recommendations on Congress knowing they would be rejected—not only on inflation control but on civil rights and repeal of the Taft-Hartley Law. During the 1948 campaign he could think of sending Justice Vinson to Moscow on a "peace mission," not long after he had publicly denounced the Soviet leaders as men whose word could not be trusted. One doesn't have to question Truman's sincerity to observe that he appears happiest when able to make a dramatic show of activity, secure in the knowledge that nothing much is going to happen.

Harsh as that estimate may sound it is Truman's only real claim to greatness. There is much to be said, after all, for the mariner who, knowing that he cannot quiet the storm, contrives somehow to stay afloat until the storm has died down of itself. The major problems Truman has been grappling with are mainly inherited. All are fearfully difficult, perhaps impossible of harmonious solution. As the President of the last center of hope in the world, Truman could hardly confess helplessness. Unable either to reconcile or to ignore the forces in conflict, he has tried to stall them off hoping that time would make decision unnecessary.

The contradictions in Truman's actions vanish when one appreciates that actually he has dreaded moving too far in any direction, of doing too much or too little. Even his acrobatic economics find their consistency in the fact that he has been afraid of both rising and falling prices. When prices go up,

Truman wants them to come down. When they start down, as in 1949, he becomes frightened of a possible recession and starts up the government's inflationary credit engines. Truman's apologists may contend that this is what is known as a "managed economy"—but the motivating force has been to put off politically painful economic adjustments.

Similarly, in foreign affairs Truman will lash out boldly when his hand is forced, as in Korea. When it comes to seeing things through, however, he will drag action, as if hoping something will turn up to make it unnecessary to go too far. Not for two years after the North Atlantic Defense Pact was signed was anything much done to implement it, although in the interval the Soviets exploded their first atomic bomb. So leisurely was the timetable for mobilization laid down in 1950, that it really represented a gamble that the Soviet Union did not intend to go to war. Our slow rate of rearming could be justified only on the basis of faith—let us hope well founded —in Stalin's desire for peace.

If over the last seven years Truman's personal standing has rocketed up and down like a roller coaster, it has not been because he, himself, has been so erratic, but because of changes in the stresses and strains of the forces in conflict.

As the costs and frustrations of continued stalemate grow more burdensome the middle ground on which Truman has pitched his political tent tends to crack and crumble. The tensions of office tell on him personally as, like Alice's Red Queen, he has to run ever faster in order to stand still. In the glaring light of threatened showdown, all his weaknesses become mercilessly exposed—the wavering evasions, the lack of any policy for achieving decision.

But if that is the source of his weakness, it also explains his astonishing recoveries from the abysmally low levels of public esteem to which he has fallen at times. The choices of action which Truman has been evading are all extremely difficult ones, such as splitting the Democratic party or letting the economy run loose to find its natural level, or precipitating a showdown with the Soviets which might cause them to back down but could also bring on war. Truman's constant gamble is that the American public, when confronted with the unpleasant implications of decisive action, will prefer to continue with his policy of calculated drift.

The secret of Truman's political vitality is that he has shrewdly planted himself on the furiously dead center of stalemate to which irreconcilables must repair if they are to make a bargain. Whenever the balance of the raging conflict shifts in favor of conciliation, Truman inherits the situation. But for how much longer can the stalemated forces be held at arm's length? Eventually won't they wrench apart whoever stands in the middle?

There we have the essential drama of Truman's Presidency. It is the drama of a man fighting stubbornly and, yes, courageously, to avoid decision. Whether, in standing against these pressures, Truman is a pitiful or heroic figure cannot be answered today. Although his place in history is set, as the man who bought time, one all-crucial question remains unanswered:

In whose favor is time working?

Is time operating to strengthen the cause of peace? Or is it merely giving the Soviet Union a breathing spell in which it may overcome its weaknesses and amass the strength to make an eventual war bloodier and more difficult to win?

Is time working to invigorate and stabilize our economy or is it merely piling the inflationary bricks ever higher for a bigger crash?

Is time, in its not always obvious workings, managing to bring into existence the conditions which will consolidate the Democrats as the nation's majority party? Or are its clashing elements being driven ever more hopelessly apart until they must split?

In short, are the processes of time in these atomic-riven days of a self-healing or a cancerous nature?

If the verdict of history vindicates Truman he will rate as one of our greatest Presidents, as much for what he did not do as for what he did. If the verdict proves hostile, Truman is likely to appear as another James Buchanan who also considered himself a crafty, dexterous politician, but who wasted the last remaining years of conciliation and left the White House with his own party ready to break up and a disunited country drifting into bloody war.

Whatever the judgment of the future, it should be clear by now that Truman is incapable of breaking the stalemate which grips us and is probably even unwilling to try. Deadlock is the essence of the man. Stalemate is his Midas touch.

And whether Truman remains in the White House after next January or is succeeded by someone else, Republican or Democrat, the same question will dominate the next administration. Is this deadlock to be broken or are we to continue to drift in irresolution?

Before attempting to answer that question it would be well to examine this stalemate carefully. Now in its fourteenth year it is no simple thing to be resolved by a mere change of tenants in the White House. Nor is the deadlock solely political in any narrow sense of the word. The harsh fact we face is that virtually all of the major political, social and economic strands of our times have become twisted into one Gordian knot which, currently at least, defies either unraveling or cutting.

There can be no question that the American people have come to one of the gravest political crises in our history. In my judgment that crisis can be summed up roughly in these terms:

The overhanging threat of war requires a strengthening of the Presidency. Only through Presidential leadership can national unity be achieved, a coherent foreign policy formulated and the resources of the nation mobilized to meet the needs of the cold war. Yet, domestically, the prevailing political currents are directed at weakening Presidential power. This attack on the Presidency does not arise primarily out of misgivings over Truman's personal capacities, although that is a factor. Mainly the conflict stems from the fact that the Presidency has become the symbol of the political revolution wrought by Roosevelt, while Congress has become the symbol of the counterrevolution which has been seeking to reverse the New Deal.

That is not to imply that the New Deal revolution was good and the counterrevolution is bad. The issues involved are not that simple. My point is that at a time when the threat of atomic war makes political unity desperately urgent, the heritage of political conflict which Roosevelt left continues to divide the nation.

Politically, we are passing through a perilous twilight period. So torn and divided is the established majority that the compromise of mutual frustration is the only harmony its clashing elements can find. Yet, there is no party realignment in sight which promises to bring a new majority into existence. At a time when the capacity of government to achieve decision was never more important, indecision appears to be what holds together the party in power.

Whatever the result of the 1952 election this problem will remain—can the American people overcome their internal dissensions sufficiently to re-establish an effective political majority? This unity will not be achieved merely through some dramatic appeal to patriotism. If many Americans today would weaken the powers of government, it is because they fear how those powers may be used domestically. Before unity can be forged, a domestic political balance must be struck which will clear the way for strengthening the government to the extent made necessary by the cold war.

Behind all our fitful political tossings, I believe, stirs the search for this balance. Essentially it is an effort to reconcile the many changes wrought by the Roosevelt Revolution. In the chapters which follow we will trace through these changes in terms of the major elements which comprise the Roosevelt coalition. We will follow this coalition through three successive stages, showing:

First, how this coalition emerged, from origins not generally appreciated, to become the new, normal majority party in the country.

Second, how it came to be deadlocked in self-conflict by its own successes and, in the process, stalemated the Roosevelt Revolution. In brief, what the New Deal did was to give the rival Democratic elements the strength with which to fight one another for control of the Democratic party.

Third, how the cold war has thrust up new issues which have aggravated the tensions within the coalition to the breaking point.

Is the Roosevelt coalition capable of meeting the challenge of the cold war? Or must it be smashed before the national unity that is so sorely needed can be attained? Can the Republicans build a new coalition which can deal with the problems of this time of troubles?

3

Revolt of the City

1. A Little Matter of Birth Rates

In the winter of 1910 Congress received the longest report ever submitted by a government investigating body up to that time. From early 1907 a special commission had been studying almost every imaginable aspect of immigration, filling forty-two fat volumes with its findings. Buried in that statistical mountain was at least one table of figures which was to prove peculiarly prophetic for our own times.

This table showed that a majority of the children in the schools of thirty-seven of our leading cities had foreign-born fathers. In cities like Chelsea, Fall River, New Bedford, Duluth, New York and Chicago more than *two out of every three* school children were the sons and daughters of immigrants.

Viewed in today's perspective, it is clear that those figures forecast a major political upheaval some time between 1930 and 1940. By then all of these children, plus baby brothers and sisters not enrolled in school, would have grown to voting age. Massed as they were in the states commanding the largest electoral vote, their sheer numbers would topple any prevailing political balance.

No matter what else had happened, the growing up of these children of the 13,000,000 immigrants who poured into the country between 1900 and 1914 was bound to exert a leveling pull on American society. As it was, the depression—striking when most of them had barely entered the adult world—

sharpened all their memories of childhood handicaps. When Roosevelt first took office, no segment of the population was more ready for "a new deal" than the submerged, inarticulate urban masses. They became the chief carriers of the Roosevelt Revolution.

The really revolutionary surge behind the New Deal lay in this coupling of the depression with the rise of a new generation, which had been malnourished on the congestion of our cities and the abuses of industrialism. Roosevelt did not start this revolt of the city. What he did do was to awaken the climbing urban masses to a consciousness of the power in their numbers. He extended to them the warming hand of recognition, through patronage and protective legislation. In the New Deal he supplied the leveling philosophy required by their sheer numbers and by the hungers stimulated by advertising. In turn, the big-city masses furnished the votes which re-elected Roosevelt again and again—and, in the process, ended the traditional Republican majority in this country.

Today this same big-city generation still stands like a human wall between the Republicans and their past dominance. It is this generation—now grown to parenthood and in many cases to home-owning, but still bound by common underdog attitudes—which the Republicans must crack to win the Presidency.

Twice before in American history a majority party has been transformed into a minority party. Each time the change was prefaced by a dramatic reshuffling of population. Jacksonian democracy tramped in to the echoes of the oxcarts which had rolled westward in the twenty years before. In 1800 only one of twenty Americans lived west of the Appalachians; when Jackson was inaugurated the transmountain country claimed one of every three Americans.

Similarly, the formation of the Republican party was preceded by a tremendous westward expansion into the Great

Lakes and Midwest regions. Between 1840 and 1860 the nation's population almost doubled, swelling another 60 per cent by 1880. If it is true that the pre-Civil War parties were overwhelmed by their inability to dam back the passions stirred by the slavery controversy, it is also true that they were unable to channel the flood of new voters.

There were two population currents which cleared the way for the New Deal:

Between 1910 and 1930 for the first time a majority of the American people came to live in cities. The second population shift might be described as the triumph of the birth rates of the poor and underprivileged over those of the rich and well born.

Searching for families of five or more, the U.S. Immigration Commission's investigators found two-and-a-half times as many among unskilled laborers as among businessmen. In Minneapolis, for example, the second generation of English stock—the backbone of Republican strength—celebrated a blessed event on the average of one every five years. Among the foreign born a new baby arrived every three years.

As late as 1925 wives of miners and laborers were still having twice as many children as the wives of bankers.

Nor was it the birth rates of the immigrants alone which were threatening the Republican majority. The other prolific baby patches were in the farming areas, particularly in the Appalachian hills and in the South. When World War One shut off the flow of European immigrants, it was into these areas of high human fertility and low living standards that industry sent its recruiting agents searching for cheap labor. Whites and Negroes were sucked north into the cities, especially after 1920 when immigration was curtailed sharply.

Between 1920 and 1930 more than 6,500,000 persons were drawn off the farms and hills; 4,500,000 came into New York, Chicago, Detroit and Los Angeles alone. They hit the cities at roughly the same time that the children of the immigrants were growing up and bestirring themselves. The human potential for a revolutionary political change had thus been brought together in our larger cities when the economic skies caved in.

Through the entire Roosevelt era the Republicans labored on the wrong side of the birth rate. Nor was there anything they could do about it, since the birth rates frustrating them were those of 1910 to 1920. During the last years of Republican victory, from 1920 through 1928, roughly 17,000,000 potential new voters passed the age of twenty-one. From 1936 through 1944, the number ran over 21,000,000, most of them coming from poorer, Democratically inclined families.

Whatever inroads into Roosevelt's popularity the Republicans made was offset largely by these new voters. In 1936, for example, nearly 6,000,000 more ballots were cast than in 1932. While the Republicans gained just under 1,000,000, Roosevelt's vote swelled by almost 5,000,000.

Except for the Polish-Americans and Italo-Americans, the wave of new voters among the immigrant groups passed its crest by 1945. Not until the 1970's will the record number of births of recent years register politically. Until then the nation's basal political metabolism is likely to remain more sluggish than during the Roosevelt years. The issues of realignment will have to be fought out primarily among existing population elements, whose instinctive voting attitudes are already largely formed.

This prospect, of no abrupt change in the make-up of the electorate, re-emphasizes the decisive importance of the big-city generation, which came of age through the Roosevelt years. Without their overwhelming urban pluralities the Democrats would not have won in either 1940, 1944 or 1948. The 1948 election was so close because Truman's vote in the twelve largest cities fell more than 1,000,000 below Roosevelt's.

Not only does this generation hold the balance of political

power in the nation. It also constitutes a radically new political force in American history. The old Republican dominance was rooted in the Civil War and the transcontinental expansion which followed. Most of the immigrants who peopled our larger cities came to these shores long after the Civil War, even after the exhaustion of free lands in the West. To their children and grandchildren the loyalties of Appomattox and the Homestead Act were details in history books rather than a family experience passed down from grandfather to grandson.

Never having known anything but city life, this new generation was bound to develop a different attitude toward the role of government from that of Americans born on farms or in small towns. To Herbert Hoover the phrase "rugged individualism" evoked nostalgic memories of a rural self-sufficiency in which a thrifty, toiling farmer had to look to the marketplace for only the last fifth of his needs. The Iowa homestead on which Hoover grew up produced all of its own vegetables, its own soap, its own bread. Fuel was cut and hauled from the woods ten miles away, where one could also gather walnuts free. "Sweetness" was obtained from sorghums. Every fall the cellar was filled with jars and barrels which, as Hoover observes in his memoirs, "was social security in itself."

To men and women who regulated their labors by the sun and rain, there was recognizable logic in talking of natural economic laws—although even among farmers the murmur for government intervention grew louder, as their operations became more commercialized and less self-sufficient.

In the city, though, the issue has always been man against man. What bowed the backs of the factory worker prematurely were not hardships inflicted by Mother Nature but by human nature. He was completely dependent on a money wage. Without a job, there were no vegetables for his family, no bread, no rent, no fuel, no soap, no "sweetness." Crop failures, plagues of grasshoppers or searing drought could be put down as acts of God. Getting fired or having one's wages cut were only too plainly acts of the Boss.

A philosophy that called for "leaving things alone" to work themselves out seemed either unreal or hypocritical in the cities, where nearly every condition of living groaned for reform. The wage earner had to look to the government to make sure that the milk bought for his baby was not watered or tubercular; he had to look to government to regulate the construction of tenements so all sunlight was not blocked out. If only God could make a tree, only the government could make a park.

Neither the Republicans nor the New Dealers seem to have appreciated how sharp a wrench from the continuity of the past was involved in the rise of this big-city generation. G.O.P. leaders persisted in regarding Roosevelt's popularity as a form of hero worship, abetted by the radio. Only Roosevelt's personal magnetism and political skill were holding together the varied Democratic elements, reasoned the Republicans. With "that voice" quieted, the coalition would fall apart. The nation would then return to safe and sane Republicanism. What this reasoning overlooked was that the Roosevelt generation had no tradition of Republicanism to go back to. For them the weight of tradition was such that if they were undecided about rival Presidential candidates, they instinctively would give the Democrats preference.

The basic weakness of the Republican party stems from this fact, that it remains rooted in an earlier historical era in which it was dominant. The resilient Democratic strength springs from being so alive—clumsily perhaps, but definitely alive—to the problems with which the newer generation has grown up.

Between the Republican and Democratic appeals, as we shall see, the issue is less one of conservatism versus liberalism than one of timeliness.

2. The Forgotten Warrior

At the height of Roosevelt's popularity, Republicans used to lament over the youthfulness of so many of the nation's voters. Since they had come of age since 1928, the complaint ran, the only Presidents they knew were Roosevelt and Hoover, who was hopelessly linked with the depression. Still, it would be a mistake to regard the Roosevelt coalition as strictly a product of the depression.

The startling fact—generally overlooked—is that through the booming twenties Republican pluralities in the large industrial centers were dropping steadily. Even when the stock market tickers were clicking most gratifyingly the forces of urban revolt were gathering momentum.

Consider the waning Republican strength revealed in the table below which totals the vote in our twelve largest cities (New York, Chicago, Philadelphia, Pittsburgh, Detroit, Cleveland, Baltimore, St. Louis, Boston, Milwaukee, San Francisco and Los Angeles). In 1920 the Republicans had 1,638,000 more votes than the Democrats in these twelve cities. This net Republican plurality dropped in 1924 and was turned into a Democratic plurality by 1928.

Year	Net Party Plurality
1920	1,638,000 Republican
1924	1,252,000 Republican
1928	38,000 Democratic
1932	1,910,000 Democratic
1936	3,608,000 Democratic
1940	2,210,000 Democratic
1944	2,296,000 Democratic
1948	1,443,000 Democratic

Two things stand out from those figures. First, it was not the depression which made Roosevelt the champion of the urban masses but what he did after he came to the Presidency. Between 1932 and 1936 the Democratic plurality in these cities leaped 80 per cent, the biggest change in any single election. Second, the Republican hold on the cities was broken not by Roosevelt but by Alfred E. Smith. Before the Roosevelt Revolution there was an Al Smith Revolution.

In many ways, Smith's defeat in 1928, rather than Roosevelt's 1932 victory, marked off the arena in which today's politics are being fought. The Happy Warrior and four-time governor of New York first hacked out the rural-city cleavage which generates so much of the force behind the present struggle between Congress and the President. It was Smith who first slashed through the traditional alignments that had held so firmly since the Civil War, clearing the way for the more comprehensive realignment which came later.

Smith split not only the Solid South but the Republican North as well. While Hoover was carrying more than 200 Southern counties which had never gone Republican before, Smith was swinging 122 Northern counties out of the G.O.P. column.

Seventy-seven of these counties are predominantly Catholic. But more than religious sympathy inspired their support of Smith. This is shown clearly by the way these counties have voted since. Fifty-seven have remained staunchly Democratic in every Presidential election from 1928 through 1948. Included are some of our heaviest voting areas—New York, Boston, Providence, St. Louis, San Francisco, Cleveland, Milwaukee and St. Paul, also Butte, Montana, and Burlington, Vermont.

Of the sixty-two Smith counties whose allegiance has wavered, most are German-American in background and therefore broke against Roosevelt in 1940 because of the war. In 1948 Truman gained over Roosevelt in fifty of these counties, with eighteen returning to the Democratic party.

Smith may be today's "Forgotten Warrior" but the line he drew across the map of American politics has never been erased.

How profound a social upheaval stirred beneath the Smith vote can be seen most clearly in the industrial East, where one finds the heaviest concentration of counties which have been Democratic since 1928. Before Smith, no other part of the country was more religiously Republican. None had a heavier proportion of foreign born. Nor were these two factors unrelated.

During the twenty years of heaviest immigration, from 1890 to 1910, coal production tripled and steel output multiplied seven times. It was in the cities with the most immigrants that Bryan's free silver crusade was beaten. To a considerable extent, in short, both the expansion of industry and Republican political dominance rested on the immigrant.

The conditions under which these immigrants worked and lived hardly requires description here. Coming to this country after the free lands were gone, they were thrust into the sectors of the economy with the sorest tensions, into the sweatiest jobs, where wages were not much above subsistence level and where labor unions were feeble. The foreign born made up 60 per cent of the workers in the packing-house plants described by Upton Sinclair's *The Jungle;* 57 per cent of those in iron and steel, 61 per cent of our miners, nearly 70 per cent of those toiling in textiles or clothing.

Probably of greater long-run political significance than their low wages was the segregation in which they lived. In one-industry coal and steel towns the separation of laborers and managers was as complete as that between serfs and lord on a feudal manor. In the larger cities, even where Gold Coast and slum were hardly a block apart, they still constituted two separate worlds. Roosevelt has often been accused of ranging class against class, as if class antagonism did not exist before the New Deal. Yet, certainly since the turn of the century our urban social structure had been a class structure.

For a long time, though, the resentment of the "other half" against those on top merely smoldered submissively. Even had the immigrants been inclined to political activity, they would have found it difficult. In 1910 one of every five among the foreign born spoke no English. Until 1920 the twelve-hour working day, still the rule in iron and steel, left little leisure time. As late as 1933, when the N.R.A. codes were being considered, Secretary of Labor Frances Perkins had to go out into the mill towns to drum up interest among the steel-workers. At Homestead a Catholic priest arranged a meeting with some Polish-American workers, all of whom came scrupulously scrubbed. They spoke no English and the meeting had to be conducted through an interpreter. Mrs. Perkins was visibly touched when several workers rose and spoke and it developed they were asking God to bless the President, much as peasants in Russia might have blessed the czar.

The rise in the educational level is a revealing index to the quickening political pulse of the urban masses. At the turn of the century only one of every fifteen youngsters was going beyond the elementary school. By 1930 every second child of high school age was in high school.

At first, this rising generation found little real identification with either of the major parties. In exchange for a favor or a two-dollar bill the newly naturalized voter would vote the way the political machine instructed. But he was as likely to follow the dictates of a Republican boss in Philadelphia as of Tammany Hall in New York. None of the Republican Presidents stirred that most vital of all political assets: vicarious identification. It was not a matter of postwar disillusionment. Far from feeling like a lost generation, the children of the immigrants were intensely idealistic. But with whom could they identify this idealism? Harding was a dirty story. Calvin Coolidge might be untouched by scandal, but the same Puritanical, small-town qualities which endeared him to Main Street made "Silent Cal" a chilling, pedagogic figure to city kids.

On the Democratic side, Woodrow Wilson had captured

the imagination of some of these underdog elements through favorable labor legislation, through his dream of peace and by championing the cause of Europe's minorities. Even today, in appealing to Czechs and Poles, Democratic politicians find it effective to invoke Wilson's memory. But this enthusiasm did not carry over to either James M. Cox, an Ohio publisher, or John W. Davis, a Wall Street lawyer. As for William Jennings Bryan, his revivalist oratory might inflame the Bible belt—but in the city he was a repellent, even comic figure. When the "Great Commoner" rose before the 1924 Democratic Convention in New York to oppose denouncing the Ku Klux Klan by name, contending "We can exterminate Ku Kluxism better by recognizing their honesty and teaching them that they are wrong," he was hissed and booed by the galleries.

By 1924, "the enemy's country," as Bryan called the East, had flung up its own Great Commoner in Al Smith. Prohibition and the Klan were the immediate weapons in the duel Smith and Bryan fought; but behind each antagonist were ranged the habits and prejudices, hopes and frustrations, prides and hatreds of two different cultures and two historical eras.

The very eccentricities and mannerisms of the two men were symbolic. The brown derby and rasping East Side accent, which stamped Smith as "one of our boys" to the sidewalk masses, sent shivers down the spine of Protestant respectability. In turn, the traits which made Bryan seem like the voice of pious morality to his Prohibitionist, rural, Protestant following—the liberal use of Biblical phrases, the resonant Chautauqua tones, the heaven-stomping energy—made him sound like the voice of bigotry to the urban masses.

Both men were mouthpieces of protest—Bryan of the over-mortgaged Bible belt, Smith of the underpaid melting pot. Whether either was understood in the other's country is doubtful. Could the factory worker really share the despair of the farmer watching a sheriff tack a foreclosure notice on the barn door? Could the farmer feel the vicarious terror of the factory masses reading of a shirtwaist fire in which 145 women were trapped and burned alive?

The year of this Triangle fire, 1911, was the year Smith first went to Albany. It marked the beginning of his fight to improve factory conditions, reduce the hours of labor for women and for other social legislation. After his relations with Roosevelt had curdled, Smith came to denounce the New Deal's "socialism." But during the 1920's he was the means by which the Democratic party absorbed the agitations— and votes—of the Socialists and their sympathizers.

What Smith really embodied was the revolt of the under-dog, urban immigrant against the top dog of "old American" stock. His Catholicism was an essential element in that revolt. The so-called "old" immigration which settled the farms was drawn largely from Protestant countries, England, Norway, Sweden and Germany. The "new" immigration after 1885 which crowded the teeming cities, came mainly from Italy, Poland, Russia, Greece and the disintegrating Hapsburg Empire. The larger part of these new immigrants were Catholic. They also included perhaps 1,500,000 Jews.

Because they came to this country late, these immigrants and their children were concentrated in the lower economic rungs. Moreover, they resented what seemed to them efforts to force conformity to an Anglo-Saxon, Protestant culture, through Sunday Blue Laws, prohibition and the Klan.

Throughout the industrialized East, the make-up of society was such that Protestantism coincided largely with the Republican party, with millowners and financiers, with the snobbish members of exclusive clubs—in short, with the upper class. Catholicism, in turn, coincided largely with discrimination and sweated labor, with immigrant minorities who were looked down upon as inferior beings—in short, the lower class.

In his campaign Smith did not draw the line of class conflict. His campaign manager, John S. Raskob, was a millionaire. So were other ardent supporters like Pierre Du Pont,

Herbert Lehman and William F. Kenny, who was reputed to have made $30,000,000 as a contractor. Still, the class and cultural cleavage was there, like a deep fault, in the granite of our national life. Smith's candidacy unavoidably split the rock along that fault.

The viciousness of the 1928 campaign is usually laid to religious prejudice. In view of developments since, one wonders whether it did not also reflect the violence of the realignment which Smith was precipitating. Generally, American elections blur social divisions. But in 1928, economic, racial, religious and cultural differences all sharpened the cleavage.

Before Smith the Democrats were little more of an urban party than were the Republicans. In Pennsylvania, for example, the three counties the Democrats won in 1920 and 1924 were largely rural and native born. These counties swung for Hoover in 1928. In their place, the Democrats captured three mining and industrial counties—Elk, Luzerne and Lackawanna—which had not gone Democratic since at least 1896. In Pennsylvania, Smith pushed the Democratic vote above the million mark for the first time. Throughout New England, whole voting elements such as the French-Canadians and Italo-Americans were swung out of the Republican party never to return.

Smith also made women's suffrage a reality for the urban poor. In better income families, women started voting in 1920 as soon as they were granted the privilege; but among the urban masses the tradition that a woman's place was in the home still held strong until 1928. That year in Massachusetts (which Smith carried along with Rhode Island) the outpouring of women lifted the number of voters by 40 per cent over 1924. The turnout in Boston was 44 per cent heavier.

Although the issues of 1928 have long passed off, the cleavage which Smith's candidacy laid bare still persists. If New England remains the most Republican of the major regions, it is also where the line between unwaveringly Republican and unwaveringly Democratic voters is most rigidly drawn. Between 1932 and 1944, New England's Democratic vote did not shift by more than 2 per cent in any election, while other parts of the country were fluctuating by 5 and 10 percent.

There are Catholic Republicans, of course, as there are Yankee Democrats, but, in the main, the bedrock cleavage in the East remains a Catholic-Protestant one. The divergence in cultures shows up in all sorts of ways. One county carried by Smith in 1928 and which has remained Democratic since is Hillsborough in New Hampshire, which was the site of the "mercy killing" trial of Dr. Herman Sanders. When Sanders went on trial, prayers for his acquittal were voiced in the Congregational Church. When he was freed, the Catholic hospitals barred him from practicing there.

But if Smith lifted the Democratic vote to new heights in some cities, he lost such Democratic strongholds as Oklahoma City, Atlanta, Birmingham, Dallas, Houston. In virtually all the Southern cities, Smith's vote fell off, as well as in cities with heavy Scandinavian populations, reflecting Lutheran distrust of Catholicism; he also lost ground wherever the population was mainly native born or Ku Klux in sympathy.

To sum up, by 1928 the masses in the cities with the most foreign born were already in political revolt. But that part of the urban population which was drawn from native American stock had still to be roused.

3. The Year of Decision

Bowls of red roses graced the speakers' table while American flags and tricolored bunting draped the walls of the banquet hall. The occasion was the first annual dinner of the Muncie, Indiana, Chamber of Commerce since the depression. Its immediate inspiration had been the news that General Motors, which had stripped its local plant three years before, was moving back. Mindful that the company was returning to escape a strike in Toledo, the Mayor assured the banqueters that "the citizens of Muncie are in no mood for outsiders to come in and agitate."

Returning to the city that June week in 1935 to begin their study of "Middletown in Transition," Robert and Helen Lynd were struck by the eagerness with which Muncie's community leaders were hailing the return of the "good old days."

But if Muncie's businessmen were ready to forget the depression as "just a bad bump in the road," that was not the feeling across the railroad tracks "in the other world of wage earners." Predominantly native born, drawn mainly from near-by farms, Muncie's "cornfeds," as the local workers were called, had seen no point in labor unions before the depression. Out of a working force of 13,000, hardly 700 had carried union cards, fewer than joined the Klan. Al Smith won a lone precinct in the city, losing one of the two precincts which went Democratic in 1924. With every fourth Muncie worker jobless in 1932, Roosevelt carried thirteen precincts, but still lost the city.

As in so many other communities, the N.R.A. brought a rush among Muncie's workers to join labor unions. At the Ball glass factory and the automotive plants—Muncie's two strongest antiunion citadels—the American Federation of Labor was petitioned to send in organizers. But the A. F. of L. was fumbling and inept, while the business community was militantly efficient. The local police force was secretly increased. Persons distributing handbills advertising a union meeting were picked up. One local newspaper front-paged a photograph of a picket in Oregon being dragged through the streets under the caption, THIS PICKET HAD REAL "DRAG" WITH COPS.

By the time the 1936 Presidential campaign opened, the drive to unionize Muncie had been broken. But the workers still had the ballot. To the Lynds the 1936 campaign "witnessed perhaps the strongest effort in the city's history by the local big businessmen (industrialists and bankers) to stampede local opinion in behalf of a single Presidential candidate." When the ballots were in, Muncie had gone for a Democratic President for the first time since the Civil War. Exulted one worker to the Lynds, "We certainly licked the big bosses."

Muncie was not the only Republican citadel which resisted Roosevelt in 1932 but fell in 1936. Twenty-three other counties, which the Republicans held in 1932, swung four years later and—like Muncie—have stayed Democratic. Among these was "Bloody" Harlan in southeast Kentucky, where efforts to organize the miners in the 1930's exploded in assassinations and pitched battles; also the cities of Philadelphia and Wilmington, the home of the Du Ponts. To defeat Roosevelt, various members of the Du Pont clan contributed more than $500,000 to the Republicans, in addition to their donations to the American Liberty League. The net effect seems only to have advertised more sharply who was on whose side.

So overwhelming was Roosevelt's 1936 victory, that its political decisiveness is often overlooked. With only Maine and Vermont remaining Republican, Roosevelt's re-election seemed primarily a vote of gratitude for lifting the country out of a desperate economic crisis. Certainly many people favored him for that reason. But 1936 was also the year of realignment in which the Democrats became the nation's normal majority party. The traditional dominance which the Republicans had enjoyed since the Civil War was washed away and a new era in American politics began.

The depression vote of 1932 still mirrored the orbit of conflict of the old Republican order. The G.O.P. cleavage had been mainly a struggle between the "progressives" of the Midwest and Far West against the industrial East. Roosevelt's first campaign was directed primarily toward splitting off this "progressive" vote. His best showing came in the Western and Mountain states. All six states he lost—Pennsylvania, Delaware, Connecticut, Vermont, New Hampshire and Maine—were in the East.

The shift in the basis of Roosevelt's appeal "from acreage to population," to use Raymond Moley's phrase, occurred in 1935. Moley credits the change to Huey Long's "Share Our Wealth" agitation and to Roosevelt's ire over the Supreme Court's declaring the N.R.A. unconstitutional. To steal Long's thunder, Roosevelt proposed a "soak the rich" tax bill, which, Moley feels, marked the beginning of the conservative-liberal split inside the Democratic party. Whatever the exact turning point, 1935 saw more social legislation enacted than in any other year in the nation's history—the "wealth tax," the Wagner Labor Relations Act, the Social Security Law, the creation of WPA, the Public Utilities Holding law, the start of the Rural Electrification Administration.

Not only in Washington but throughout the country 1935 was the year of decision. To go back to the old order or to move forward to something different? That was the question posed for decision in 1935, in countless different ways, in every phase of life.

In the early New Deal days how things were done had been less important than getting the stalled economy going again. By 1935 recovery had progressed to the point where there no longer was any question that the country would be saved. The new issue was: Would the "good old days" of unchallenged business dominance be restored? Or was America to be reshaped?

The more articulate business groups had one answer. As in Muncie, they were ready to resume their annual Chamber of Commerce dinners as if there never had been a depression. But the same processes of recovery which restored the courage of businessmen also enabled the leaders of organized labor to recover their nerve. Early in 1933 John L. Lewis, Phil Murray and Tom Kennedy lamented to Roosevelt that the United Mine Workers had barely enough members to pay the union's expenses. "Go home and have a good night's sleep," Roosevelt consoled them. "If I don't do anything else in my administration I am going to give the miners an opportunity to organize in the United Mine Workers of America."

Taking Roosevelt at his word, Lewis nearly emptied the UMW treasury to hire organizers, sending them out to tell the miners, "The President wants you to join a union." By 1934 Lewis could stand before the A. F. of L. convention and boast that the UMW was again a fighting force of 400,000 miners. By 1935 he was ready to demand that the A. F. of L. embrace the principle of industrial unionism or let a new labor movement organize the mass production industries.

The hard right to the jaw which Lewis swung at Bill Hutcheson in Atlantic City that October was symbolic of the fact that at least one group of labor leaders were determined not to go back to the old order.

When the first sit-down strike broke in November 1935, it came—significantly—not among workers of immigrant origin, but among the rubber workers of Akron. That city had drawn so many hillbillies from near-by states that it was often jokingly called "the capital of West Virginia." Before taking their place in the picket line, some rubber workers knelt in prayer. After the last "Amen," they picked up their baseball bats and lead pipes and moved into formation around the factories.

This fervor for unions which swept the native American workers—some observers likened it to a religious revival— was of crucial political importance. Al Smith, as we have seen, stirred a new sense of political consciousness among workers of immigrant and Catholic origin. But the native workers off the farms and hills had always held suspiciously aloof from those of immigrant stock.

The hillbillies had their own sense of group solidarity. Flint, Michigan, had its "Little Missouri" and "Little Arkansas" residential settlements. In Akron, the West Virginia State Society had 25,000 members and put on an annual West

Virginia day picnic. Marked off from the older inhabitants by their accents, manners and dress, the "snake-eaters" were the butt of ridicule and jokes, which were fiercely resented. A judge in Akron suspended sentence on one man on condition that he return to West Virginia. A newspaper reporter wrote up the incident, "Judge Sentences Man to West Virginia for Life." At the next election the hapless judge was badly beaten by the votes of outraged mountaineers.

The formation of the CIO marked the fusing of the interests of the immigrant and native-stock workers. That, I believe, is perhaps the most telling accomplishment of the CIO. Its political importance can hardly be exaggerated. The mass production industries had been the ones in which racial and religious antagonisms among the workers were most divisive. Carnegie-Illinois, for example, had sprinkled clusters of different nationalities in each of its mines, reasoning correctly that a Balkanized working force would be more difficult to unionize. In some industries immigrants and Negroes had first been introduced as strikebreakers or because they would work for lower wages than native-born workers. The failure of the Knights of Labor in the 1880's was largely a failure to unite the immigrant working groups. Much of the A. F. of L.'s reluctance to embark on a real organizing drive in the mass production industries reflected the dislike of the "aristocrats of labor" in the skilled crafts for the immigrant "rubbish."

By 1935, of course, the immigrants had made considerable progress toward Americanization. But the key to the change was the rise of a common class consciousness among all workers. The depression, in making all workers more aware of their economic interests, suppressed their racial and religious antagonisms. Put crudely, the hatred of bankers among the native American workers had become greater than their hatred of the Pope or even of the Negro.

This struggle between the old nativist prejudices and the newer class consciousness still remains one of the crucial behind the scenes battles in the mass production unions. Class feeling or racial-religious feeling? The future of American labor rests largely on which holds the ascendancy.

This rise in class consciousness among native-American workers was a nation-wide development. In Muncie the Lynds reported the first evidences of class feeling among the workers, stirred by the sense that the government could do something for them. In "Yankee City" (Newburyport, Mass.) W. Lloyd Warner tells of a similar change among the so-called "River-brookers," the proud, clannish, Yankee-stock workers who had always refused to join unions with immigrant workers. When the new shoe union staged the first successful strike in Yankee City's history, the Riverbrookers supplied the leadership.

Negroes were another voting element which was determined to go forward rather than back. In some cities as many as four out of five Negro families were on relief. "Don't Buy Where You Can't Work" campaigns were being pressed to force white storeowners to hire Negroes. In Harlem the accumulated tensions of the depression years were exploded suddenly by a trivial incident.

On March 19, 1935, a sixteen-year-old boy snatched a ten-cent bread knife from a five-and-ten cent counter—"just for fun" he later told the police. Two white clerks and the white manager chased the boy to the rear of the store. When they grabbed him, he bit their hands and broke away.

The boy was a Puerto Rican, yet the rumor spread that a Negro had been lynched in the store. Pickets appeared. A soap-box orator on one street corner attracted a growing crowd. When a funeral hearse happened to drive by a woman shrieked, "They've come to take the boy's body!" The Negro mob went on a rampage. When the riot was over, one man was dead—three others died later of injuries—and a hundred or more whites and Negroes had been shot, stabbed or stoned.

The grisly tragedy was lightened only by the action of a

Chinese laundryman. When he saw the mob surging through the streets, heaving stones into store windows, he hastily thrust a sign into his window, "Me colored too."

New York City had had four previous race riots, without anything much happening afterward. The 1935 riot, however, set off a series of far-reaching changes. Harlem's shopowners hastily put on Negro employees. Before the year was out Tammany Hall had named its first Negro district leader. Mayor Fiorello La Guardia had appointed the first Negro magistrate. In 1932 most Negro voters in the country were still Republican. In 1936, in many cities two of every three Negro voters were for Roosevelt.

And so it went all through the country. It would be impossible to trace in full all the different ways in which the question —whether to go back or forward—was being asked of the American people. Sometimes the query was put bluntly in so many words. More often it was implicit in the logic of events or in reminders of the depression. At the end of 1935, more than $780,000,000 was still tied up in closed banks, 3,000,000 persons were still on relief; one survey of a group of garment workers showed that half of them had not bought a new coat for four years.

Lifelong Socialists had to ask themselves—did they return to the ivory tower of a futile third party or did they defend their immediate interests by rallying behind Roosevelt? Sidney Hillman and David Dubinsky, whose unions had been saved by the N.R.A., formed a new American Labor party to enable New Yorkers to vote for Roosevelt and still remain independent of the Democrats. Norman Thomas polled 884,000 Socialist votes nationally in 1932 and only 187,000 votes four years later.

On the other side of the political barricades the realignment was equally sharp. In 1932 one fourth of the Democratic campaign funds was contributed by bankers. In 1936 bankers accounted for a mere 3 per cent of the Democratic party's war chest. (Their total contributions to the Democrats were only about a third of the $750,000 spent by organized labor.)

Particularly in rural areas, the 1936 vote showed that sizable numbers of voters were ready to return to the Republicanism of their ancestors. Winston County, which had seceded from Alabama during the Civil War to remain loyal to the union, swung back to the Republican party in 1936; so did thirty-two counties in Missouri, all but eight bone-dry by tradition. Less than a dozen wheat counties in the whole country had stayed Republican in 1932. Four years later, most of the wheat counties were on their way back to the Republican party.

In the industrial centers, however, the political allegiances that had grown out of the Civil War were uprooted for good. In New York, New Jersey and Pennsylvania, alone, the Democratic vote leaped by roughly 1,800,000. Despite the depression, in 1932, Roosevelt failed to carry a dozen cities with 100,000 or more population—Philadelphia, Scranton and Reading in Pennsylvania; Canton, Youngstown and Columbus in Ohio; Gary, Duluth, Des Moines, Grand Rapids and Springfield, Massachusetts. Every one swung for Roosevelt in 1936 and except for Grand Rapids have remained Democratic since.

A dramatic glimpse into the nature of this hidden political revolution will be found by comparing the 1928 and 1936 vote in our major cities. While Smith won six of every ten voters in some cities, in others he drew only three out of ten. This disparity had narrowed by 1932, but wide divergencies in voting still prevailed in different parts of the country. With the 1936 election, as the table below shows, the voting of nearly all our major cities hit a common level.

Whether the cities are heavily foreign born or native American in make-up, Catholic or Protestant, with large numbers of Negroes or of whites up from the South, did not make too much difference in their 1936 vote. Nor whether the city had a strong labor tradition like San Francisco or an open

shop tradition like Los Angeles, nor whether it was located
on the East or West coast or in the Midwest.

	Cities High Smith			Cities Low Smith	
City	Dem. % 1928	Dem. % 1936	City	Dem. % 1928	Dem. % 1936
Lawrence	71	73	Flint	19	72
Boston	67	63	Wichita, Kan.	24	64
Lowell	64	61	Los Angeles	28	67
Fall River	64	67	Akron	31	71
New York	60	75	Des Moines	31	55
New Haven	57	65	San Diego	32	65
Milwaukee	53	76	Seattle	32	64
New Bedford	52	65	Duluth	32	71
Cleveland	52	76	Canton	34	66
St. Louis	51	66	Spokane	35	71
San Francisco	49	72	Detroit	37	65
Chicago	48	65	Indianapolis	39	57
Pittsburgh	47	67	Philadelphia	39	60
Baltimore	47	67	Youngstown	39	74

A new nationalizing force had clearly been injected into
American politics. In the past American political realignments
have always followed sectional lines. The Revolt of the City,
however, had drawn the same class-conscious line of economic
interest across the entire country, overriding not only regional
distinctions but equally strong cultural differences.

This development was not without its irony. In drawing the
line of cleavage between worker and "economic royalist,"
Roosevelt unquestionably sharpened the sense of class division
in American society. Yet, in doing so, he subordinated the old
nativistic prejudices of race and religion, which had divided the
lower half of American society for so long, bringing these
lower income elements a greater degree of social unity than
they had ever shared before. Was Roosevelt dividing or unifying the country? That question is worth coming back to later
after we have delved more deeply into the implications of the
rise of the urban masses.

4. By Fire and Water

If the 1936 vote marked the emergence of the new Roosevelt coalition, the third term election brought the crucial trial by fire and water which demonstrated the coalition's durability.

In both 1932 and 1936 Roosevelt would still have been elected without his heavy urban pluralities. In 1940, however, with the war and the third-term issue cutting heavily into his rural strength, the margin of victory that accounted for at least 212 electoral votes was supplied by the dozen largest cities in the country.

In every city I visited while doing a postelection survey I found that the Roosevelt vote broke at virtually the same economic level, between $45 and $60 a month rent. Below that line his pluralities were overwhelming. Above it, they faded away. In Pittsburgh, for example, Roosevelt got three fourths of the vote in wards whose rentals averaged under $40 a month and only four tenths of the vote where rentals were above $65 a month. Minneapolis, whose social make-up contrasts sharply with Pittsburgh, showed much the same results —about 40 per cent of the vote for Roosevelt in the highest income ward, but seven of every ten voters in the lower rental areas.

The sharpness with which the balloting stratified in city after city—Chicago, Boston, St. Louis, Seattle, Cleveland— left little room for any appreciable shift of votes because of the campaign put on by Wendell Willkie. When I asked one auto unionist in Detroit why the third-term issue had made so little difference he replied, "I'll say it even though it doesn't sound nice. We've grown class conscious." With other unions there may have been less bitterness but the division between worker and "economic royalist" was as sharply drawn. In a Minneapolis ward, inhabited largely by teamsters, the pastor of one church had been outspoken in condemning the third term. He admitted bitterly, "I don't suppose I changed a single vote." John Lewis, who had endorsed Willkie, could have echoed him.

This class consciousness, it should be noted, was not confined to workers. The balloting revealed as much class feeling among the higher income Republicans. If Roosevelt solidified the lower classes, he also welded the upper class.

The one sharp break from "economic voting" came on the basis of ethnic background, reflecting the varying impact upon different groups of Hitler's War. Roosevelt's heaviest losses came in German-American and Italo-American wards, where resentment was strong against his "stab in the back" reference to Mussolini's attack on France. The highest income areas voting for Roosevelt were Jewish. In Brooklyn he carried streets with $15,000 homes—a comfortable valuation in 1940— and apartment houses with doormen. Where low income status coincided with the nationality background of a country invaded by Germany, the vote for Roosevelt was prodigious. Polish-American wards in Buffalo went Democratic nine to one, with individual precincts running as high as twenty to one, his heaviest pluralities in the whole country.

Curiously, the ethnic elements most bitterly antagonized by Hitler were largely those contributing the heaviest numbers of new voters. In Buffalo, in 1940, the Polish-Americans mustered enough votes to elect a Polish-American judge for the first time. One Democratic ward leader, John Kryzinski, a tavern keeper, was foaming with enthusiasm at the significance of this victory.

"Out in ritzy Humboldt Park they get two voters to a family," he snorted contemptuously. "I get six out of my house. I got neighbors who give me eight. We elected a judge this year. The way things are going in eight years we'll elect a mayor."

Nine years later Buffalo did elect Joseph Mruc its first Polish-American mayor.

In every city one could see the same inexorable spread of numbers and the same leveling pressures. Almost it seemed, in fact, that the Republicans had decided to abandon the cities to the Democratic masses, taking refuge in the suburbs. In St. Louis the Twenty-eighth Ward had stayed Republican in 1932. By 1940 this G.O.P. stronghold had been reduced to three precincts. Along Lindell Boulevard and Skinker Road, "For Sale" signs were propped in front of mansionlike homes with graveled driveways, flagstone walks and antique-fabricated lampposts. Some of the more imposing residences were being razed to make way for apartment houses. In the old days at the Pageant, the neighborhood movie house, seats were reserved. When I saw it, the lobby was placarded with handbills advertising double features on Wednesdays and Thursdays, with three features for a quarter on Fridays and Saturdays.

In Harlem, as well, the spirit of 1936 had quickened. Along 125th Street Negroes were working in hundreds of establishments which as late as 1935 had been manned completely by whites. Garment workers, janitors, bartenders, waiters and waitresses, Pullman porters, laundry workers, newspaper men, retail clerks and redcaps were flocking into labor unions with a sense of deliverance. To the Negro, unionism promised more than a wage boost. It also seemed the trumpet which would eventually tumble the Jericho walls of discrimination. Some Harlem unions were holding daily classes to teach Negroes selling, typing and stenography, to be able to rebuff employers who protested, "I can't hire Negroes, they're not experienced."

Probably 50 per cent of Harlem's Negroes were still getting relief of some kind. Older Negroes, clinging to the Republican party, might shake their graying heads and mutter, "Our people are selling their birthrights for a mess of pottage." Younger Negroes had a different slant on WPA. "The really important thing about WPA is that it is a guarantee of a living wage," explained Carl Lawrence, a reporter on the *Amsterdam News*.

"It means Negroes don't have to work for anything people want to give them. This helps lift the standards of all Negroes even those not on WPA."

The fall of France in 1940 had spurted the armament program, and the defense boom had been building up steadily in the months before the election. With the boom in employment, a highly significant thing was happening. Older people, who had been thrown out of work during the depression, were not being re-employed. The jobs were going to their children, while the older folk stayed on relief or lived on their savings, plus some help from their children. It hardly had been planned that way, but the New Deal was cushioning a wholesale shift in the working population, by easing the older generation of depression casualties out of the way to make room for a new generation.

In the Charlestown area of Boston one half of the voters were under forty. The ward leader himself, William Galvin, was thirty-six. Two younger brothers* had got out of high school during the depression and had gone into the CCC camps. When employment in the Boston Navy Yard expanded, they got jobs as electrician's and pipe fitter's helpers. From the CCC to the Navy Yard—to these two youths, the government had brought advancement as real as any they could have achieved under a private employer.

As a reporter in Washington I had shared the general belief that the New Deal was hastily improvised and animated by no coherent philosophy. When one translated its benefits down to what they meant to the families I was interviewing in 1940, the whole Roosevelt program took on a new consistency.

The depression had thrown grave strains upon lower income families. Many family heads had lost their jobs, never to be employed regularly again. In some instances, the children were old enough to take over the breadwinning, which often robbed the deposed patriarch of his self-respect. In other

* Another brother has since become Undersecretary of Labor to Maurice Tobin.

families the parents had to struggle along until the children grew of age and took over.

In varied ways the New Deal eased these family strains. Through the HOLC a million homes were saved. Many home-owners were too old to have been able to buy a new home, if they had lost their old ones. With their children grown older, I found, many were renting out part of the house, often to a married son or daughter.

Into the CCC camps went 2,750,000 sons of the cities. No longer a drain on the family larder, they even sent some money back home. Children in high school might get NYA aid. Those who went to work usually did so in low-wage industries where the effects of the wage-hour law were most noticeable.

These and other New Deal benefits did not solve all the family problems by any means. They did ease the adjustments that had to be made as the unfortunates of one generation grew unemployable and another generation finally found its opportunity in defense employment.

The recovery from the depression low helped Roosevelt politically with all groups. It was particularly important in the cities because that recovery coincided with the hatching out of the birth rates of 1910 to 1920 and the rise of a new generation. The very size of the Democratically inclined families helped knit them to the New Deal. Even persons who had done rather well for themselves were likely to have a less fortunate family member lower down the economic ladder being bene-fited by the New Deal. Old-age pensions and other aid eased the burden of having to care for parents too old to work. In-stead of being dragged by family burdens, the rising generation was able to solidify its gains.

How much of all this was "planned that way" and how much of it just happened can be speculated upon endlessly. One can also speculate about what might have happened if Roosevelt had not run for a third term and if the war in Europe had not broken out when it did.

Both Garner and Farley have written that they opposed a

third term to keep the Democratic party from degenerating into a personal vehicle for Roosevelt and Roosevelt alone. If Roosevelt runs again, Garner told Bascom Timmons, his biographer, "after he is off the ticket the Democratic party will fall to pieces." Despite Garner's deserved reputation for political shrewdness, he seems to have misjudged the forces at work. But for the third term, it is questionable whether many of the elements who had thrown their strength to the Democrats for the first time in 1936 would have solidified in the party. Early in 1940, for example, Ralph Bunche was still writing of the Negro vote as being "essentially Republican."

Paradoxically, the New Deal also appears to have grown stronger politically after it was abandoned. The outbreak of the war put an end to social reform. But the war boom made unnecessary any additional New Deal measures. In fact, the war succeeded in doing what the New Deal never could accomplish; it brought the country out of the depression.

Unemployment never fell below eight million in 1939 and growing numbers of people wondered whether there ever would be full employment. In the "little steel" strike of 1937 organized labor suffered a serious setback. If the recession of 1938 had dragged on, labor might have had to retreat, instead of entrenching itself as a permanent force in the mass production industries. All through the 1930's surplus sons and daughters had been held back on the farms because of a lack of opportunity in the cities.

The defense boom sparked anew the migration from farm to city. It also sparked new vigor into the marriage rate. In the middle 1930's one of four youths in their late teens and early twenties had never had regular work. By 1939 the marriage rate had risen from the depression low of eight to nearly eleven per thousand population. In 1941 it leaped to almost thirteen per thousand.

Economically speaking, then, the defense boom was the happy ending which saved the New Deal and made it a success story. The ten years of full employment which followed the outbreak of Hitler's War solved the economic problem of the Roosevelt generation, solidifying them in the Democratic party. But in the process this generation changed markedly. Not only had it aged and taken on new responsibilities, but much of this generation had climbed from poverty into the middle class. The rise of this new middle class—whose significance is still only dimly sensed even by professional politicians—is worth examining.

4

The Frontier Reappears

1. The New Middle Class

Outwardly at least there seemed nothing unusual about this Cleveland street. Each two-story frame dwelling had its lawn in the front and garage in the rear. If stained-glass windows and scrolled, oaken doors in some houses hinted at a lost elegance, the lady cigar trees shading the sidewalks and the "No Through Trucks" sign at the corner stamped the street as still fair-to-do, middle class. Driving by one would hardly give these houses a second glance. Yet it was here that Thomas E. Dewey lost his chance at the Presidency.

To have beaten Truman, Dewey should have swept streets like this one, with homes ranging in value between $15,000 and $20,000. Actually, he managed only to break even. Of the three precincts converging upon the West Boulevard Church, Truman carried one by eight votes, while Dewey squeezed through in the other two by seven apiece. Perhaps nowhere else in the whole country was the vote so close.

In the 1920's this area was overwhelmingly Republican. The fact that it has now become a break-even zone in the raging political war is one of the more portentous developments of the Roosevelt Revolution.

The Democrats generally have been thought of as the "poor man's party" and, at the outset of the New Deal, they certainly were mainly an aggregation of economic "have-nots." The rising prosperity of the last twenty years, however, has subtly transformed the internal make-up of the Democratic coalition, lifting many of its members to a "have" status. The 1950 census showed half again as many homeowners as in 1940, making more homeowners than apartment renters in the country for the first time since 1890. Despite the lapse of the G.I. Bill of Rights, college enrollment, as well, has been half again as high as before the war. The median family income has risen from $1,325 in 1939 to $3,420 in 1950.

In view of the usual sharp division in voting along economic lines, one might expect people to turn Republican as they mount to better income heights. There has indeed been some of that, particularly in the last few inflation-haunted years. But in the main, as the poor and underprivileged have prospered and climbed they have remained loyal to the Democratic party. The new middle class, which has developed over the last two decades, seems as Democratic by custom as the older middle class elements are instinctively Republican.

In the case of the three West Boulevard precincts in Cleveland, for example, an afternoon of random doorbell ringing the week after the 1948 election netted seven persons who had voted for Dewey and nine who had favored Truman. The Dewey ballots invariably were among the older folk, who had never voted anything but Republican. Mostly they were old-timers in the neighborhood. Some had retired. Several had been compelled to rent out the upper floor. But reduced economic circumstances had not altered their political allegiance. As one widow, who took in boarders, remarked, "I've lived to seventy as a Republican and I'll stay one."

Oddly, the Democratic voters, although primarily younger people, were almost as tradition-bound in their voting. Mainly skilled workers, a few teachers, a merchant, almost all had moved into the neighborhood in recent years, rising from poorer circumstances to home-owning status. With them they had brought political attitudes shaped by their struggle to mount the economic and social ladder.

"I'm a Democrat—that and labor," replied a diemaker, in explaining why he had voted for Truman. Another typical response, from the wife of a truck driver, was "We were high school kids during the depression but remember how tough it was." A second housewife, a few doors away, confessed she had not made up her mind how to vote until the last two weeks of the campaign. She finally decided for Truman because "it seemed the safe thing to do."

Truman rather than Dewey seemed the conservative candidate to many voters in these Cleveland precincts—a reaction I got in middle-class precincts in other cities and in the farm belt. The 1948 voting was done in the shadow of threatened depression and Dewey's vague campaign talks left deep fears about what he might do in case of economic collapse. The harshest fact about the 1948 voting from the Republican viewpoint was how many ordinarily conservative persons feared a Republican victory.

To an appreciable part of the electorate, the Democrats have replaced the Republicans as the party of prosperity. In Arlington, a fairly well-to-do suburb outside of Boston, I asked one middle-aged man why he hadn't turned Republican when he moved into suburban surroundings. He replied, "I own a nice home, have a new car and am much better off than my parents were. I've been a Democrat all my life. Why should I change?"

The essential difference between the Republican-rooted middle class and the newer Democratically inclined middle class is hardly one of conservatism versus liberalism, in the true meaning of these terms. What really separates these two middle classes is the factor of timing—of when each arrived at the state of middle-class blessedness. Because of the timing of their rise, the newer middle-class elements probably had tougher going during the depression and differ in occupational and business interests. Having achieved their gains in a period of expanding governmental authority, they are not as hostile to "Big Government" as the older middle-class elements. They also are apt to be of different ethnic or religious backgrounds.

The ethnic differences are not crucially important in themselves. What makes them so significant politically is that having come to this country in roughly the same period, the so-called "new" immigrants and their offspring shared common experiences in this country. All have been part of one of the epic population movements in history—of the upsurging out of the slums toward the middle class which has swept our major cities over the last fifty years and which still is going on.

To map the growth of almost any of our larger cities since the turn of the century is to map this upward, outward push of the masses toward the greener suburbs, propelling the older residents before them. And the story of the Democratic party in the big cities is really the story of the social and political revolution which marched along with this exodus from the slums.

The exodus was not accomplished in a single, mass evacuation, but through successive moves, from one neighborhood to the next. Each new neighborhood represented a higher rung on the social and economic ladder. And as they climbed, the masses were transformed. By the time the heights of middle-class status had been scaled, the immigrant generation which had begun the trek had died off or had become grandparents, relegated to the role of baby sitters, and a new native-born generation had come into its own.

A similar clocklike progression through successive frontier zones marked our westward expansion. So alike, in fact, are the dynamics of the two movements that one is justified in asking: Did the frontier ever really pass from American life? True, the supply of free land was virtually gone by 1890. But did the frontier really die with the exhaustion of free lands? Or did it merely sink from sight temporarily, to reappear in a new form in our developing industrial civilization?

2. The Old Tenement Trail

Possibly because it lacked the excitement of the Indian wars or because it still is so close to us, the saga of this twentieth-century odyssey of America's urban masses has gone unsung. Yet the parallels between the old western frontier and the new urban frontier are striking.

To Frederick Jackson Turner, who made American historians frontier-conscious, the ever-receding frontier was the zone of most rapid and effective Americanization. At the outer edge, "where civilization and savagery met," was where "men of all races were melted down and fused into a new race." Each new zone of frontier settlement was a "beginning all over again" which took Americans ever further away from dependence on Europe's economy and ways.

That holds equally true for the new frontier. For the urban masses each advance into a new neighborhood has also been a "beginning over again," which took them ever further from their European origins in the case of the immigrants, or, with Negroes, from the Plantation South. There has been much pooh-poohing of social climbing, without appreciation of the fact that it is a vital part of the Americanization process. The move to a "nicer" neighborhood would often be celebrated by a shortening or Anglicizing of names. Items of alien garb would be dropped; foreign accents would lighten. There would be more American food in the grocery stores, less orthodoxy in worship, more intermarriage with other ethnic elements and—as an ironical index of Americanization—more divorce.

The role of the railroads in opening up the Western lands has been duplicated first, by the subway and streetcars and, currently, by the automobile, in making ever newer housing accessible. The role of the pioneer woman was repeated in the immigrant mother who, with the sieve of drudgery, rescued the savings which enabled the family to climb to higher rental reaches. The immigrant mother was also the guardian of respectability on the urban frontier.

Like the Old West, the ever-changing urban frontier has been more "a form of society" than a geographical area. And as the story of America's social evolution could be read page by page in the successive frontier zones through which the pioneer pushed, so the march of the urban masses can be charted by tracing the neighborhoods through which these groups have climbed.

For example, when the late Arnold Bennett wrote his impressions of the United States in 1911, he closed his narrative with an account of a visit to New York's Lower East Side. The "astounding populousness" of the streets—some of which had more inhabitants per square foot than the most crowded areas of Bombay—roused the famous novelist to helpless indignation. On Rivington Street the "very architecture seemed to sweat humanity at every window and door." The thought of the "picturesque, feverish and appalling existences" endured by these "sickly-faced immortal creatures who lie closer than any wild animal would lie" stirred Bennett to protest to his American companions. They retorted, "Well, what are you going to do about it?"

The sequel to Bennett's visit can be read in any of several Old Tenement Trails which had their beginning in the dreary, cold-water flats of the East Side. The northward trail mounted first to Harlem or Yorkville, where hot water and steam heat were at least available, even if one had to bang the pipes before the janitor stoked the furnace. The next jump was out of Manhattan to the East Bronx, where trees stepped out of poems onto the streets; then to the West Bronx, crossing that Great Social Divide—the Grand Concourse—beyond which rolled true middle-class country. West of the Concourse, janitors were called superintendents; apartment houses had lift elevators and parquet floors, which needed no scrubbing. The migration then swept north paralleling the Concourse, the mink coats growing thicker as one mounted to Fordham Road and beyond.

Having run the length of both Manhattan and the Bronx, in recent years the Tenement Trail has swung abruptly eastward to the expensively filled-in marshes of Queens, which is currently the outermost fringe of New York's housing frontier. Here today will be found many of the "sickly-faced immortal creatures" whom Bennett saw. But how they have changed! Because they spent their youth in rootless tenements which knew no community life, they have been buying homes and have become doubly civic-minded in their eagerness to build a community in which their children might escape the deprivations of their own childhood.

From Rivington Street to Forest Hills in Queens is only a few miles. Historically, the spanning of that distance was a social revolution.

This same process of social exploration can be repeated with any of the former minority elements and in all of our larger cities. By going up and down the ladder of neighborhoods through which these different elements have climbed, one can see the progress they have made and the setbacks they have suffered—their clashes and reconciliations with other ethnic elements, and their assimilation into American society generally.

Do you wonder how the manners and habits of Negroes alter when they reach the middle class? In the North Bronx, around Gunhill Road, can be found a group of Negroes, mainly white collar and professional people, who have bought homes in recent years. As if feeling themselves on trial, they are as unlike the Harlem stereotype as imaginable in their habits. Their tastes in clothes and furnishings are sober. They pay cash at the neighborhood stores. At nearby Evander Childs High School their children rate tops scholastically. "Their drive to get an education is terrific," observes Dr. Hyman Alprin, Evander's principal. Oddly, every Negro child in the school takes Latin, as if seeking some mark of culture.

Or, one can follow the trek of the Irish in Boston, from the hilly streets of Charlestown out to Cambridge, on to Arlington and Newton; or of the Czechs in Chicago from South Lawndale, to Cicero and Berwyn. In Detroit the "uptown" upsurge has been eastward toward Grosse Point; in Milwaukee it has been northward along Lake Michigan and westward towards Granville.

If land hunger was the propelling force behind the agrarian frontier, the drive behind the urban frontier has been the hunger for social status. The changed nature of present-day political issues is largely a reflection of this contrast between the earlier agrarian frontier and its urban counterpart.

As the pioneers moved westward the obstacles they had to overcome were primarily physical and natural—breaking the sod in the semiarid plains, clearing the wilderness, driving railroad spikes across an untracked continent. Along the urban frontier the obstacles have been primarily man-made. The mountain barriers which have to be scaled are those of rents and restrictive covenants. Unemployment is the drought which could wither one's labors. The swiftly flowing rivers which have to be forded and bridged are those of class and social distinction, none the less treacherous because they are intangible.

The politics of westward expansion were bound to be sectional, since some parts of the country unavoidably lagged behind others and the newer settlements were often indebted, colonial offshoots of the older creditor areas. In contrast, the urban migration was bound to quicken class and social conflict, mirroring the uneven progress toward acceptance by different social groups.

In today's perspective, the Republican-dominated era can be said to have centered around one enormous historical fact: the spanning of the continent and the creation of a nation-wide economy. In the perspective of the future, we may look back upon today's Democratic era as an adventure in social unification, in the creation of the kind of nation-wide social structure which an industrialized civilization requires.

In any case, the reappearance of the frontier in a new urban form has been one of the most important political forces of our time. It explains the divisions between the old and new middle class. It generates the explosive force behind the civil rights issue, as will be shown in our next chapter. It also has been transforming the big-city political machines, dooming the old-style political boss.

For the Democratic machines the spoils of office over the last twenty years have been fat indeed. Yet the reigns of the bosses have been growing progressively shorter. Fewer and fewer are dying with their patronage boots on. Usually this is credited to the fact that a beneficent federal government has replaced the political clubhouse in dispensing relief and other favors. Of equal, if not greater, significance has been the simultaneous coming-of-age of most of the old underdog elements.

As its large families have grown to voting age and as it has developed its own leadership, each minority group has been demanding an ever-increasing share of political recognition. Today, the plight of the Irish Democratic bosses, who managed most of the big-city machines, is not unlike that of the wearied rulers of the British Empire, who are everywhere on the defensive before the rising "nationality" elements they once ruled.

Tammany Hall, once as Irish as St. Patrick, fell to the Italo-Americans in 1947. A year earlier the Kelly-Nash dynasty in Chicago was superseded by Jacob Arvey, a Jew. In 1949, a coalition of dissident Irish, Italo-Americans and Polish-Americans terminated the thirty-two year, "I Am the Law" role of Frank Hague in Jersey City.

Currently, the most dramatic illustration of this trend is the rise of the Italo-Americans. In 1948 eight Italo-Americans were elected to Congress, twice as many as in any previous year. Two of these congressmen were from Newark, which in 1949 named an Italo-American mayor. Hoboken, Passaic and Paterson are among the other larger New Jersey cities which have elected Italo-American mayors since the war's end. Compared with 1936 more than twice as many Italian names are answering the legislative roll calls in Pennsylvania, New Jersey, New York, Connecticut, Rhode Island and Massachusetts—the six states with the heaviest Italo-American concentrations.

The intensifying Irish-Italian feud which has accompanied this rise wracks not only the Democratic party but also the Catholic Church whose hierarchy in this country is mainly Irish. It rocks gangland, too. The struggle between James Pendergast and Charles Binaggio in Kansas City ended in violent murder. Of the gangsters cited by name in the Kefauver Crime Report, almost one half are clearly Italian.

That does not mean that Italians are peculiarly susceptible to criminal activity. The battle to control the nation's rackets now being pressed by Italo-American racketeers is part of the same "coming of age" process* which is reflected in the growing frequency of Italian names on big league baseball and college football teams. Until 1929 not a single Italian name was listed on Walter Camp's annual all-star football team. Since then there has been hardly a year in which there wasn't at least one Italian name on the all-star list.

How does an immigrant group erupt virtually simultaneously in so many varied ways? As a case history let us look at tiny Rhode Island where the Italo-Americans have registered their greatest advance in the country.

3. A Passion For Respectability

One blustery January morning in 1935 the great American flag which hangs in the lobby of the Chicago *Tribune* building was hastily pulled down. When it was put back some time

* Both Frank Costello and Joe Adonis have attributed their interest in politics to the desire to gain greater recognition for Italo-Americans.

later the flag had only forty-seven stars. On orders of Colonel Robert McCormick, the *Tribune*'s lordly publisher, one star had been removed.

McCormick was demonstrating his imperial displeasure at a Democratic *Putsch* in Rhode Island during which—in just fourteen and one-half minutes—the entire state government was reorganized and the venerable Republican judiciary was thrown out of office. In view of this outrage, the *Tribune* publisher felt Rhode Island was no longer worthy of statehood. Later that afternoon, when he was advised that mutilation of an American flag is punishable by a fine of ten to one hundred dollars or thirty days in jail, McCormick grudgingly ordered the star replaced, thus restoring Rhode Island to the union.

In Rhode Island the coup which provoked the McCormick ire has come to be known as "the bloodless revolution." It toppled Yankee political power in the state and marked the definite ascendancy of the Irish. For more than half a century Irish and Yankees had feuded implacably. Since neither was strong enough to rule alone, the balance of voting power rested with the state's two other major population elements— the French-Canadians and the more numerous Italo-Americans. In the 1934 election the Irish finally managed to win the Italo-Americans. This victory enabled them to put through their *Putsch*.

Originally the Italian vote in Rhode Island was Republican. How it was lost furnishes an instructive insight into what has been ailing the Republican party.

Some Italian immigrants voted Republican because Garibaldi and Mazzini had called themselves Republicans. By far the most important reason, however, was an almost literal faith in the McKinley slogan of the "full dinner pail," the belief that prosperity and the Republican party went together. As long as jobs were available, the bulk of immigrants were content to follow the suggestions of their *padroni* on how to vote.

The Republicans did little to hold this "Italian vote." In 1912 they gave the Italo-Americans their first political recognition by naming Antonio A. Capotosto, as assistant to the attorney general, a $1500-a-year post. The Republican leaders then seem to have felt they had done all that was needed. No other major Italo-American appointments were made.

This indifference to Italo-American aspirations might not have been particularly important before World War One, when the leading Italian politicians were mainly undertakers and the mass of inarticulate immigrants were still struggling to make ends meet. In 1910 the Providence Board of Trade could find only one schoolteacher of Italian descent in Providence's schools, only one policeman, one fireman and two lawyers. The war, however, lifted the status of the whole Italian group.

Wars have always boosted the lot of the underdog in this country. The youth who has risked his life for his country doesn't take to being treated as a second-class citizen when he comes home. More important than the psychological ferments which wars bring are the economic opportunities they open.

With more jobs than workers, wages soar. Occupations barred to particular minorities are flung open. Jobs become available for all members of a family capable of work. This is particularly important for the poor people with their larger families. The family overhead does not change much with three or four breadwinners instead of one, but the income spurts spectacularly. The more thrifty families save their surplus earnings. On the strength of those savings they keep their children in school longer, even pushing them on through college. They also flee their ethnic ghettos for nicer residential areas.

In Chicago, for example, the Italians were a static, immobile force until 1920. More than half of all of Chicago's Italians could be found within a two-mile radius of the city's center, where they first had settled. By 1930 the Italo-Americans had pushed out through the city, so that a majority lived 3.3 miles from the city's center.

Providence saw this same bursting of the confines of Federal Hill—as the local "Little Italy" is known—into Silver Lake and other better residential wards. Wherever they moved, the Italo-Americans displaced older groups. With the displacement came a struggle to wrest political control from the established politicians, who generally were Irish.

This new Italo-American mobility, in other words, was not only physical, but economic, social and political at the same time. The record of admittances to the Rhode Island bar is revealing. From 1906 through 1924 only eighteen Italo-American lawyers passed their bar examinations, an average of one a year. In 1925 alone seven made the grade. Thereafter the average ran four to five a year. Since 1947 the number of new Italo-American lawyers in Rhode Island has averaged eight a year. Italo-American political activity has quickened proportionately.

From these "rising young lawyers," who began to appear in the 1920's, were bound to come the future Italo-American political leaders. Yet the Republicans remained distinctly cool to them. The Democrats welcomed them eagerly but, at first, had little to offer beyond the publicity of being a candidate on a losing ticket. The Republicans controlled all federal and state patronage as well as much of the patronage in the cities, where voting was restricted by property qualifications.

The first break in the Republican power structure came in 1928, when the property qualification on voting was repealed. With an enlarged electorate, the Democrats swept most of the city councils in 1930. They shrewdly used the spoils of office to give recognition to all of Rhode Island's minorities—Italo-Americans, Jews, French-Canadians and others. With Roosevelt's triumph in 1932 the patronage at the disposal of the Democrats swelled anew. Again, it was used to cement the Democratic following among the minority groups in preparation for the assault on the Statehouse, which finally fell in 1934.

In 1928 a Providence tailor named Salvatore Pastore rented a store and enthusiastically started an "Al Smith for President" club. His oldest stepson, Lucio, became the club's secretary, but another stepson, John, would have no part of the venture. Studying law at night, John was still uncertain whether he wanted to be a Republican or a Democrat. By 1933, though, there no longer could be any doubt as to which party promised the greatest opportunity to a struggling young Italo-American lawyer. One Sunday John Pastore stood outside St. Bartholomew's Church until Tommy Testa, the rising Democratic power in the ward, came out. "I want to go into politics," Pastore told Testa, whom he had never met before.

Thirteen years later, at the age of thirty-nine, Pastore had become the first elected governor of Italian origin in the United States and, in 1950, the first Italo-American to sit in the U. S. Senate.

The details of Pastore's spectacular rise through Providence machine politics need not be recounted here. They are less important than two other factors: (1) his entrance into politics was timed perfectly to synchronize with the coming of age of the Italo-Americans, and (2) he, himself, was an almost perfect embodiment of that awakening.

Although as a child Pastore had to work after school, his family was not one of the poorest in Federal Hill. His father, Michele—unlike the usual run of unskilled, illiterate, Italian immigrants—learned the trade of tailoring in Italy before coming to America in 1899. Shortly after John was born, Michele opened a shop at home, moving to larger quarters at 14 Pallas Street, off Broadway, then a showplace street. The Pastores seemed well on their way up the economic ladder. Then, one May morning in 1916, John was awakened by his mother, screaming that his father was dying. The Pastore house touched on the residence of Dr. Horace Williams and Mrs. Pastore shrieked from the rear window, "Williams! Williams!" Illustrative of his respect for authority, even while fighting for his dying gasps, Michele rebuked his wife, "You must call him Dr. Williams or he won't come!"

John, then nine years old, dashed barefooted for the doctor. When they returned, Michele was dead.

Mrs. Pastore was carrying her fifth child. After its birth she moved back to Balbo Avenue, going to work as a seamstress in a department store. Federal Hill, at the time, was a pretty tough neighborhood. Street fights between Irish and Italian gangs were common. Whenever there was a "crime wave" the police would swoop down and round up anyone found loitering on the street corners. Mrs. Pastore's constant dread was that her children, lacking a father's stern hand, would grow up unruly and get into trouble. Middle-class respectability became a veritable passion with her.

One Christmas a neighbor sent the Pastores a food basket. John's mother made him return the basket and wept the rest of that day, mortified that anyone could think them in need of charity. "Make yourself liked, make people respect you" was her constant exhortation to her children. She discouraged their playing in the streets, took them to Mass regularly and dressed them more neatly than any of the neighbor's children. Even though it meant scrubbing and ironing twenty-odd shirts a week, on top of her work at the store, she made Johnny and his brothers wear fresh shirts every day.

His mother's influence can be seen today in Pastore's almost fantastic meticulousness in the matter of dress. He rarely will remove his jacket even while playing bridge in the privacy of a friend's home. He buys twenty-five neckties a year and often dons fresh shirts twice a day.

Such fastidiousness may seem an unimportant personal quirk. Actually, it holds the key to why some immigrant families rise out of the slums and others do not. In checking Pastore's career I searched out many of his childhood acquaintances. Those who have proven most successful—the doctors, lawyers, dentists and the like—were all subjected to the strictest discipline as children. To set them apart from the "tough" boys, their parents overdressed them to the point where many were considered "sissies." As for the boy who had been the "toughest kid on the block"—he was now an iceman.

The fact that Pastore, rather than some other Italo-American, became governor was a matter of luck. When Pastore entered politics the outstanding Italo-American in the state was Louis Cappelli, one of the first Italo-American lawyers to throw in with the Democrats. In 1932 Cappelli became the first Italo-American to run for a state-wide post, as secretary of state. In 1940, and again in 1942, when J. Howard McGrath was elected governor, Cappelli was his running mate. But lieutenant-governor was as high as the Irish leaders would permit any Italo-American to climb. Somewhat embittered, Cappelli settled for a post on the Superior Court. To replace him another Italian name was needed. Pastore, then an assistant to the attorney general, was chosen. Within a year McGrath had resigned to become solicitor general in Washington and Pastore found himself governor.

But for McGrath's resignation, one shrewd Rhode Island politician has estimated that the Italo-Americans might have had to wait another ten years before gaining the governorship. Although they didn't like the idea, the Irish Democratic leaders could not deny Pastore the chance to run for governor in his own right. When Pastore was born in 1907 the Italians were only one thirteenth of the state's population. By 1915, one of every five babies born in Rhode Island was Italo-American. In 1938, the state legislature declared Columbus Day a legal holiday, less in tribute to Columbus' discovery of America than to its discovery that every fifth voter in the state was Italo-American.

Over the years, as well, Italo-American economic power had grown steadily. In 1910 the Providence Board of Trade valued all the property owned by Italo-Americans in the city of Providence at $5,000,000 with another $4,000,000 in savings. Nearly forty years later, when I visited the Aurora club, the social center of Italo-Americans of wealth, I was given a list of a score of millionaire members. Included were the heads of four of the five leading construction companies in the state; the owners of purportedly the world's largest knife, ring and shoe buckle factories; a manufacturer of artificial flowers who had parlayed a $200 investment into a business grossing $700,000 a year. One of Rhode Island's leading portrait painters told me that about a fifth of all his commissions were coming from *nouveau-riche* Italo-Americans, where ten years previously he had none.

Most of these wealthy Italo-Americans were Republicans. But when Pastore ran for governor in 1946 they raised a special campaign fund of $60,000 for him. Had Pastore been running a few years earlier, before the Second World War solidified Italo-American economic power, he might not have had this financial backing. Nor would nearly so many Italo-Americans have been old enough to vote.

As it was, he squeaked through by a scanty 22,000 plurality, the slimmest for any Rhode Island governor since 1932. While the turnout of other voting groups dropped 10 per cent, Dave Cameron, the Providence *Journal*'s astute political reporter, calculated that the Italian vote jumped 5.5 per cent.

Pastore's later re-election as governor by the largest plurality in Rhode Island history and his overwhelming victory for U.S. Senator were tributes to his excellent record while in office. His 1946 victory, however, marked a dramatic joining of what can be put down as the prime essentials for the political arrival of any minority group—the growth to voting power of its heavy birth rates, plus a rising middle class to provide the necessary leadership and financial support.

4. Jacob's Ladder

What is often described as "The March of the Masses" is usually thought of as a radical, even insurrectionary development. The very phrase murmurs suggestions of mob rule and political lynching. Yet, with the Italo-Americans we have seen that their political upthrust was sparked not by hard times but by boom times. Their leadership came not from the most oppressed and discontented, but from those with the strongest middle-class drive.

The same pattern holds for other minority elements as well. None were stirred to political uprising when their grievances were heaviest. It was as they emerged from the social cellar and got their first whiffs of the fresher, middle-class air that their political spirits quickened. The key to the political progress of any minority element in this country would seem to lie in just this success in developing its own middle class. Sheer numbers alone are not sufficient for political power—witness the ineffectiveness so far of the Mexican-Americans in the Southwest. To be effective, numbers must be supported by economic, educational and social progress.

The climbing masses can hardly be described as a conservative force. But are they as radical as they appear? Since their emergence stirs class conflict, it is easy to view their rise as confirming Karl Marx's dire prophecies of class warfare. Actually we are witnessing an almost complete refutation of the Marxian thesis. Our class struggle, if it can be called that, arises not from the impoverishment of the masses but from their progress. It is evidence not of the failure of the American dream but of its successes.

Despite all the talk of monopolistic control of American economic life and the supposed end of opportunities, even

the most downtrodden elements have been able to climb.
And if the urban masses are challenging the *status quo,* their
challenge, essentially, is a demand for acceptance into our
predominantly middle-class society.

The trends of our times seem to be strengthening this
midde-class bias of American politics. Not so long ago political appointees were more often graduates of saloons and street
gangs than of universities. Old-timers in the Bronx can
remember an amusing pair of local Irish judges who not only
knew no law but couldn't even read. One of these judges,
after hearing a case, would take down a thick lawbook, pore
over it learnedly and announce, "This is a fine point of law,
I will reserve decision."

At lunchtime he would hotfoot it to a higher court, get
coached on the law, return and announce his verdict.

The second judge, equally unlettered, kept making a
spectacle of himself until he decided to imitate his colleague.
After hearing one case, he reached up to the nearby shelf,
took down a fat volume and thumbed through it. Making
quite a show of learned deliberation, he announced, "An
exceedingly fine point of law is involved. I think I'll reserve
decision." The spectators burst into laughter. The book the
judge had consulted so learnedly was the telephone directory.

Today college training or its equivalent is required for an
increasing proportion of appointments. To register its political strength a minority group has to have its own lawyers
or leaders with equivalent training. In turn, the broader the
middle-class base developed by any upclimbing element,
the more clamorous become its demands for political recognition.

Patronage is peculiarly important for minority groups,
involving much more than the mere spoils of office. Each
first appointment given a member of any underdog element
is a boost in that element's struggle for social acceptance.
It means that another barrier to their advance has been lifted,

another shut door has swung open. Whenever Roosevelt nominated a Negro to a white collar post in the federal government, for example, he transmitted a vicarious thrill to every young Negro who thought instinctively, "Maybe there's a place up there for me or my child."

The opening of these new opportunities, in turn, stimulates the political consciousness of the group, encouraging its leaders to eye the next highest post on the patronage ladder.

In most northern cities, the Democrats have actually developed a ladderlike succession of posts, through which the political progress of various minority elements is recognized. Just as one can judge how far any minority has climbed economically from its position on the residential ladder, so one can measure its effective political power by its place on the patronage ladder.

The earliest stirrings of any group usually are appeased by an appointment as assistant district attorney, which entails little more than that some members of the group be educated as lawyers. A county judgeship, on the other hand, requires a candidate who has succeeded in a lower post, a large enough vote to withstand the competing claims of other minority blocs, and the economic backing to finance a campaign. Similarly, with elected posts, the solid vote of an ethnic element may win an aldermanic district or a seat in the legislature or even in Congress. But no minority group can be said to have arrived politically until its members can appeal beyond their own ethnic boundaries, to win a county-wide or city-wide election.

This system of succession obstructs as well as advances minority progress. By compelling each element to serve its apprenticeship in lower posts, the machine bosses have been able to slow and temper the rise of the underdog elements. Largely through this system of seniority and by playing off one ethnic element against the others the Irish have been able to cling to a much larger representation among office-holders than their voting strength would warrant.

The emphasis on hyphenated candidates, or what has come to be known as "League of Nations" politics, is often condemned as "un-American." Yet it is really an integral part of the Americanization process, serving as a means through which minority elements are assimilated into the structure of government. This was true during the Republican era, when the sons of the Norwegian, Swedish and German immigrants banded together to wrest greater recognition from the Yankee bosses who then controlled the Republican party. It holds equally true today.

Another fundamental difference between the Republican and Democratic parties is that they have been the vehicles for the political advancement of quite different ethnic elements. The Republicans, by political necessity, became sensitive to the aspirations of the "old" immigrant elements, who settled so largely on the farms. The Democrats, in turn, have been more alive to the aspirations of the "new" immigrant elements who crowded the teeming cities.

The cultural chasm between the two parties can be measured roughly by the record of federal judicial appointments since 1920.

Harding, Coolidge and Hoover, in their twelve years in the White House, named 207 federal judges, not including members of the Supreme Court or territorial judges. The religious background of 21 of these judges is unrecorded. Of the others, 170 were Protestants, 8 were Catholic and another 8 were Jewish.

In sharp contrast, of 197 judicial appointments made by Roosevelt, 52 were Catholic and 7 were Jewish. The religion of 6 appointees is unrecorded. Through the summer of 1951 Truman had made 127 judicial appointments of which 38 were Catholic, 12 were Jewish and 2 unrecorded as to religious background.

Through the Republican period, in summation, one out of every twenty-five appointments went to a Catholic; under Roosevelt and Truman more than one out of four. In some parts of the country no Catholic had ever been named federal judge before 1933.

A glance over the names of the Roosevelt-Truman appointments reveals that the overwhelming bulk of Catholic appointments are Irish, a vivid testimonial of the extent to which the Irish have dominated the Democratic party. Truman's appointments, however, show a significant quickening of the pace of recognition for non-Irish elements. Roosevelt named the first Italo-American, Matthew Abruzzo, to the federal bench in 1936; he appointed the first Negro federal judges, William C. Hastie and Herman E. Moore during his second term.

Truman promoted both Hastie and Moore, naming a third Negro to the federal bench, Irvin C. Mollison. Truman also appointed two more Italo-Americans, Paul Rao and Alfred Modarelli; and the first Polish-American, Arthur A. Koscinski. Truman has also named more Jewish judges than Roosevelt, who made no more Jewish appointments than his Republican predecessors.

Through the 1920's the Republicans generally were either unaware of or indifferent to the aspirations of the climbing urban masses. This apathy no longer holds. Particularly in the Eastern states, Republican governors now are competing vigorously for the vote of the urban minorities. Governor Alfred Driscoll made New Jersey the first state to end segregation in its militia. New York State Republicans are no less careful than the Democrats to "balance" their ticket with an Italian and Jewish name. The 1950 New York City mayoralty election was marked by the unusual spectacle of all four parties having Italo-American candidates.

For the immediate future, the prospects point to an intensification of "League of Nations" politics. The closeness of recent elections and the more vigorous competition of the parties should insure that. In addition, virtually none of the underdog groups has obtained the full recognition of its numbers. The Polish-Americans and Italo-Americans are still enlarging their proportions of the electorate. The migration from the South is increasing Negro numbers in the Northern cities far more rapidly than the white population. Some elements which have not yet developed their own middle-class spokesmen will be doing so in the coming years.

Time, inevitably, will narrow the gap between the make-up of the governing groups and the ethnic elements they command. This will occur not only in our political parties, but in labor unions, in the churches, in teaching and other professions, in short throughout society.

To sum up, despite the revolutionary changes it brought, the Roosevelt Revolution appears to have strengthened rather than weakened the traditional middle-class basis of American politics. The drive behind the climbing urban masses remains the essentially conservative hunger for middle-class social standing. The leadership of most of the former minority elements is mainly a middle-class leadership. The political apprenticeship each rising element has to serve also makes these elements more dependent on their ability to create a middle-class economic base, from which the resources can be drawn to climb still higher on the ladder.

The fact that both major parties are now actively competing for the vote of the various minority elements holds out the further promise that, in time, the cultural differences which now divide the big-city Democratic following from the Republicans will be steadily blurred. How quickly that happens will depend largely on another development of the urban frontier, to which we now turn—the agitation over civil rights.

5

Civil Rights Melting Pot

1. The Negro Problem Changes

In 1945 New York became the first state to enact legislation outlawing discrimination in employment because of race, creed, color or nationality. Six states and two dozen cities have followed suit, so that fair employment practices laws now cover about one fourth of the total population. Going beyond employment, the scope of civil rights legislation has been expanded to include educational practices, the National Guard, municipal employment, housing built with public funds and discrimination in hotels, theaters and other places of public accommodation.

If these statutes have been enacted in the last seven years, it has not been because there is more discrimination in the United States than in previous years. Probably there is less. These laws are on the statute books because those who suffered discrimination in the past—the children of the "micks," "wops," "kikes," "niggers," "polocks" and other abused groups—are in the mood, and at last have the political strength, to do something about it.

Civil rights are popularly thought of as a Negro problem. But what makes the civil rights issue so explosive is not simply that Harlem is on the march. The significant fact is that Harlem's awakening coincides with the "coming of age" of all the other urban underdogs. The old darky, laboring through rows of cotton, has been replaced by the new

Negro on the assembly line or in the law office. And, simultaneously, the sluggish, submissive immigrant has passed from the American scene and his place has been taken by a new native-born generation—most of whom have gone through high school, and who are determined that the insults and indignities they suffered will not be visited upon their children.

The old minorities have become the new majority—that sums up the change which has taken place in our Northern cities. Irish, Jews, Poles, Czechs, Scandinavians, Italians, Greeks: the elements differ from place to place, but in the main the Democratic strength in the North has been drawn from the children and grandchildren of these one-time immigrant groups, plus Negroes, hillbillies and poor whites up from the South and border states. Has any political party ever had a more heterogeneous following? Can such dissimilar, clashing elements remain a united political force?

That question rather than the Negro vote alone represents the political stakes of the civil rights issue. Will the spirit of Ku Kluxism flare anew among the older American elements? What of the century-old, Catholic-Protestant hatred? Will the children of the immigrants turn upon the Negro as a threat to their own harshly earned social status? Or, having known the pains of discrimination, will they succeed, where the "old" Americans have repeatedly failed, in finding some solution to our most difficult social problem—that of color.

In the long run the fate of the Roosevelt coalition is likely to hinge upon the outcome of this battle for racial and religious tolerance among its own elements.

The test is peculiarly a test of the urban frontier. Migration brought all these elements together in the cities in the first place. Their frictions today arise from rubbing against one another, as they climb the social ladder simultaneously. A generation ago, when these underdog elements were still sunk in poverty, they lived in segregated ghettos and had relatively little to do with one another. Each was concerned almost exclusively with its own struggle for acceptance. Now that all have broken out of their molds of segregation to some degree, they face a double challenge—not only of continuing their separate advance, but also of finding a new pattern for living together.

With the appearance of the Negro on the urban ladder, the Negro problem has been transformed. Wherever he appears, the Negro, of course, carries with him his own peculiar struggle for emancipation from the shackles of color. But in the Northern and Western cities the Negro has also been the latest immigrant, replacing the Europeans as the primary source of cheap labor. In his current struggle to climb the social and occupational ladder, the Black Immigrant and his children are fighting the same struggle for economic and social advancement which all the earlier immigrant elements have had to wage.

Through the Negro, in other words, two of the greatest of American social conflicts are being fused—the battle to liquidate the heritage of slavery, and the immigrant's striving to become Americanized and assimilated. It is the mixture of these two conflicts—once quite distinct—which is boiling the civil rights melting pot so furiously.

The resulting tensions will be better appreciated if we bear in mind the distinctive dynamics of the urban frontier. Where the western frontier was an escape for the least successful, the climbing trek in the cities has always been led by the most enterprising and most successful. As the better income families pulled out for newer housing on the city's outskirts, landlords in old neighborhoods would decide it no longer paid to keep up their properties. Housing would deteriorate, rentals would drop, bringing in still poorer people and pushing out all who could make the next rental grade.

Once this cycle of deterioration got under way, it quickly acquired its own momentum. The poorer the neighborhood the greater the danger that one's sons would be drawn into street gangs and become criminals. An even more impelling drive to get out would be the presence in the family of a girl nearing marriageable age. In a "nicer" neighborhood she would meet "better class" boys, and run less risk of wedding into the trap of poverty.

The rhythm of the urban frontier, in short, has been the rhythm of the crowd running away from itself, with neighborhoods booming and declining in a regular cycle as the masses chased through them. At their heels, as each group struggled upward, could always be felt the pressure of the next climbing group threatening to overtake and engulf them. There was no standing still. Either one climbed or one fell victim to the pursuing slum.

The main reason why city slums seem self-perpetuating is that the strong fight constantly to leave, while those remain who have lost the struggle to climb. Slums, crime and broken homes go together in a single process of grim selection. The battle to climb is fought as a family unit. The weaker the ties of a family the greater its chances of being stranded.

The urban frontier has always seethed with the frustrations of those left behind and the aspirations of those beginning to rise. In the past the colliding groups were primarily white. The explosive new element which accompanies the climbing Negro is the added tension of color. Wherever he moves, the Negro whips up the already existing fears of being engulfed in a slum. He spurs the already strong tendencies of the older residents to take flight. The Negro's own struggle for acceptance is aggravated. So is the despair of those white residents who must stay behind, while relatives and friends move to "nicer" neighborhoods of social prestige.

The fact that the Negro has been caught up in the migration from the slums, which was described in the previous chapter, must be put down as another of the more far-reaching changes unloosed by the Roosevelt Revolution.

Probably never again will the march of America's masses be free of the frictions of color. The forces of racial and economic protest in our cities can be expected to swirl together —either to merge their grievances in a new form of urban radicalism or to vent their fury on one another in mutual hostility.

One can already see this new belt of political insurgency taking shape in our larger cities, the crude equivalent for our times of the old zone of agrarian protest in the West. The insurgency of the Grangers and Populists followed the line of newest settlement, which was where the frustrations of the frontier fell most heavily. Farmers there had not had time to get rooted financially; they were most distant from markets, or most vulnerable to crop failure, having pushed beyond the precarious zone of adequate rainfall.

The frustrations of the urban frontier, however, fall most heavily on the older residential areas, along the line where expanding Negro settlement pushes in on those unable to rise higher on the social ladder. Along this racial "middle border," where the rainfall of social status is so uncertain, the emotions stirred by the civil rights issue assume their most violent form. Most of the anti-Negro incidents of recent years have occurred in this zone of new Negro residential penetration. Here, also, will be found the boldest experiments in racial relations.

Time will show whether such a zone of political protest actually is taking shape in our cities. An analysis of Henry Wallace's vote, however, shows that his strongest following came in exactly such economically depressed, transitional racial zones.

2. An Experiment in Race Relations

In February, 1948, something of a national sensation was created by an obscure, young Bronx lawyer, named Leo Isacson. Running for Congress under the Wallace banner,

Isacson trounced his Democratic opponent in staunchly Democratic territory by a two to one majority. The incident, which ruined the Florida vacation of Democratic boss Ed Flynn, was generally explained away as a protest against Truman's Palestine policy, the district being about 40 per cent Jewish. What this explanation overlooked was that the East Bronx where Isacson swept to victory—and where Wallace later got one of every five votes cast—is a dying Jewish neighborhod where the chill of being trapped penetrates everywhere.

In 1935 Clifford Odets used the East Bronx as a setting for his *Awake and Sing,* a tragedy of a Jewish family whose social rise had been cut short by the depression. Then, although it had begun to deteriorate economically, the East Bronx was still fairly homogeneous racially. As late as 1938 its school population was only 3 per cent Negro. Over the next dozen years, though, out of Harlem poured something like 50,000 Negroes and another 75,000 Puerto Ricans. The mold of residential segregation was abruptly smashed, scores of apartment houses becoming mixed in their occupants.

Between 1940 and 1948, the years of the heaviest Negro-Puerto Rican inpouring, juvenile arrests tripled. One housewife I interviewed recalled this period as "a time when we couldn't sleep because of street rows. If we complained to the police, they told us, 'Madam, we're doing everything we can. We even have orders to shoot to kill.'"

Those who could fled the area. Their flight, in turn, quickened the influx, trapping those who could not flee. In one public school in a single year there was an almost complete turnover of the student body, from predominantly German and Jewish in background to Negro and Puerto Rican. "The principal was ready to throw himself out of the window," recalled Frank Whalen, the associate superintendent in the area. "We had to put in a new principal and a whole new staff of teachers."

By 1948 the East Bronx had become an almost perfect example of the new zone of political insurgency developing in our larger cities.

In a day's random interviewing, I could not find a single family which was not desperate to get out of the area. With their wartime savings some could afford higher rentals but at that time no housing was open anywhere in the city. Others would not have been able to move even if housing were available.

One woman, in her late thirties, had moved in with her parents "temporarily" on her marriage fifteen years before. She and her husband were still living with her parents. They had never had a home of their own. "I don't worry about my boy," she said, "but my daughter is now twelve years old and we must get into a better neighborhod soon." Later I ran into her husband. He had taken a second job at night, selling dresses, to earn enough to be able to move when housing opened up.

Two other mothers still escorted eleven-year-olds to and from school.

Mention of politics brought angry outbursts: over rising prices—"our living standards are lower now than during the war"—against landlords, about the housing shortage, over Palestine. With one exception all who said they would vote for Wallace added, "if only Eisenhower were running," indicating clearly their mood was primarily one of political protest. An Irish woman, whose three children attended parochial school, explained, "Everyone in the house voted for Isacson. We probably will vote for Wallace. We're not Communists. We want to give someone else a chance."

In other cities conditions like those in the East Bronx have exploded into race riots. Here, though, the result has been an organized effort to develop a segregation-free community. Generally, once Negroes move into an area, the whites move out and the area soon becomes solidly black. In the East

Bronx a concerted effort is being made to prevent the creation of such a black belt.

At Morris High School, the residential zone has been redrawn to bring in more white children—perhaps the first time this has been done in any American city. Usually, school districts are rezoned to take white children out of a school with large numbers of Negroes. The man mainly responsible for the new approach is Dr. Jacob Bernstein, the mild-toned, graying principal of Morris. A mixed school works best, Dr. Bernstein believes, when slightly more white than colored. "If Negroes make up only 10 to 15 per cent of the students they feel insecure and there is trouble," he explained. "When the percentage swings to where it is three-fourths or more Negro there is trouble again because the Negroes feel they are in a Jim Crow school."

Early in 1948 Morris' student body had become almost 60 per cent Negro and 20 per cent Puerto Rican. By 1951 Bernstein had brought the complexion of the school down to 30 per cent Negro and 12 per cent Puerto Rican.

A deliberate program has been pressed at Morris to get white and colored children to intermingle. To break down inhibitions against dancing together, students are brought together at first through square and folk dances. Co-operative homework projects are assigned to mixed students in the hope that it will take them into one another's homes. The job placement service makes recommendations solely on the basis of ability. If a Negro child is refused a particular job, Bernstein will not send a white child instead. One insurance company rejected two Negro stenographers on the ground that other employees would refuse to work alongside of them. Bernstein persuaded the company to hire the girls for a six months' trial. No difficulties developed.

Since 1946 one East Bronx department store, the Sachs Quality Store, has maintained a teen-age canteen where boys and girls of diverse complexions get together on Saturday nights. The children dance to phonograph records, colored and white children mixing freely. At one party several Negro girls tried to coax a shy, Negro lad out of a corner. Finally, a blonde, blue-eyed, Irish girl took him firmly by the arm and put him through his first waltz.

The dances, which are chaperoned by adults, are held in the department store's community auditorium, which is used on weekdays by varied community groups. Free coffee and cake are served all comers. The day I visited the auditorium the walls were hung with prize-winning posters in a racial relations contest held in nearby schools.

That this store has taken on the sale of tolerance as a side line can be credited to Hitler. In the late 1930's a strong Coughlinite Christian Front movement developed among the poor Irish in the South Bronx under the leadership of Joe McWilliams. Spreading Hitler's anti-Semitic propaganda, McWilliams organized demonstrations picketing Jewish-owned stores. With other merchants and community leaders, Sachs joined in forming a South Bronx Committee on Tolerance. McWilliams had hardly been driven from the Bronx when the influx of Negroes and Puerto Ricans began.

"We decided that if we weren't hypocrites," recalls Phil Michaels, the Sachs store manager, "we would have to show we believed as strongly in civil rights for Negroes as for ourselves against the Christian Front."

"We also wanted to keep the Bronx from becoming another Harlem," added Will Sachs. "We remembered the race riots in Harlem in 1935 because white storeowners wouldn't hire Negroes. We didn't wait to be pressured into employing Negroes. We went out and recruited them."

Tolerance is not easily measured and it is impossible to say how much progress has really been made in the East Bronx. Most of the people living in the area are unaware that they are part of a living experiment in race relations. Living side by side with Negroes has lifted some prejudices. At one school, where Negroes and Puerto Ricans are predominant, a white woman was elected president of the Parents Association. Shortly afterward she had to call the members of her executive committee together and invited them to her home. At first her neighbors were aghast at the sight of Negroes and Puerto Ricans coming into a white woman's house. Soon it became an accepted practice to rotate meetings, holding them in a different member's house, regardless of race or color.

As housing has opened elsewhere in the Bronx and Queens, white families have tended to flee from the East Bronx. New municipal housing is being erected in the area. By law such projects are open to whites and Negroes alike. Some East Bronx leaders want to go further. They have proposed the use of quotas to keep the new housing projects 60 per cent white. Conceding that quotas have always been a hated weapon of discrimination, George Gregory, the director of Forest Neighborhood House, argues, "Quotas can also be made a weapon of tolerance to avoid the creation of black ghettos."

Despite these and other efforts the odds are almost overwhelming that in time the East Bronx will become another Harlem. Still, the significance of what is being attempted there should not be lost sight of. Although it may fail it does point up a problem, which is growing steadily more acute and for which no solution is even in sight.

3. The Great Migration

Since the war's end in all our major cities Negroes have been breaking out of their overcrowded black belts into new residential areas. Wherever they have penetrated they have raised the same question—are the whites to flee all these areas, creating a host of new black ghettos, or can a new frame of tolerance be worked out under which Negroes and whites can dwell side by side?

In some cities the emerging Negroes have been met by bombings and fiery crosses. The sale to Negroes of homes in white neighborhoods has provoked at least one murder and several small-scale race riots, such as the one which flared last year in Cicero, Illinois. These incidents may have slowed Negro infiltration but they have not halted it.

Many areas into which Negroes are moving will become black belts. Yet, it is also unlikely that the old pattern of residential segregation ever will be fully restored. Even as white families try to run away from the Negroes, some Negroes will be running along with them.

The basic fact is that in our major cities—Chicago, Detroit, Cleveland, Los Angeles—the Negroes have advanced sufficiently economically so that appreciable numbers will continue to be strung along the social ladder, climbing alongside of the less successful whites.

By 1946, according to U.S. Census estimates, 85,000 Negro families in Northern cities were earning $5,000 or more a year. The full employment of the postwar period has enabled the Negroes to keep the foothold in heavy industry which they obtained during the war. The general increase of purchasing power among the Negro masses continues to lift ever larger numbers of Negroes into the middle class.

With every other minority element the strengthening of its middle class has intensified the urge both to climb socially and to gain greater political recognition. Negroes can be expected to behave the same way.

As it is, the flight of better income families to the suburbs already has left sizable blighted areas in the heart of all of our larger cities. These blighted areas have become the breeding ground of the current alliance of gamblers and politicians. In many of these areas racketeering is almost the only form of "free enterprise" left to attract the more ambitious youths.

To the middle-class aspirations which propel the Negro up the social ladder must be added the pressures of Negroes migrating from the South and crowding into already bursting black belts. Over the last census decade alone the number of Negroes outside the South leaped almost 60 per cent, from 2,960,000 to 4,600,000. In the industrial states, which have drawn almost all of this migration, the number of nonwhites, predominantly Negroes, has risen five to ten times as rapidly as the white population:

State	% Non-White Rise	% White Rise
Michigan	109	18
California	106	51
Oregon	73	39
Washington	64	36
Connecticut	62	16
Illinois	60	8
New York	55	8
Indiana	44	14
Pennsylvania	38	4
Ohio	38	14
Missouri	28	3

(Based on preliminary reports of the 1950 Census.)

Nor have the forces behind this Great Migration of the Negroes spent themselves. In the South the mechanization of agriculture, which displaced more than 500,000 Negroes between 1940 and 1950, continues to gain momentum. Eventually, the bulk of the Negroes in the country must expect to be drawn off the land into a nonagricultural economy. This urbanization of the Negro, which is going on apace in both the South and North, lends special urgency to the civil rights issue.

The established code of Negro-white relations in the South is primarily a rural one, reflecting the paternalistic relationship of master and black on the plantation. There, the Negro had a definite economic place, which, even if harsh, was at least fairly assured. In the cities, the relationship of

Negroes and whites is impersonal, in the South as in the North. Also, the Negro is being forced to find a new place for himself economically, and discrimination is far more critical in urban than rural living.

In many industries, for example, one cannot get a job unless one belongs to a trade union. Should unions be allowed to restrict their membership because of racial or ethnic prejudice? To rise on the occupational ladder the members of any minority element must have the opportunity to acquire skills at lower working levels. If Negroes are denied vocational training, as in many colored high schools in the South, or if they are barred from apprenticeship training, their opportunities are prejudiced for years to come.

The more complex society becomes the more the relations of groups and individuals become a matter of regulation by law. The color problem is no different. As a larger proportion of the Negro population is drawn into industrialized life, it becomes ever more important for Negroes to have their rights defined by law.

The displacement of the Negro from the agricultural South has transformed the Negro problem in still another way. What was once the peculiar concern of the South has become a national problem. As a result of the last war, areas of the country which never knew more than a few Negroes, suddenly acquired heavy black concentrations. Between 1940 and 1950 the number of Negroes in Los Angeles nearly tripled; in San Francisco it increased nearly ten times, and in Portland, Oregon, five times.

When Southerners cry, "Leave us alone to handle our racial problem in our own way," they fail to realize that the Negro is no longer merely *their* problem. The basic weakness of States' rights, as a means of dealing with race, lies in its assumption that the color question is still a local matter, when in fact it has become nation-wide in scope.

Racial relations in the North may become even more combustible than they are in the South. The South has a safety valve for its racial tensions. If Negroes refuse to accommodate themselves to segregation they can get out—go North. But the Northern and Western cities cannot shift the burden. They represent the end of the racial line.

4. *"Balance of Power"?*

That the Democratic party should have become the political arena for this new national color problem may seem strange at first thought. Obviously, no more violent political opposites could be found than the Southern "Bourbon" and Northern Negro. For them ever to have been brought together in the same party seems to defy all logic.

The mystery disappears if we bear in mind that the controlling force shaping the Negro's new political role has been the Great Migration from the South which began with the First World War. While nine of every ten Negroes in the country still lived in the South, as at the turn of the century, the Negro remained suppressed politically, submerged hopelessly beneath the hatreds of the Civil War and Reconstruction. The Great Migration not only brought the Negro back into national politics, but moved him into a wholly new orbit of social, economic and political conflict.

Once in the Northern cities, as we have seen, the Negro got caught up in the same fight to rise out of the slums which agitated all of the urban masses. If he was not to be isolated racially in his struggle to rise on the social ladder, his politics had to become the politics of the other climbing masses.

The basic reason why the Republicans have been unable to recapture the Negro vote lies in their inability to identify themselves with the climbing aspirations of the black masses. Dewey's record in behalf of the Negro surpassed that of any previous New York governor. The first governor to sign a fair employment practice law, he made more Negro appointments than any of his predecessors. He saw to it that more of the liquor licenses issued in Harlem went to Negroes instead of white proprietors. But, if Dewey could appeal to the Negro's race consciousness, he could not surmount the Negro's consciousness of being part of the lower economic class.

Instead of weakening with time, the Negro's attachment to the Democratic party has been growing stronger. In some cities like Detroit, Negro wards have been turning in heavier pluralities than any other Democratic voting element. The 1950 elections saw less of a break among Negroes than among any other major group in the Roosevelt coalition.

Senator Taft, for example, was able to cut in heavily upon organized labor and other ardent Roosevelt supporters. But in eight Negro wards in Cincinnati, Toledo and Cleveland, Taft got fewer votes than Dewey did.

Taft's victory, in the face of Negro opposition, raises the question whether the so-called "balance of power" strategy of Negro political leaders is working out as they planned. According to this theory, the Negro vote is so large and so strategically spread through the states with the big electoral votes that it constitutes the margin of victory in any close Presidential race. The strategy evolved by Negro leaders was to use this balance of power to force both major parties to compete for the Negro vote.

Actually, though, the Negro vote has not been balanced between both parties. It has virtually solidified in the Democratic party. At the same time some Republicans like Taft and Senator Richard Nixon of California have been able to win handily with the bulk of Negroes against them.

In their own states, neither Taft nor Nixon has much to lose politically by alienating the Negroes. They may decide that it is smarter politics for the Republicans to seek coalition with the conservative Southerners than to try to recapture the Negroes.

Political realignment is a two-edged sword. To the degree

that the Negro becomes entrenched in the Democratic party, to that degree the Republicans can be expected to seek to put together a victorious coalition without Negro support.

Up to now the northward Negro migration has unquestionably swelled the Democratic voting strength in the cities. The long run consequences of further migration are not so clear. The few referendums on civil rights issues which have been held indicate that expanding Negro numbers may aggravate anti-Negro prejudice outside the South.

In California a proposal for an FEPC law was approved by only 30 per cent of the voters in 1946. The defeat has been blamed on the fact that the proposal was sponsored by extremist leftist groups. But the sharpness with which the vote divided along class and social lines leaves little doubt that the referendum was a revealing test of the intensity of racial prejudice.

In Los Angeles I found a number of precincts where the vote broke with dramatic abruptness. On one side of a street a precinct would show a heavy majority for FEPC. On the other side of the same street another precinct would be violently opposed. Searching out these streets I found that they marked off the borders of Negro residential expansion. The precincts in which Negroes were threatening to buy homes showed the widest difference between their support of Truman and FEPC. Several gave Truman as much as two thirds of their vote and FEPC only one vote of every four.

Significantly, in all of these precincts the residents were of "older American" stock. Where Negro penetration cut into largely Jewish or Mexican areas, the result was a heavy vote for FEPC. The five precincts in all Los Angeles which Wallace carried were heavily Jewish areas into which Negroes had begun to move (much like the East Bronx). Each of these five precincts voted more than 75 per cent for civil rights. None of the five gave Dewey more than 10 per cent of the vote.

Clearly, the political impact of the civil rights issue varies sharply with the voter's ethnic background. Among Negroes, Mexicans and Jews, their support of FEPC and of the Democratic party does not differ much. Other Democratic voters, from Southern and Midwestern states, tend to break strongly against FEPC. Bell Gardens, inhabited mainly by Okies, gave Truman nearly three fourths of its vote, but tallied only 27 per cent for FEPC.

In contrast to this division among the Democrats, opposition to FEPC apparently solidifies the Republican ranks. Of more than 3,000 precincts in Los Angeles, I could find only eleven which Dewey carried in 1948 and which showed a majority for FEPC. All eleven are heavily Jewish. No non-Jewish Republican precinct showed a majority for FEPC. At least as far as Los Angeles is concerned, the traditional Republican sympathy for the Negro has largely vanished.

San Francisco reveals a similar pattern. The staunchest Republican area in the city, the Twenty-first District, voted 63 per cent for Dewey, 69 per cent against FEPC and 70 per cent for Nixon against Helen Douglas in 1950. The precincts showing a majority for civil rights were Negro, Chinese or Mexican, while the heaviest break against FEPC came among Democratic voters of Irish background.

Curiously the attitude of the San Francisco Irish toward FEPC (unlike other ethnic groups) does not seem to change with economic status. A sampling of two groups of predominantly Irish precincts, one moderate and the other higher in income, shows little difference in the FEPC vote. Among Italo-Americans, on the other hand, the civil rights vote was almost twice as heavy in the low as in the upper income precincts.

The attitude of the Irish in San Francisco should not be taken as typical, necessarily, of the Irish all over the country. Those who settled in San Francisco did not experience the discrimination which the Irish in New England had to endure.

Also, Irish workers in San Francisco have a long tradition of hostility to Chinese and Japanese immigration.

The same tendency for the Democratic vote to split over civil rights was evident in Portland, Oregon, where an ordinance forbidding discrimination in places of public accommodation was defeated in 1950 by 74,444 to 61,058. Portland's Republicans, however, seem more tolerant racially than their California cousins. Of sixty-two Portland precincts which went 50 per cent or better for the civil rights ordinance, twenty-five were carried by Dewey in 1948. There were only four Republican precincts among the twenty-nine, voting less than 35 per cent for the civil rights ordinance.

Of these twenty-nine precincts, with the lowest civil rights vote, all but three voted strongly in favor of public housing in 1949. The pro-housing precincts were also heavily for Truman. The economic ties binding Portland's Democratic voters are clearly stronger than the bonds of racial tolerance.

These civil rights votes leave little doubt that the struggle for racial and religious tolerance among the varied Democratic elements is anything but won. Our analysis of the 1936 election showed that one major factor in the formation of the Roosevelt coalition was the suppression of the racial and religious antagonisms among the urban masses under their stronger feeling of common economic interest. Today, wherever the Negro appears on the urban ladder, he puts to test the relative strengths of the economic ties binding the Roosevelt elements and the racial prejudices tugging them apart.

Which will prove stronger ultimately cannot be foretold today. Although the Negro, stirring as he does the same issues wherever he migrates, is serving as a nationalizing force in American politics, it is not yet clear whether he will prove a unifying or disrupting influence. The answer will depend on what is done in race relations in both the North and South.

Roughly a third of our 15,500,000 Negroes live outside

the South today. Over the next two decades it is possible that nearly half of our Negroes will come to live north and west of the Mason-Dixon line. If this thinning of Negro numbers in the South encourages the growth of tolerance there, then the spread of Negroes through the country will prove a unifying force. Solution of the Negro problem will become attainable. But, if as Negroes disperse through state after state, the South remains "solid" and "unreconstructed," then the political strains could prove intolerable.

In which direction is the South moving, toward a new national balance or toward a perpetuation of the old sectional unbalance? We shall try to judge that in the next chapter.

6

The Conservative Revolution

1. Who Beat Frank Graham?

Almost everywhere in the South today one sees evidence of economic and social revolution. Cattle graze in fields once devoted exclusively to cotton and tobacco. Tractors chug past abandoned tenant shacks, dramatizing the fact that machines are at last freeing the South from its ancient dependence on cheap, subservient hand labor. Each tractor replaces from two to five families; each cotton picker harvests as much cotton as twenty to thirty hand pickers. In another decade or two, some experts estimate, the South will need only one half to one third of its present labor to plant and harvest its crops.

In the cities into which those displaced from the land are drifting the pace of change seems equally hectic. One statistician has figured that for every working day since 1940 several new plants have opened in the eleven Southern states. Roughly a million new jobs have been created in manufacturing employment and another million new jobs in trade. Bank deposits have quadrupled. Average incomes have tripled.

Revolutions are supposed to sweep aside the old order and to usher in a new scheme of things. The revolution currently reshaping Dixie Land has been making the South more not less conservative politically.

For our study three aspects of this conservative revolution are particularly significant—the failure of labor's Southern organizing drive, the rise of a new, politically insurgent middle class in the Southern cities, and the paradox of a dramatic extension of Negro rights being accompanied by an intensification of the race issue politically.

The swirling together of these three trends was primarily responsible for the defeat two years ago of Senators Frank P. Graham in North Carolina and Claude Pepper in Florida, the most crushing setbacks Southern liberalism has suffered since the coming of Franklin Roosevelt.

Graham's defeat was the more spectacular. No man had been more representative of liberalism in Dixie Land. Under his presidency the University of North Carolina had become the pioneering center for courageous self-examination of the South and its problems. Graham had battled for labor's right to organize when to do so was to invite being branded a Bolshevik. A devout Christian, who neither smoked, drank nor cussed, he had fought efforts to forbid the teaching of evolution in North Carolina and had defended Bertrand Russell's right to speak his atheistic philosophy. As a member of President Truman's Civil Rights Commission, along with Mrs. M. E. Tilley, Graham had represented what was believed to be the more enlightened South.

As for North Carolina, for decades every book on the South had pointed to the Tarheel State as the inspiring exception. More industrialized than any other Southern state, it had gone furthest in narrowing the gap in expenditures for white and Negro schools; its poll tax as a prerequisite for voting was lifted in 1920; not for fifty years had the issue of white supremacy been raised in an election campaign. Having had fewer slaves and less of a landed aristocracy in the pre-Civil War period, North Carolina was supposed to be relatively free of race fixations.

This reputation seemed borne out by the May 27, 1950 primary, in which Graham ran 53,000 votes ahead of his closest opponent and came within one per cent of the needed majority. On June 24, however, Graham was defeated by 18,000 votes. What had happened to North Carolina's famed progressiveness in those few weeks?

After the first primary, I made a detailed study of the vote, sampling the largest cities and several agricultural counties. When the runoff results were announced I went back through these same cities and farming areas, looking up many of the people with whom I had talked only a few weeks earlier.

Until the last few days Graham seemed certain to win. In Lenoir County his campaign manager, Judge Albert W. Cowper, a devoted former student, checked his precinct workers daily through the runoff. Each day he got the same report, "Graham is a cinch to win"—each day that is until the Thursday before the Saturday voting. That Thursday, when some residents of Kinston, the Lenoir County seat, unrolled their afternoon paper, out dropped handbills in shrieking type:

"WHITE PEOPLE WAKE UP"

(A reproduction of the handbill appears on facing page.)

That evening one of Cowper's workers, a filling station operator, telephoned, "It's going like a brush fire. I can't stop it." The man sounded so disturbed Cowper drove out to see him. For two hours Cowper argued with the man, going over each specific racial charge being made and supplying the facts to refute it. When Cowper left, exhausted, he felt the situation had been saved. Not until after the election did he learn that the filling station owner had broken and swung to Willis A. Smith, Graham's opponent.

In those last three days—Thursday, Friday and Saturday— one couldn't pick up a newspaper in North Carolina without seeing an advertisement proclaiming, "The South Under Attack" or "End of Racial Segregation Proposed." One couldn't listen to the radio for long without a spot announcement cutting in, "Do you know that 28 per cent of North

WHITE PEOPLE
WAKE UP
BEFORE IT'S TOO LATE

YOU MAY NOT HAVE ANOTHER CHANCE

DO YOU WANT?

Negroes working beside you, your wife and daughters in your mills and factories?

Negroes eating beside you in all public eating places?

Negroes riding beside you, your wife and your daughters in buses, cabs and trains?

Negroes sleeping in the same hotels and rooming houses?

Negroes teaching and disciplining your children in school?.

Negroes sitting with you and your family at all public meetings?

Negroes Going to white schools and white children going to Negro schools?

Negroes to occupy the same hospital rooms with you and your wife and daughters?

Negroes as your foremen and overseers in the mills?

Negroes using your toilet facilities?

> Northern political labor leaders have *recently ordered* that all doors be opened to Negroes on union property. This will lead to whites and Negroes working and living together in the South as they do in the North. Do you want that?

FRANK GRAHAM FAVORS MINGLING OF THE RACES

HE ADMITS THAT HE FAVORS MIXING NEGROES AND WHITES — HE SAYS SO IN THE REPORT HE SIGNED. (For Proof of This, Read Page 167, Civil Rights Report.)

DO YOU FAVOR THIS — WANT SOME MORE OF IT?
IF YOU DO, VOTE FOR FRANK GRAHAM

BUT IF YOU DON'T

VOTE FOR AND HELP ELECT

WILLIS SMITH for SENATOR
HE WILL UPHOLD THE TRADITIONS OF THE SOUTH

KNOW THE TRUTH COMMITTEE

Carolina's population is colored?" or "The Southern working man must not be sacrificed by FEPC!"

Photographs of Negro G.I.'s dancing with white girls in English night clubs were left at filling stations where farmers like to gather and chat; other leaflets listed prominent Negroes like Richard Wright and Walter White who had white wives. But the main issue stressed at the "whispering campaign" level was the threat of an end to racial segregation in the public schools. Between the two primaries the Supreme Court, winding up its work for the summer, ruled that Pullman dining cars could not segregate Negroes and that the universities of Texas and Oklahoma would have to admit Negroes. The anti-Graham forces seized upon these decisions to drum, "Vote for Graham if you want your children sitting in Negro schools."

The mob mood that was built up in the final days of the campaign was not unlike that preceding a lynching. In Wilmington a precinct worker telephoned the Graham manager and demanded hysterically, "Come and take all your literature out of my house! My neighbors won't talk to me!" Graham stickers came off automobiles as people found it uncomfortable to say they were for him. In Raleigh, an eight-year-old schoolboy, who spoke up for Graham, was beaten up as "a nigger lover" by other children. A Durham election official, favorable to Graham, was awakened during the night by the jangling telephone. When his wife answered, she was asked, "How would you like a little stewed nigger for breakfast?"

In some counties, where Graham campaigners were routine party hacks, an abrupt urge developed to go fishing. "After all Graham had a big lead," explained one, "I didn't think he needed the votes I could round up. Why should I make enemies of the people I have to live with?"

The day before the voting, Graham was scheduled to speak at High Point to some millworkers. His party stopped at a filling station. Five men were sitting around. Introducing himself, Graham offered to shake hands. The men turned their backs. Muttered one, "We're all Willis Smith men here. We'll have nothing to do with nigger lovers here."

Appeals to reason were of no avail, as was shown in Beulahville, a tiny trading center for tobacco growers in Duplin County. The town lawyer, Grady Mercer, was an ardent Grahamite. When Mercer went to the University of North Carolina, he was so poor he literally had only one pair of pants —the pair he was wearing. Ashamed, Mercer sat in the last row and never got up to speak. Noticing this, Graham, then teaching history, went up to Mercer and put his arm around him. He befriended Mercer, even bought him a second pair of pants.

Graham carried Beulahville handily in the first primary but afterward, as race got talked up more and more, he was asked to come to the town. One charge being circulated against Graham was that he had appointed a Negro to West Point. Actually, Graham had given competitive examinations to all eligible youths. A Negro, Leroy Jones, had placed as an alternate, but the appointment, itself, went to a white youth, William Hauser. Graham brought Hauser with him, hoping by this example to show how untrue the whole racial campaign was. When he finished speaking and left, an angry murmur riffled through the Beulahville crowd, "Why didn't he bring the nigger he appointed? Who was he trying to fool, showing us that white boy?"

On the day of the voting the Raleigh *News and Observer*, edited by Jonathan Daniels, a strong Graham advocate, ran an eight-column streamer across page one: LIBERALISM, CONSERVATISM VOTE ISSUES TODAY. That may have been the issue at Graham's headquarters but the issue troubling most of the voters was probably reflected in a long-distance telephone call which Graham received the morning of the voting from a Greensboro textile worker. "I want to vote for you," the worker told Graham, "but tell me honestly if I do will my kids have to go to school with Negroes? I don't want that!"

That same morning in Kinston one voter on his way to the polls shouted to a neighbor, "Come on, let's vote for a white man!" Later that afternoon in Halifax County, a friend sat down to write a sorrowful note to Jeff Johnson, Graham's campaign manager, in Raleigh, "I've never seen such a mess. . . . The most respected man in town is for Graham but is afraid to open his mouth. . . . men are disgusted and won't vote at all. . . ."

An analysis of the vote revealed two dramatic reversals from the first primary. In the agricultural east, heavily populated by nonvoting Negroes, eighteen counties which Graham won in the first primary swung against him in the runoff. Since these black-belt counties were particularly sensitive to racial hatred the change was not unexpected. What was surprising, in fact, was why the racial feeling did not break through in the first primary.

That racial bitterness was there all the time seems clear from an incident in Lenoir County. In the first primary a Negro ran for one of eighteen posts as magistrate, a minor post akin to justice of the peace and paying no salary. After the Negro filed, eighteen white candidates were persuaded to run to make sure the Negro would be beaten. Later most of these whites did not even bother to take office. Strong as this racial feeling was, it did not turn upon Graham in the first primary. Why?

The explanation is that in the first primary local officials were also being elected. Fearful that their candidates for sheriff and other county offices might be singed, the local politicos dampened the racial fires. This happened throughout the state. Gov. Kerr Scott was supporting Graham, and the county candidates didn't want the force of the state administration thrown against them. With these local contests out of the way, the "Hessians," as the paid party workers are sometimes called, were free to make their deals with the Smith forces. The same "better elements" in the community who kept the racial lid on in the first primary let it blow in the runoff.

The second major voting shift came in the cities. Here, in the first primary, Graham ran behind Truman in labor precincts, but considerably stronger among Negroes and in the middle class, carrying some precincts which went for Dewey in 1948. In the middle-class precincts of Greensboro, for example, Graham got 15 per cent more votes than Truman, while in the labor "boxes" his vote was almost a third under Truman's.

Labor had no liking for Willis Smith, a former president of the American Bar Association and who was accused of having opposed a forty cents an hour minimum wage. But many workers couldn't bring themselves to vote for Graham either in the face of charges that he favored an FEPC law which would force the hiring of Negroes in place of white workers. Torn in their feelings, many workers stayed home.

In the runoff Graham suffered a further falling off in the labor vote, but not of decisive proportions. The big break against him came in the economically conservative middle class. In Asheville, all four precincts which Dewey won in 1948 went for Graham in the first primary. All four swung against Graham in the runoff.

Another pro-Dewey precinct which favored Graham in May but turned in June was Box Thirteen in Greensboro. Flanking the Women's College of North Carolina it is a semi-suburban, residential area, with homes ranging between $8,000 and $25,000. After the first primary, I found this precinct strongly opposed to Truman and the Fair Deal. All whom I interviewed were ready to vote for Eisenhower on a Republican ticket in 1952. Their support of Graham was not for his economic ideas, but as a personal tribute to his reputation as the South's most progressive educator.

What shifted this precinct was the insistent drumming on the fear that white and Negro children might have to attend the same schools. One worker for Willis Smith had written an eloquent campaign letter, picturing the threat to family security in inflationary policies which robbed savings of their value and which taxed away so much of one's earnings. She showed the letter to the wife of a doctor, who campaigned for Graham in the first primary. The doctor's wife read it and exclaimed, "That's a fine letter! It expresses my sentiments exactly."

Then, as she turned to leave, the doctor's wife added, "You know I don't want my daughter to go to school with Negroes."

That the racial emotions of "poor whites" in the South are readily inflamed has always been known. The surprise in Graham's defeat was the revelation that the cry of "Nigger" could inflame even the well-educated, well-to-do middle class. No longer will it suffice to attribute racial prejudice in the South merely to poverty and inadequate education. Frank Graham was defeated not by a foul-mouthed Theodore Bilbo but by a nationally honored lawyer, who was chairman of the Board of Trustees of Duke University. It was not only the bigots who turned against "Doctor Frank" but many "progressive" North Carolinians.

2. *"Operation Fizzle"*

Future historians are likely to record the defeats of both Graham and Pepper as the first trial runs of a Republican-Southern political alliance. True, the contests were Democratic primaries and neither Willis Smith nor George A. Smathers, the ex-Marine who defeated Pepper, ever talked openly of coalition with the Republicans. Still, a precinct-by-precinct breakdown in the major cities shows a remarkably close parallel between the vote cast against Graham and Pepper and the Republican-Dixiecrat showing in 1948.

In Wilmington, North Carolina, there were two precincts which Dewey won and eleven more in which the Dixiecrat-Republican vote exceeded Truman's. Graham lost all thirteen precincts. Again, in Guilford County, which includes Greensboro and High Point, Graham lost seventeen precincts. All but four had gone for Dewey. In two of the four, Truman's vote lagged behind the combined Republican-Dixiecrat vote. In only two of the seventeen precincts did Truman have a clear majority.

The parallel with 1948 emerges even more sharply in Florida. All ten Florida counties which Dewey won were swept by Smathers, as were the twelve precincts which Dewey carried in Jacksonville, all fourteen Dewey precincts in Tampa and all but two of the twenty-two Dewey precincts in Miami. The exceptions were in Miami Beach where Jewish neighborhoods voted against Truman but favored Pepper.

In another thirty-eight precincts in Miami, Tampa and Jacksonville, the combined Republican-Dixiecrat vote exceeded Truman's. Smathers took all but three of these precincts. He also swept the three counties which were won by Thurmond in 1948. How much of an upset was Pepper's defeat, considering that Truman would have lost Florida (also Tennessee and Virginia) had the Republicans and Dixiecrats united against him?

Race alone did not effect this merger of Dixiecrat and Dewey voters. Packaged in with the racial issue were opposition to "communism," to the CIO, to government spending, to health insurance, and to the "drift toward socialism." Twice tested, first in Florida and then in North Carolina, this package of issues is likely to serve as the ideological war chest for any Republican-Southern coalition that may be attempted in 1952.

The emergence of this Dixiecrat-Republican voting coalition in the 1950 primaries must seem a particularly sardonic development to Southern liberals, considering how high were their hopes only a few years ago. In 1944, when the Supreme Court opened the white primary to Negroes, Southern liberals rejoiced in the belief that the means were at last in sight for winning Democratic control. These hopes were fanned brighter in 1946, when the CIO launched its drive for a million new members in the South.

Four years and $6,000,000 later, though, "Operation Dixie"

had proved to be "Operation Fizzle." The South's largest union, the Textile Workers of America, was weaker in 1950 than in 1946.

Some labor leaders have blamed the failure of the Southern organizing drive on the Taft-Hartley Law, which freed employers of the compulsion of bargaining with unions and enabled employers to use the labor-board machinery to force elections under conditions unfavorable to labor. A number of other factors contributed to the CIO's frustration.

Wages and working conditions in the South on the whole have been good in recent years. Where unions have won concessions, unorganized plants generally match the benefits. Some newer textile mills are air conditioned; a number of manufacturers have introduced profit-sharing and pension plans. For many Southern workers, only recently removed from the land, mill employment represents an appreciable boost in living standards.

Unionism has made some headway since the New Deal. The Southern branches of some national industries, like steel, auto, aviation and paper, are unionized. Even in cities reputed hostile to labor one finds more widespread respect for workers today than ten or fifteen years ago. In Rome, Georgia, when the Celanese workers went on strike in 1934, their credit at the stores was cut off immediately. Within four days the strike was broken. One merchant, who was particularly brutal in denying workers credit, was boycotted afterward and had to go out of business.

In 1948 the Celanese workers struck again. This time the merchants on Main Street tried to remain neutral. One bank suspended all collections on frigidaires and other appliances which had been bought on the installment plan. The Georgia Power Company waived collection of its electric bills for ninety days.

Through most of the South today there is a general readiness to admit that unionization has brought some good. There were significantly fewer outcries against lifting the minimum wage to seventy-five cents an hour than when the forty cents an hour minimum first was instituted. Many local merchants have come around to thinking that it is good business for workers to earn more and to be able to spend more. But merchants hate strikes, which interrupt payrolls and hurt business. They also dread that if their communities acquire the reputation of being a "labor town" new industry will be scared off.

This hunger for new industry has become the core of anti-union feeling in many parts of the South. The craving for more factories is not confined to a few rich men. Since reconstruction days, industrialization has been glorified as the South's salvation. "Bring the mills to the cotton" became a common slogan after the Civil War, as employment was sought for Confederate veterans and displaced farmers who drifted into the towns. In some communities local citizens chipped in fifty cents or a dollar a week to raise the necessary capital for building a mill.

This drive for new industry was motored both by feelings of sectional nationalism and race consciousness. One of the chief talking points was the need to save the white man from being degraded to the level of the Negro.

Nor has the hunger for new industry slackened over the years. In *Southern Legacy*, Hodding Carter jokingly observes that, as a crusading editor in Mississippi, he has found he can lambast with relative impunity such things as Bilbo, the poll tax and prohibition, but that the subject on which his readers are likely to feel most strongly is the effort to attract new industry. Virtually every economic study of the South stresses the need for intensified industrialization to balance the South's high birth rate and poverty. Some Southerners may concede in principle that it is not quite fair to lure factories southward with free taxes and other concessions. But even progressive-minded Southerners feel that, if the South is to catch up with the rest of the country, it must preserve its competitive advantages in bidding for new industry.

The fever for new industry probably runs strongest among

the rising middle class in the Southern cities. The young lawyer searching for clients, the college graduate seeking a supervisory post in the mills, merchants and salesmen with something to sell, bankers hunting new investment outlets for growing deposits, doctors building their practice, all the numerous property holders who hope the cities they live in will grow out to the land they own and strike them rich—all are building their dream castles upon the growth of industry.

Most of the new plants established in the South since the war's end have been built with Northern capital. With this spread southward of new factories, the prestige of business has risen appreciably and political attitudes generally attributed to business have found growing acceptance. To some extent this holds true for the whole country. The tendency of people to identify their own interests with that of business is bound to rise during a period of large-scale business investment, just as it fell with the slump in investment during the depression decade.

In large part what has really been happening in the South since the war's end can be described as a race between Northern industry and Northern labor to extend their influence southward—with industry clearly victorious. Instead of a militant labor movement the first fruits of increasing industrialism have been a rising urban middle class, which is virtually Republican in political sympathies. It is this new middle class, the branch plant managers and their college-trained supervisors, merchants, doctors and lawyers, newspaper publishers, and realtors, all seemingly so conservative, who are the real political rebels in the South today.

3. A Two-party South?

Southern politics are usually pictured as a conservative-liberal struggle, with the liberals representing the wave of the future and with the conservatives resisting all change. This widely held theory hardly explains what is going on. The strongest single force for political change in Dixie Land today is the newly developing urban middle class who, by Northern standards, would be classed conservative.

From this middle class are coming the strongest pressures for two-party politics. The liberals, feeling themselves weak, are actually hugging the one-party system with might and main. Their sole hope for gaining power locally lies in the possibility that a premature conservative bolt will leave them to crow with the Democratic rooster.

The supposedly conservative middle class, on the other hand, feels disfranchised nationally and gerrymandered locally. In Washington they see a hostile government whose taxing and spending policies they consider destructive and yet which they cannot even vote against, since in national elections the ballots of the South do not count. Within their own states, the urban middle class are woefully underrepresented in the state legislatures, which are rigged against the cities in favor of the rural areas. Fulton County, which includes Atlanta, pays one fourth of all the taxes collected in Georgia and has one eighth of the state's population. Yet, it has only three of 205 representatives in the lower house of the legislature.

As the mechanization of agriculture drives more and more people off the farms into the cities, the Southern legislatures are becoming ever more unrepresentative. And as the South's industrial development quickens, the urban middle class becomes increasingly restive in a one-party system which denies them effective political voice.

Since 1940 the Republican Presidential vote in the South has leaped 50 per cent. The 1,360,000 votes Dewey drew in the eleven Southern states in 1948 were only 1,500 less than Hoover got when he split the Solid South. By far the heaviest Republican increases have come in the most urbanized states— Texas, Florida, Virginia and North Carolina—and in the cities in those states. Roanoke, Staunton and Winchester in Virginia went Republican in 1948 while Alexandria, Fredericksburg and Charlottesville almost did. The Republican tally in Houston and Dallas has more than doubled since 1940.

Checking the precinct returns in key Southern cities, one finds that the voting follows roughly the same economic lines as in Northern cities. As one climbs the economic scale, Democratic support weakens, with the Republicans carrying the better residential districts like Myers Park in Charlotte, Miami Shores in Miami, Irving Park in Greensboro or Highland Park in Dallas. The Dixiecrats, as well, tend to cluster most thickly in these same areas. As far as the Southern cities are concerned—and this is confirmed by the Pepper and Graham elections—the basis for genuine two-party politics already exists.

On Welfare State issues this urban middle class hews strongly to conservative views. Still, this same "country club" middle class has led in pressing for state laws unmasking the Ku Klux Klan. It has taken sizable strides away from the Old South.

In Charlotte, N. C., to give one illustration, there is general agreement that the leading local rebels are Frank and Marian Sims. Through the twenties and thirties they warred incessantly against the Klan and against the "Bible belt" taboos which caused the late W. J. Cash to complain that life in Charlotte was "one continuous blue law." The Simses crusaded against the Sunday blue laws which were lifted in 1941; they led the fight to repeal prohibition which finally carried in 1947. When Charlotte was swinging against Al Smith in 1928, the Simses supported him. However, the Simses have no particular sympathy for organized labor and on national political issues have been anti-Roosevelt and anti-Truman.

In contrast, the leader of Charlotte's "dry" forces, Francis Clarkson, a fundamentalist, is an ardent New Dealer and one of the few Charlotteans regarded as friendly by trade unionists. To round out Charlotte's political gallery, the number one

Dixiecrat locally, Dave Clark, publisher of the Textile Bulletin, is also a fundamentalist and a "dry," as race conscious in his Scotch-Irish, Presbyterian way as Walter White of the National Association for the Advancement of Colored People is in his.

Few Southern cities are more forward-looking and bustling than Charlotte and few are more Republican in their real political sympathies. Both Charlotte newspapers supported Dewey who received 34 per cent of the vote to Truman's 44 per cent, with 21 per cent going to the Dixiecrats. Graham fared even worse than Truman, despite the fact that Graham's father had been Charlotte's superintendent of schools.

Not race but economics explains Charlotte's anti-Graham vote. The principal trading center for the Piedmont Carolinas, Charlotte boasts branch offices of more than 400 national concerns.

Graham's worst showing in the city—hardly 25 per cent— came in Myers Park, unquestionably the most culturally progressive part of Charlotte. For forty years Myers Park has remained the area to which every Charlottean has aspired, so much so, one local quip runs, "Charlotte believes in the Brotherhood of Man, the Fatherhood of God and the Neighborhood of Myers Park."

For all its smugness, Myers Park supports a successful Little Theater, an art museum and a nature museum. The pastor of the swanky Myers Park Presbyterian Church is often referred to as "Jazzy" Jones, an unthinkable levity in the hellfire and brimstone days.

The very fact that there are so many Republican voters in Myers Park and similar middle-class districts in other Southern cities is evidence of how far these areas have moved from the Old South. While most Southerners still vote as their fathers did, the growing urban middle class feels sufficiently emancipated to break with the one-party tradition.

In the North, revolt against tradition tended to make one a Democrat. In the South it tends to make one vote Republican.

To explain what is agitating the South politically requires a different interpretation from the usual conservative-liberal conflict. My own belief is that what is really at stake is the political unification of the South with the rest of the country. Is the South to be integrated politically with the nation as a whole? On what terms? Under whose auspices? Those are the real issues of Southern politics today.

Viewed in that light, the South is being tugged politically at least three different ways. The more traditional Southerners, including the Dixiecrats, can be said to represent the elements which oppose unification on any basis. Both the so-called "liberals" and the middle class in the cities are pressuring for unification with the rest of the country, although on different terms.

In any Republican-Southern alliance that may develop, it is important to watch which emerges topmost, the forces tending to hold the South in sectional isolation or those pushing the South toward political integration with the rest of the nation. The latter voting stream includes many liberalizing elements, particularly in regard to the Negro. One strong factor in the brewing political revolt of middle-class Southerners is that they react much as do voters in other parts of the country to what they regard as "government by crony" and "mink-coat liberalism." Their attitudes are not too different from the independent, middle-class voter in the North.

Economically, much of the unbalance which caused Roosevelt to describe the South as the "nation's number one economic problem" has been narrowed. In 1938 per capita income in the South was roughly 50 per cent of the national average. Currently it is running better than 70 per cent of the national average. Wage differentials with the non-South have been narrowed; the growth of new industry has brought a better balance with a more diversified agriculture. Roughly the same proportion of children now attends school in the South as in the North.

Politically, however, the South, as presently constituted, still is indigestible for the rest of the country. For the Democratic party to become conservative enough to please its Southern wing would require so drastic a transformation of its following in the Northern cities that, whatever its name, the party would not be the same and could not hold a majority in the nation. Similarily, although a temporary Southern-Republican understanding is possible, a lasting alliance would force such an upheaval among the Northern Republicans as to transform that party.

Fundamentally, the South cannot be merged politically with the rest of the nation as long as it retains a one-party system. Unification can be achieved only after different Southern voting elements have been chopped into two parties and realigned with complementary voting elements in the country as a whole.

No monopoly of any kind is broken quickly and a two-party system certainly will not appear overnight in the South. When the break does come it can be looked for first in the more urbanized states and in Presidential voting before state and local elections. Before a genuine two-party system is established, there is also likely to be a transition period, during which an effort will be made to find some means of defeating the Democrats nationally, while holding the Democratic monopoly locally. Through their hold in Congress, the Southerners would hope to capture control of the defeated Democratic party. Actually, we are going through this transition stage right now.

Probably the crucial factor which will determine how quickly or slowly a two-party system develops is the changing status of the Negro, who has always been the basis of the one-party South.

4. The Negro Gains—and Loses

All the Negro leaders I have talked or corresponded with are agreed that the last fourteen years have brought impressive gains to the Southern Negro. At the turn of the century a Negro was being lynched in the South on an average of once every three or four days. By 1938, the year of the antilynching filibuster, the number of lynchings had been reduced to six. In 1950 there were two not entirely clear cases and, important to note, in both instances trials were held and members of the lynching mobs sent to jail. In 1951 only one lynching, in Florida, was recorded.

Since 1938 tuberculosis deaths among Southern Negroes have dropped roughly 40 per cent. A record number of Southern Negroes are going to college with, thanks to the Supreme Court, more than 1,500 sitting alongside of white students in Southern universities.

Still, Negro progress has not been as golden as it glitters. The last census decade brought a reduction of roughly one third in the number of Negro farm laborers and Negro women employed as domestic servants, while Negroes in factory and kindred employment doubled. This migration from the farms to the cities has unquestionably improved the Negro's lot. Still, relatively few new industrial opportunities have been opened to the Negro. His gains reflect primarily higher wages—no small lift in itself—and the ample employment available for unskilled labor, plus the boom in the construction and lumbering industries, where Negro skills are thickest.

Actually, industrialization is making the Negro less important economically in the South. In many fields, where the Negro performs the bulk of heavy work, his labor still is indispensable. However, while Negroes made up one fourth of the South's total labor force in 1940, they constituted only one fifth of that labor force in 1950. Over the last census decade, almost 2,000,000 workers were added to the South's labor force. The number of Negroes in that labor force dropped by 300,000.

The changed attitude toward the migration of Negroes northward is revealing. During World War One all sorts of obstacles were put in the way of Negroes desiring to move North. In recent years, little effort has been made to hold the Negro in the South. If anything his exodus has been encouraged.

Partly this reflected a desire to see the proportion of Negroes lightened. It also testifies to the fact that mechanical cotton pickers and tractors are available to take the Negro's place on cotton plantations. The new industries are finding most of the labor they need in part-time farmers and in the white persons being displaced by the agricultural revolution; also in the natural rise of the labor force because of the South's heavy birth rate. The automobile makes it possible to tap sources of labor which were inaccessible during World War One.

The last few years of booming opportunity would have been relatively easy ones for sprinkling Negroes through the whole industrial structure in the South on the basis of freely competitive abilities. Had that been done it would have marked an enormously important contribution to effecting a balance in racial opportunities between North and South—a balance which is indispensable for any ultimate solution of the racial problem.

Some Southern employers were prepared to hire Negroes for unsegregated jobs. "I would put on Negro clerks but I don't know what would happen to my business," observed one Atlanta merchant. "If there were a Fair Employment Practice Law I could point to that and say the law requires me to hire some Negroes."

The existence of an FEPC statute might also have proven a decisive factor in encouraging Northern companies, opening plants in the South, to introduce Northern hiring practices.

In Memphis and New Orleans, International Harvester works white and Negro employees side by side, with Negroes serving as foremen and subforemen, where their skills justify it. Virtually all other Northern firms which have moved South have followed the local custom of segregating Negroes to specific jobs, usually of a menial nature or lowest in skills and pay.

The Southern filibuster which blocked the enactment of an FEPC law has strengthened the white-supremacy bias of the Southern economy. One of the more striking features of the economic revolution sweeping Dixie today is the degree to which the South has been able to transfer its traditional, agrarian-rooted racial attitudes to the new emerging industrial society.

How precarious is the place of the Negro in this newest of "New Souths" will not become clear until the present boom slackens. The Negro, of course, will be hit hardest by unemployment. Moreover, the full effects of the mechanization of agriculture have still to be felt. As large numbers of Negroes continue to be displaced from the land, their plight will become particularly acute if industrialization is not creating enough new jobs to absorb them.

Politically, as well, one finds a similar paradox of spectacular gains for the Southern Negro being accompanied not by conciliation but by rising racial antagonism. Through the Supreme Court the Negro has won notable advances in recent years. But the immediate political effects of the High Court's decisions have been to all but throttle political "liberalism" in the South.

The defeats of both Pepper and Graham can be credited largely to heavy Negro voting, which spurred an even heavier anti-Negro outpouring. In Florida, where union membership is weak, the CIO undertook to register large numbers of Negroes. One anti-Pepper editor told me he thought this action hurt Pepper more than any other single factor. Anti-Pepper newspapers splashed their front pages with photographs of

Negroes lined up to register. The Tampa supervisor of registration told me a photographer had to wait half an hour before he could find enough Negroes together to snap a picture which could be captioned, "Negroes Swarm to Register." In the whole state, 31,000 additional Negro registrants were added to the voting lists in 1950. There were 89,000 new white registrants.

Only about 60 per cent of the registered Negroes actually voted against close to 75 per cent for the white registrants.

The abrupt increase in Negro voting has led to the spread of considerable misinformation about Negro political influence in the South. Both white-supremacy politicians and Negro leaders have issued wildly exaggerated claims, the Negroes to build up the idea that Negro voters are a force to be reckoned and bargained with, the white-supremacy agitators to scare the white voters.

Here and there, as in Savannah and Atlanta, the Negro vote has represented the balance of victory in close municipal elections. Negroes have been able to use this fact to gain local improvements long overdue them, like a new playground or school, the hiring of more Negro policemen, or paving the road to the Negro cemetery. The fact that Negroes vote also results in more respectful treatment generally at the hands of the police and in the courts, and even in obtaining some government posts. In the matter of elective office, Negroes are still struggling, mostly without success, for a voice at local government levels.

Particularly in the larger cities, some Southern politicians have begun to bid for the Negro vote, often in furtive fashion. The Mayor of one Southern city told me of going to pay his respects to Bishop Grace. When the Negro leader came downstairs, he had a photographer with him. His Honor, the Mayor, could hardly squirm out of posing with Bishop Grace. "I was scared until after election," recalled the Mayor, "that some newspaper would get hold of that picture and print it."

If competition for the Negro vote has tended to dampen

race-baiting in local contests in the larger cities,* on state and national issues the political play is still to the anti-Negro galleries. Nor is this likely to change while the struggle for Democratic control nationally rages as fiercely as it does now. Until the Southern political leaders have resolved their dilemma of whether to remain in or bolt from the Democratic party, the race issue is bound to be kept militantly alive, since it is obviously the best "cover" for any departure from Democratic regularity.

The very fact that racial relations in the South are changing must also be put down as a powerful psychological factor strengthening political conservatism in the South. From my own talks with Southerners, I got the feeling that one reason why so many have frozen stiff in their attitude toward racial reform is a dread uncertainty of what lies ahead. Except for one fervent Alabama Dixiecrat, none of the Southerners I talked with believed that the Negro could be kept indefinitely in his present status. But even among the better-educated Southerners there was a chilling fear of what would happen after Negroes had obtained their rights? What would the change in race relations bring? Where would it all end?

A woman who was working in the University of Texas cafeteria told me of her reaction the first time a Negro student came down the line. "I felt so funny inside," she recalled. "I had never served a Negro before. They had always served me. I didn't know what was going to happen."

Nothing happened, of course, and this woman now takes serving Negroes for granted. Innumerable day-to-day, person-to-person adjustments of that kind will have to take place before the heritage of fear and hatred of the Negro in the South is overcome. In the immediate years ahead, the more the status of the Negro is liberalized, the more likely white

* The cityward Negro drift is making for a curious political contradiction. Nationally, the Negro has allied with the Democrats but in state politics in the South the Negro's interests parallel more closely those of the urban Republicans in their struggle against the anti-Negro rural areas

Southerners are to solidify politically to guard against "things going too far."

For better or worse, the prevailing pattern of racial relations in the United States has become one of progress through friction rather than conciliation. The South still is geared to export its racial problem, as it has been doing for more than thirty-five years, while the North is geared to return those exports to the South in the form of Supreme Court lawsuits. Consciously or unconsciously, each region is increasing the racial pressure upon the other, the South through the continued northward migration of Negroes, the North through the counter flow of civil rights agitation.

Racial relations are too infinitely complex for this duel to be brought to a quick end. Still, the tensions in deadlock have risen to the point where both sides appear to be moving toward some sort of political showdown.

5. The Dread School Decision

The line of showdown can be seen in the case before the Supreme Court involving the schools in Clarendon County, South Carolina. In all the other school cases brought before the Court, Negro leaders sought to prove that Negro educational facilities were not equal to those for whites and therefore violated the "separate but equal" doctrine enunciated by the Court in the Plessy vs. Ferguson decision of 1896. In pressing this "separate but equal" strategy, Negro leaders reasoned that since the South was too poor financially to equalize its school facilities, segregation would fall of its own weight.

With the Clarendon case, Negro strategy has shifted to a direct assault on the principle of segregation. If Negroes and whites are to have equal educational facilities, the NAACP lawyers now contend, they must attend the same schools.

The filing of the Clarendon suit brought announcements from Governors Byrnes, Herman Talmadge of Georgia and

Fielding Wright of Mississippi that their states would close their schools before mixing the races. If the Negro leaders have decided that the time has come to press for an end to segregation, the Southern political leaders seem equally ready to draw the showdown line on the segregation issue and to rally the South behind them.

Probably no other single issue would stir as violent an emotional storm in the South as to outlaw segregation in elementary schools. An antilynching law has always commanded support among some Southerners, who are shocked by sadistic lawlessness. FEPC does not unduly disturb many elements, like farmers and the middle class, who are not in job competition with the Negro. But, as Graham's defeat showed, the whole of Southern society would be aroused by the thought of Negro and white children going to school together.

The political impact of a decision ending segregation might be similar to that of the Dred Scott decision, which plunged the pre-Civil War Democratic party into such furious conflict that the party was torn apart.

However, the present Supreme Court, is not the Dred Scott Court. In the Dred Scott case the High Court did not have to go as far as it did. Dred Scott, a slave, had raised the issue whether he acquired liberty when his master took him onto free soil and whether he retained that liberty on being returned to Missouri. Having decided that Dred Scott was bound by the laws of Missouri, and therefore a slave all the time, the Supreme Court could have halted right there. Instead, it plunged on to decide that Congress did not have the power to exclude slavery from any territory, declaring the Missouri Compromise unconstitutional.

The present Court seems to be trying to avoid another Dred Scott decision. In all of the so-called civil rights cases of recent years, the Court has dealt with each particular case in the narrowest frame possible, avoiding any opinion on segregation itself. In line with this strategy the Court could rule that since Negro schools in Clarendon are obviously unequal, white schools in the county should be opened to Negro children. This would put a chink in the wall of segregation but would leave the wall standing.

Since the Court's civil rights decisions have been unanimous, they can hardly be credited to any one man. Still, the contrasting approaches between the present Court and the Dred Scott Court do mirror, with remarkable faithfulness, the different personalities of the two chief justices.

Roger B. Taney, who wrote the Dred Scott decision, was an intense man, a devout Catholic, who prayed daily for guidance. Born in the tobacco-planting, slave-holding section of Maryland, he freed his own slaves. Like Andrew Jackson, whom he helped in the fight against the Bank of the United States, Taney didn't care whether he made political enemies. Head-on attack was his idea of political logistics.

Vinson, in contrast, belongs to the same border state school of politicians from which Truman was drawn and whose essential political strength has always rested in conciliation. The soft-drawling Kentuckian was brought into top government circles by Byrnes, when the latter was searching for administrators with tact and skill to compose the differences between Congress and the President. He was named Chief Justice by Truman largely to heal the breach between Justices Hugo Black and Robert Jackson. A phrase Byrnes once applied to Vinson is a good caption of the man, "Able and subtle."

In dealing with the Negro, the present Court has been as subtle as the Taney Court was intense.

Should Vinson's name be brought before the 1952 Democratic convention it would be an almost unbelievable bit of historical stagecraft. The three principal actors at the convention, Truman, Vinson and Byrnes, would be men whose careers have revolved around the spinning deadlock within the Democratic party.

With a characteristic Vinson touch, the Supreme Court on

January 28, 1952 sent the Clarendon case back to the lower court for further factual findings. This adroit maneuver probably puts off the dread school decision until after the 1952 elections. Still, although the Supreme Court has managed to sidestep the issue so far, eventually it will have to rule on the direct question of whether segregation is constitutional. If segregation is upheld Southern attachment to the Democratic party will be strengthened. If segregation is outlawed, the pressure for Southern revolt against Democratic regularity will grow. In short, the effect of the Negro drive for greater rights in the South unavoidably is to strain Democratic unity to the limit and to push the South toward coalition with the Republicans.

While the Democratic party was exclusively a "white man's club" it retained the aristocratic glamour of the Old South. Voting Democratic and being respectable were synonymous, a feeling which was fortified by the fact that the few Negroes who voted in the South were Republicans. The fact that almost a million Negroes have registered in the Democratic primaries in the South is serving as a powerful pressure upon the Southern whites to drive themselves out of the Democratic party.

The curious dilemma of the Dixiecrats is that only by preserving the one-party system, as one explained, "can we hope to keep the Negroes from voting and circumvent the Supreme Court's rulings." Yet, in fighting to defeat the national Democratic administration, the Dixiecrats have been pinning the hated "nigger" label on the Democratic party, weakening its traditional claim to Southern respectability. Should the Dixiecrats or like-minded Southerners come to feel that the fight to disfranchise the Negro is hopeless, a mass exodus from the Democratic party could develop rather quickly.

To sum up, today's insurgent political pressures in the South stem from two different aspects of the conservative revolution —racial and economic change. Both groups of insurgents find themselves in the same plight—in disfranchising the Negro locally, they have disfranchised themselves nationally. Both insurgent groups find themselves under growing pressures to make their votes count nationally. To do so, they must bolt the Democratic ranks and make common cause with the Republicans in the North, directly or covertly.

The historical irony in the dilemma confronting the Southern insurgents is worth noting. The prime objective of the one-party system has been to suppress the Negro as a political issue. In doing so all efforts in the past to give Southern politics economic and social focus have also been suppressed. Such class-conscious uprisings as the Populism of the 1890's flared briefly beneath the racial bell jar but soon were snuffed out for lack of political oxygen.

Today it is the class-consciousness of the well-to-do and upper classes which is struggling to free itself of the frustrations of the one-party system. It is the white-supremacy advocates who find that as long as the South has no alternative but to vote Democratic, it cannot fully counter the rise of Negro political power in the North. As a result of the Roosevelt Revolution the basis of Southern politics has been turned topsy-turvy. Where the old pull of Southern sectionalism was to remain apart from the rest of the country the South's sectional interests today are impelling it to move into the national mainstream. The immediate problem of the dominant Southern political leaders is to find the issue or man strong enough to override the tradition of Democratic regularity and the economic ties binding many Southern workers and farmers to the administration.

Their task will be more difficult if Truman does not run, since he has been the personal target for so much of their agitation.

If General Eisenhower is the Republican choice, the Democratic convention is likely to split wide open. Armed with the feeling that in Eisenhower they have an alternative candidate whom they can support, many Southern delegates would come to the Democratic convention in an uncompromising mood. They could be expected to be unyielding in their demands for repudiation of the 1948 civil rights plank and for restoring the rule requiring a two-thirds vote of the convention delegates to nominate a presidential candidate. Acceding to these demands would drive other Democratic elements into revolt.

But what will be the result of any attempt to form a nationwide conservative coalition? Can it win the Presidency? Or will it realign not only the South but the rest of the country and go down in defeat? Would a Southern bolt be sure to defeat the "Trumancrats" as Byrnes and Senators Harry F. Byrd and Richard Russell feel? Or could such a bolt boomerang and help elect the Democrats?

The answers to those questions hinge less on the Southerners and Negroes than on other voting segments like the farmer, labor and the middle class. It depends not simply on economic and racial matters but on other issues like corruption and foreign policy. Let us now see what effect the world crisis has been having on the Roosevelt coalition.

7

The Myth of Isolationism

1. Who Votes Isolationist?

The small monoplane swooped low over the cemetery. Leaning out of the cockpit, the pilot emptied the contents of the urn over the side of the plane. Dipping the plane's wings in a last salute, he turned and flew off into the horizon.

The flyer was Charles A. Lindbergh, Jr., then still an obscure, twenty-three-year-old barnstormer who had not yet become a national hero by winging across the Atlantic. The rite he had performed had been in response to the request of his father who had wanted his ashes scattered over the family plot near Melrose, Minnesota.

For ten years the elder Lindbergh represented the Sixth Minnesota District in Congress. In 1918 he undertook a campaign for governor which stamped him the nation's leading isolationist—a role his famous son assumed twenty-odd years later in the Second World War. The story of father and son, cast in such similar roles, has been related often. Perhaps the real drama has lain all along in the flat countryside over which the ashes of the elder Lindbergh fell. For Stearns County is in many ways the classic isolationist county in the whole United States.

Relatively well-to-do dairying country, Stearns is not only where the Lindbergh family homesteaded but the birthplace of William Lemke, who was Father Coughlin's candidate for President, and of Sinclair Lewis. Sauk Center, in the northern part of the county, provided the setting for *Main Street*.

Normally Democratic in politics, Stearns cost Wilson Minnesota in 1916. Four years later it gave Harding 86 per cent of its vote. That Stearns's residents were not balloting for "normalcy" became clear in 1924, when Robert La Follette carried the county, and again in 1928 when Al Smith swept it. In 1940, after the outbreak of the Second World War, Roosevelt's share of the county's two-party vote dropped 34 percentage points.

What makes Stearns and similar areas so strongly isolationist? What part has isolationism played in the story of the Roosevelt Revolution and in the prevailing political deadlock in the nation? Is it still a major political force even in these days of atomic bombs and supersonic guided missiles?

True, hardly any politician will confess himself as openly isolationist these days. Senator Taft has protested, "How can we be isolationists when we are involved in wars and treaties and every kind of international relationship?" But if the label itself is in disrepute—"Nationalist" and "America First" being preferred—there is ample evidence that one wing of the Republican party has been gambling its Presidential hopes on a resurgence of isolationist sentiment.

To politicians, the existence of a sizable body of voters with a known prejudice must exert an almost irresistible attraction, much like a low-cut gown on television. For many Republicans the prospect of an isolationist comeback is particularly tantalizing. They cannot help recall that the last and, in some respects, most luxurious era of Republican power began in 1920 when isolationist sentiment almost wrecked the Democratic party. They must also remember that the emotions stirred by Hitler's war wrested eight states from Roosevelt in the same general region where Truman scored his surprising gains four years ago. The sudden fury with which the dominant Republican leaders in Congress began hammering on foreign policy after the 1950 elections reflected a belief that at last they had a winning issue.

But did the 1950 vote really mark a resurgence of isolationist feeling in the country? Who are the isolationist voters? What made them isolationists in the first place? Does their make-up explain why the very politicians who are so set against European entanglement seem hell-bent in favor of Asiatic involvement?

To some degree all Americans share the traits commonly associated with isolationism—a hatred of war, a suspicion of foreigners, dislike of militarism and a reluctance to have one's sons drafted. To sift out the isolationists, I took as a basis the Presidential votes in 1920, when the League of Nations was at issue, and in 1940, after World War Two had broken out.

Obviously, everyone who voted Republican in those years was not an isolationist. But counties where Democratic losses were three, five and even eight times the national average, clearly had the highest isolationist potential. From the available statistical data I winnowed out what these counties had in common. To penetrate beyond the statistics, I visited a number of these areas in nine states, talking first-hand to voters of every type, to see whether the Korean War had stirred the same emotional responses as had the last two wars.

What I found raises the question whether isolationism, as generally pictured, ever really existed. Possibly because it seemed to concentrate in the Midwest, the belief developed that isolationism grew out of the physical insularity of the American interior. Midwesterners were presumed to be less sensitive to events abroad than coastal residents and more likely to feel that the United States could live alone and get away with it.

The cure, it was reasoned, was to make Americans more world-minded, to emphasize how the world was shrinking under the ever-expanding range of modern weapons and to dramatize this nation's inseparability from the rest of the world.

This concept of isolationism, must be discarded. It is a myth. The hard core of isolationism in the United States has been ethnic and emotional, not geographical.

By far the strongest common characteristic of the isolationist-voting counties is the residence there of ethnic groups with a pro-German or anti-British bias. Far from being indifferent to Europe's wars, the evidence argues that the isolationists actually were oversensitive to them.

This ethnic factor emerges even more strongly in World War Two. Throughout the country in 1940, Roosevelt's proportion of the major party vote dropped roughly 7 per cent from 1936. There were twenty counties where his loss exceeded 35 per cent—five times the national average. Nineteen of these counties are predominantly German-speaking in background. Another thirty-five counties showed a Democratic drop of 25 to 34 per cent in 1940. In all but four, the census tables reveal German as the first or second strongest nationality of origin. This is also true of at least 83 of the 101 counties where Roosevelt's 1940 vote dropped between 20 and 24 per cent.

In Kansas, Iowa, Nebraska, North and South Dakota this German-American defection was strong enough to swing those states Republican. Nor was the Midwest alone affected. In states as different as Texas and Ohio, Washington and Wisconsin, Minnesota and Indiana, Idaho and Missouri, the sharpest Democratic declines came in German-background counties.

Surely, it will be argued, nationality ties become insignificant after three generations in this country. Impressive evidence of the Americanization of the German-Americans can be marshaled. But does the influence of ethnic and religious background on voting ever really disappear?

Take our oldest ethnic element, the Yankee descendants of the original English settlers. In 1940, despite his loss in the country as a whole, Roosevelt increased his vote 7 per cent in Maine, more than 3 per cent in New Hampshire and Rhode Island, almost 2 per cent in Vermont and Massachusetts. Boston's Brahmin stronghold of Beacon Hill gave Roosevelt 3 per cent more of its vote than in 1936.

Why was the South so consistently stronger for aid to Britain and for war with Germany than any other section of the country? Was it because the South is so rural? But Northern interventionist sentiment was strongest in the cities. Did backwardness and poor education explain the South's war-mindedness? Then, why do the most strongly isolationist counties in the Midwest rank low in school attendance?

What differentiates the South most sharply from the rest of the country, as John Temple Graves has pointed out, is the absence of any Germanic tradition. Never having received significant numbers of European immigrants, the South was not divided in its reaction to the war by conflicting emotional attachments. Nor did the South have an opposition political party to make an issue of intervention.

The two factors, then, primarily responsible for American isolation are:

First, the existence of pro-German and anti-British ethnic prejudices.

Second, the exploiting of these prejudices by an opposition political party.*

Disloyalty is not involved. That should be stressed. Isolationist voters sent their sons to war and those sons served as patriotically and heroically as any Americans.

The 1948 election showed that many voters may not even be consciously aware of how ethnic feelings influence their voting. Although there were exceptions, Truman's greatest gains generally came in the same German-American counties where Roosevelt suffered his heaviest losses in 1940. Truman

* Strongly Republican areas in the South, like East Tennessee, have shown "isolationist" feelings.

made no special appeal to these German-Americans (even after the swing took place, he did not know what had happened). Still, German-Americans all over the country shifted together, as if in response to some subconscious instinct.

The commonly accepted belief that Truman's astonishing victory was caused by a shift of farmers toward the Fair Deal—a "green revolution" as it has been termed—must be modified. Did the farm belt ever turn against the New Deal? The Midwest's defection from the Democratic party in 1940 was largely a revolt of German-American farmers against involvement in war with Germany. With the war's end and Roosevelt's passing, many of these same farmers returned to the Democratic fold.

Nor was this German-American swing merely an agricultural one. My postelection surveys in 1940 and 1948 showed the same pattern for German-American precincts in the cities.

In view of the closeness of the 1948 election, the German-American swing can definitely be credited with giving Truman his margin of victory. Ohio's twenty-five electoral votes, for example, were carried by only 7,107 votes. In six largely German-American counties in western Ohio alone, Truman picked up more than 6,700 votes over Roosevelt's 1944 showing, while the Republicans lost 13,000 votes.

There is an irony worth noting in the strategic importance of the isolationist vote. At a time when American power represents the balance of freedom in this war-threatened world, the balance of voting power in the United States could rest with the former isolationists.

2. Merchants of Revenge

The fact that Truman regained so much of the vote which Roosevelt lost because of the war is further evidence of the passing of the old Republican-dominated political era. In 1920 the bulk of American voters were still Republican by tradition. The isolationist swing which followed the First World War was strengthened by a reassertion of the country's normal Republicanism which had been broken by Theodore Roosevelt's Bull Moose insurgency. The return of so many one-time isolationists to the Democratic fold in 1948 must be taken as indicating an underlying Democratic allegiance, which was broken only temporarily by the war.

Between the two world wars, as a matter of fact, the nature of isolationism was drastically transformed and decidedly weakened. Two main factors appear responsible:

First, the ethnic base of isolationism shrank appreciably. In World War One, Americans of Swedish descent were almost as fiercely antiwar as were the German-Americans, while Norwegian-Americans were only a trifle less so. Prior to our entry into the Kaiser's War, the bulk of the Swedish-language press and Swedish Lutheran clergy assailed Russia as Sweden's "traditional enemy," while hailing Germany as a champion of Protestant and Teutonic civilization. Normally Republican, many Scandinavian counties swung to Wilson in 1916 because "he kept us out of war."

The worst Democratic setbacks in 1920 came in areas of Swedish, German, Norwegian and Irish background, with a smaller drop among Italo-Americans. In large part it was a vote of revenge. The war had precipitated a hysterical movement to eradicate everything German. With the war's end, the German-Americans proceeded to settle old scores. When Harding was nominated German language newspapers stressed that his father-in-law was of German stock and spoke German fluently. The German press drummed at the theme that "a vote for Harding is a vote against the persecutions suffered by German-Americans during the war."

With a shrewd eye to the Italian vote in New England, Henry Cabot Lodge (Grandfather of the present Massachusetts Senator) had argued that Fiume was as essential to Italy's welfare as New Orleans was to the United States. Irish hatred of Britain was also spilled against the Treaty of Versailles and the League of Nations. In 1917 Wilson tried to persuade Britain to grant Ireland home rule, but British statesmen had not yet learned that England's security might depend on America's melting-pot politics.

Contrast the drastically altered ethnic line-up in 1940. Some lingerings of pro-German and anti-British feeling showed up in Swedish and Irish sections. Many Italo-Americans resented Roosevelt's criticism of Mussolini's attack upon France. But in the main the German-Americans were left as the hard isolationist core.

Offsetting their influence was the strength Roosevelt drew from voters of Polish, Norwegian and Jewish extraction because of Hitler's anti-Semitism and his invasion of Poland and Norway. Roosevelt's 1940 vote held up so much better in the cities than in the rural areas partly because the "new" immigrants, drawn so heavily from the Central European countries which Hitler ravaged, were concentrated in the urban centers.

The second major difference between the two waves of our isolationist past lies in the altered economic background. World War One broke upon America after a long period of agitation against monopolies of all kinds and the "money trust" in particular. The isolationism of that day merged with the forces of economic protest. By 1940, however, isolationism had become a weapon through which the conservative Republicans hoped to defeat Roosevelt's New Deal.

Reflecting this change, the favorite argument of the isolationists was abruptly reversed. The "leftist" isolationists liked to justify their opposition to war on the ground that it stifled reform at home. The later isolationists have attacked war as a disguised effort to press social reform.

This transformation in the economic bias of isolationism is worth tracing, if only for the light it sheds on the political chemistry by which foreign and domestic issues find a common solvent. The process is perhaps best exemplified in the story of the Non-Partisan League in North Dakota. The League was born in 1915, not of agricultural depression but of semicolonial revolt. Virtually a one-crop state, North Dakota was really a tributary province of Minneapolis and St. Paul. Alex McKenzie, the Republican boss who ruled the state, lived in a St. Paul hotel. Twin City bankers pulled the life-strings of credit. Twin City millers bought most of North Dakota's wheat, grading and pricing it—unfairly, the farmers felt.

To break this chain of dependence, the Non-Partisan League, whose founders had been Socialists, proposed state-owned terminal elevators and flour mills, a state bank and state-owned packing plants and cold-storage warehouses. With our entry into the war, there is no question that the League's opponents fomented accusations of disloyalty in hopes of discrediting the League's socialistic program. But it is also true that the League's leaders exploited the emotions stirred by the war for their own political advantage.

In almost every state into which the Non-Partisan League sought to extend its influence, the strongest single ethnic element was German. From the outbreak of the war until the United States entered it, German-American leaders had fought to embargo the shipment of American-made arms and had kept up an insistent attack on the profits being earned in the munitions traffic.

While the Liberty Loan drive was on, Arthur C. Townley, whose high-pressure salesmanship built the League, made speeches demanding the "conscription of wealth." As casualty lists grew longer, he told audiences:

"We have been dragged into war by the American autocracy; dragged into a war we did not want and we are told it is a war to liberate the people from the control of autocracy. Who started this war? I will tell you. It was the big-bellied, red-necked plutocrats. Their big bellies will stop more bullets than the bodies of our slim, young men, whom they are taking from their families."

Neither Townley nor William Lemke, generally considered the brain behind Townley, were naïve men who would be unaware of the appeal of such speeches among German-Americans. Lemke, himself, was a devout German Lutheran, who neither smoked nor drank, and whose father fought with the Prussian Army against France in 1870. The Lemkes had followed the land boom from Minnesota to the cheaper lands of northwestern North Dakota, where the family fared well enough to send Bill to the State University. A classmate there recalls bull sessions at which Lemke would quote from Karl Marx on class hatred and say, "If I can find out what people hate most I can build a new political party around it."

Lemke had not always been an isolationist. Searching for a short cut to wealth, he organized a land company which bought tracts of range land in Mexico, which were to be sold to land-hungry North Dakota farmers. The Mexican Revolution burst this imperialistic dream castle. Lemke vainly tried to have Wilson intervene in Mexico, which may partially explain his bitterness toward Wilson.

Townley, as well, turned to politics on the bounce from disastrous speculation. Leasing more than 7,000 acres from the Northern Pacific, he embarked on a bold venture in large-scale flax growing, using gas engines instead of horses. When the flax bubble burst, Townley turned first to socialism and then to organizing the Non-Partisan League. He would have his organizers chug up to farmhouses in Fords, then not too common. He would accept as membership fees checks postdated to come due in the future. Fat commissions were given for recruiting new memberships.

One fellow worker recalls Townley's instructions on how to talk to a prospective member, "Find out the damn fool's hobby and talk it. If he likes religion talk Jesus Christ; if he is against the government damn the democrats; if he is afraid of whisky preach prohibition; if he wants to talk hogs, talk hogs—talk anything he'll listen to, but talk, talk until you get his God-damn John Hancock to a check for six dollars."

When, in 1917, the League staged a meeting to protest the government's action in fixing the price of wheat, the list of speakers featured La Follette and others who had voted against declaring war.

Actually, it would have been surprising if the agrarian hatred of the "money interest" and pro-German sentiment had failed to merge. All American politics are a politics of coalition—an incessant search for issues and appeals which will unite different groups of voters. Subconsciously, if not consciously, the German-Americans must have been searching for some means of voicing their opposition to the war. Unable to stand in naked opposition, they could parade their protest in the clothes of economic grievance.

Inevitably, the hatred of war and money became the chief issues of the 1918 elections. The most violently dramatic contest came in Minnesota, where Charles Lindbergh, Sr., sought the Republican nomination for governor with Non-Partisan support. Born in Sweden, Lindbergh had spent his years in Congress agitating against the "money trust," which he blamed for the 1907 panic. A successful lawyer, he was a strong advocate of regional economic independence. Instead of paying premiums to Eastern insurance companies, he urged farmers to form their own company and keep their capital within their own region. In a book entitled *Why Is Your Country at War and What Happens to You after the War and Related Subjects* he blamed the war on profiteers and international bankers.

Lindbergh's campaign attacks were applauded by the German-Americans who felt that America had been tricked into war. Other Minnesotans, angered by such talk, broke up League meetings, cut the tires of the automobiles of

League organizers and painted the houses of League sympathizers yellow. Since many German-Americans had been the targets for similar "loyalty" demonstrations, these actions tended to solidify their identification with the Non-Partisan League.

Although Lindbergh lost the Republican primary he carried thirty counties. They clustered mainly in two parts of the state—western Minnesota, whose wheatgrowers shared the grievances and Scandinavian background of North Dakota's wheatgrowers, and south central Minnesota, the area of heaviest Germanic concentration. In the November general election, when the Farmer-Labor emblem appeared on the ballot for the first time, five of the eight principal German-American counties went for the new party. (None had gone for Theodore Roosevelt in 1912.) These same five counties favored La Follette for President in 1924.

Nearly a third of the counties which La Follette carried for President, show up on the list of counties where Roosevelt suffered a loss of 20 per cent or more in 1940. The 4,800,000 votes which La Follette got in 1924 were often described loosely as the irreducible minimum of liberal strength in America. Much of that vote, representing approval of La Follette's opposition to war with Germany actually had nothing to do with liberalism.

This alliance of leftist economics and isolationism projected itself through the whole interwar period. Many progressives felt their cause had been betrayed by the war—a feeling which probably was strengthened by the antiliberal hysteria which followed the Armistice. Along with the Midwest's "colonial" resentment against the East went a feeling that to concern oneself with foreign affairs was to neglect unsolved problems at home. William Borah, Hiram Johnson, George Norris and most of the other "Sons of the Wild Jackass," who plagued the Old Guard Republican leadership through the 1920's, were strong for government intervention at home but against all intervention abroad.

Nor was Franklin Roosevelt much of an internationalist at the outset. During his 1932 campaign, reportedly under pressure from William Randolph Hearst, Roosevelt disavowed the League of Nations. In 1935 when Father Coughlin and the Hearst press launched their campaign against joining the World Court, Roosevelt shied from fighting the issue too strongly for fear of losing the support of the isolationist progressives for his domestic program.

This leftist phase of isolationism reached its climax with the "Merchants of Death" investigation headed by Senator Gerald Nye. Ignoring the obvious lesson of history that the causes of any war are exceedingly complex, Nye hammered on the thesis that we had been dragged into the war by foreign loans and munitions profits. Bankers generally were in low esteem at the time and the public was ready to believe the worst of the "profit system."

Nye's thesis was widely hailed as a sensational revelation of suppressed truth. Few commentators noted how closely his charges paralleled the Non-Partisan League's wartime propaganda, or that Nye, himself, was a product of the politics of North Dakota, where opposition to the first war still rankled in voters' memories.

When the Neutrality Act was passed in 1937 the New York *Herald Tribune* suggested its proper title was "An Act to Preserve the United States from Intervention in the War of 1914-18." An even more appropriate title would have been, "An Act to Prove That Those Who Opposed Our Entry into the War of 1914-18 Were Right."

3. Strange Peacefellows

The advent of World War Two shattered the old isolationist tradition and, in doing so, sorely weakened the Roosevelt coalition. In his 1932 campaign Roosevelt made a particularly strong bid to pull the progressives out of the Republican party and the bulk of the German-Americans had swung for him. With the approach of the second German war though, the isolationists were spun on their political heels and tugged rightward in opposition to the New Deal.

It was this abrupt shift which killed the old third party movements in the Midwest. An analysis of the counties which were the principal sources of votes for the La Follette Progressives in Wisconsin and the Farmer-Laborites in Minnesota reveals that both parties served as halfway stations for two distinct streams of insurgents—those who were leaving the Republican party in protest against big-business domination, and those who had forsaken the Democratic party in vengeful memory of "Wilson's War." Wrenching these two voting streams apart, Hitler's war moved the economic liberals into the Democratic party and the isolationists into the Republican party.

This splitting of the leftist-isolationist alliance began as early as 1936, with the formation of Father Coughlin's Union party. The "radio priest" set out to unite all the dissident elements in the country. He claimed the support of Huey Long's "Share Our Wealthers" and Doc Townsend's Old Age Pension movement. Coughlin also worked strenuously to picture his Union party as the heir of the old third parties.

For his candidate, he picked that veteran Non-Partisan Leaguer, William Lemke, who adopted the campaign nickname of "Liberty Bell" Lemke. The slogan provoked the observation that "the liberty bell also was cracked," but the liberty bell had been the symbol of the 1924 La Follette Progressive movement. Most of the planks in the Union party's platform were lifted from the 1932 platform of the Farmer-Laborites in Minnesota. To this program, Coughlin added his own frenzied attacks on international bankers, Jews and Communists and his praise of Mussolini and General Francisco Franco.

Which of all the hatreds and crackpot grievances that Coughlin and Lemke drummed upon brought any noticeable response from the voters?

The very smallness of the vote given Lemke—890,000, or less than 2 per cent of the national total—makes its concentration particularly revealing. Lemke's best showing in any state, of 13 per cent, was in North Dakota, which can be credited primarily to local pride and to Lemke's personal political machine. Outside of North Dakota, Lemke got more than 10 per cent of the vote in thirty-nine counties. Twenty-one of these counties are more than 50 per cent Catholic. In twenty-eight of these thirty-nine counties the predominant nationality element is German.

The only four cities where Lemke got more than 5 per cent of the vote are also heavily German and Irish Catholic. He got 11 per cent of St. Paul's vote and 9 per cent in Dubuque, whose Archbishop Francis Beckman was later to become a leading "America Firster." In Boston the Union party drew 8 per cent of the vote, while in Cincinnati, Lemke's best showing, of 12 per cent, came in heavily Catholic Price Hill. In Chicago, English-baiting former Mayor William Hale Thompson, running on the Union ticket, could get only 100,000 votes.

Drawn primarily from Irish and German Catholics, Lemke's following represented the most belligerently isolationist voters in the country. By 1936 Hitler had already marched into the Rhineland and it was clear that he and Roosevelt were locked in an epic duel. By the fall of 1936, as well, the Spanish Civil War was raging and a sizable part of the Catholic clergy in the United States was denouncing the Spanish Republicans as "Communists" and supporting Italian and German intervention in Spain.

That foreign policy rather than economics explains the Lemke vote is confirmed in Minnesota. There Lemke's worst showing came in the strongest Farmer-Labor counties—

although he had virtually copied the Farmer-Labor platform! The six Minnesota counties where Lemke got more than 15 per cent of the vote are all predominantly Catholic or German.

By following the Lemke vote through the 1938 and 1940 elections one can see the Minnesota Farmer-Laborite party breaking up before one's eyes. The counties where Lemke got his highest percentage in the state gave Elmer Benson, the Farmer-Laborite candidate for governor in 1938, less than a fourth of their vote. The counties where Lemke was weakest averaged better than 40 per cent for Benson.

Since even the staunchest Farmer-Laborite counties swung against Benson, it is plain that a general revulsion against Farmer-Laborite rule was sweeping Minnesota in 1938. But this revulsion was strongest in the German-background counties. Also the 1938 break of the German-American counties continued on into the 1940 Presidential elections, while the lowest Lemke counties came back to support Roosevelt heavily.

The same fate overcame the Wisconsin Progressives. The twenty-two Wisconsin counties where Roosevelt suffered a drop of more than 20 percentage points in 1940 gave Phil La Follette 45 per cent of their vote for governor in 1936. Since this was a three-cornered race, La Follette carried nineteen of these counties. Two years later he lost all but one, drawing only 31 per cent of their vote.

"Governor Phil" had opened the 1938 campaign with the bold announcement of the formation of a new nation-wide third party. I spent an afternoon with him that summer and can still remember the messianic gleam in his eyes as he talked of 1860 being about to repeat itself. Recalling how the Democrats and Whigs had been smashed by their inability to solve the slavery question, La Follette saw unemployment as the issue which both the Republicans and Democrats were unable to solve and which necessitated a new party.

Paraphrasing Lincoln, La Follette observed, "A nation cannot exist half boom and half broke." There was no mistaking that "Governor Phil" imagined himself in the role of Lincoln, and that he expected his National Progressive party to inherit Roosevelt's following in 1940. (At the time, a third term for Roosevelt was not an active prospect.)

La Follette was correct in sensing that the times called for political realignment. His tragedy lay in his failure to understand that the third parties, not the two major parties, were being torn apart. While the bulk of the Progressives floated with the liberal, economic stream into the Democratic party, La Follette, himself, followed the isolationist current into the Republican fold, where he emerged as a champion of economic conservatism. He was not alone in this strange conversion. Burton Wheeler, who had run for governor of Montana in 1920 with Non-Partisan League backing, John T. Flynn, even "Liberty Bell" Lemke—all once arch foes of Wall Street—became equally bitter foes of the new "road to socialism." War, it would seem, makes strange peacefellows.

Neither the Wisconsin Progressives nor the Minnesota Farmer-Laborites were able to survive the second German war. Nor could Henry Wallace, for all his talk of peace in 1948, stir even a friendly rattle from the ghosts of the leftist isolationism of the 1930's.

This breakup of the old third parties is another crucial factor in our present political deadlock. In the 1938 Congressional elections the Republicans picked up enough seats to put control of Congress into the hands of the anti-New Dealers. The heaviest Republican gains in 1938 came in Minnesota and Wisconsin, where the collapse of the Progressive and Farmer-Laborite parties boosted the Republican vote spectacularly.

The so-called conservative coalition which has dominated Congress for the last fourteen years, in other words, has not been simply an economic coalition. One important source of its strength was opposition to intervention in the war against Germany.

This is worth bearing in mind, for it indicates that the Republican hold in the Midwest is far more precarious than most G.O.P. leaders realize. Truman's 1948 victory was a dramatic warning that if the one-time isolationists return to the Democratic party, Republican strength in the Midwest could drop abruptly. The hold on Congress of the anti-New Deal coalition might even be threatened.

4. *What's Left of Isolationism*

The shiftings of the isolationists between 1940 and 1948 point to what must be the raging conflict in their own ranks. It is primarily a tugging of the emotions aroused by war and foreign policy against the economic appeal of the New and Fair Deal. While the crash of battle deafened all other thoughts, the German-Americans and many Irish-Americans were inclined to vote Republican. With the end of the war their economic interests pulled many back to the Democratic fold.

The strength of isolationism, in other words, is not a constant force. It can be expected to rise or fall with changes in the economic situation and to concentrate most heavily where the pull of the Fair Deal is weakest—namely the rural areas.

Isolationism is also most persistent in areas of cultural insularity. The most isolationist of all Americans are unquestionably the "Russian-German" farmers, whose ancestors settled in Russia in Catherine the Great's time, migrating here after 1890. Particularly numerous in the wheat country— they introduced hard wheat to America—the Russian-Germans with their offspring probably number 400,000 today. Wherever their voting can be checked, in Nebraska, Kansas, the Dakotas and the Big Bend region of Washington, the same pattern emerges.

North Dakota has the heaviest concentration of Russian-

Germans and they have been a major factor in keeping it the most isolationist state in the Union. McIntosh County, for example, gave the Democrats the smallest percentage of the vote in the whole country in 1920—only 4 per cent—and showed the highest Democratic drop in the nation in 1940— 48 percentage points. The number of Roosevelt voters fell from 1,900 in 1936 to 318 in 1940.

The Russian-German counties were also the backbone of Senator Nye's political strength. Of the thirteen counties Nye carried in 1944, twelve were counties where Roosevelt suffered his heaviest losses in 1940. From these same counties has come the margin of victory in the Republican primary for Senator William Langer, one of the thirteen Senators voting against the North Atlantic pact.

This Russian-German isolationism may reflect somewhat a traditional opposition to military service. To attract their forebears into Russia, Catherine the Great exempted them from conscription. Revocation of this privilege was one factor impelling them to leave Russia. Still, the most pacifist Russian-Germans—the Mennonites—have swung less violently in voting than those of Catholic and Lutheran faiths. In Kansas, the counties of McPherson, Harvey, Reno and Marion, where the Mennonites are thickest, have fluctuated only moderately compared to heavily Catholic Ellis County.

More important than any pacifist tradition appears to be the cultural isolation in which the Russian-Germans live. During a century in Russia, their ancestors picked up few Russian characteristics beyond a liking for cabbage soup, watermelon seeds and vodka. Organized on theocratic lines, their communities remained German. Intermarriage with Russians was taboo.

An attempt was made to settle the Russian-Germans in similar closed communities in the United States, but Congress refused to modify the homestead laws. Still, they have clustered sufficiently to remain ethnic islands in the American

sea. The church is usually the center of community life.
Families of nine and ten are common. Divorce is rare. In 1910
a woman in one community was caught stealing some sausage.
Her punishment, as recounted by the North Dakota *Freie
Presse*, was reminiscent of New England in the time of Cotton Mather. The woman had to stand in the school grounds
with the stolen sausage draped around her neck and a cooking
kettle on her arm, while children pranced around taunting,
"*Wurst! Wurst!*"

As late as the last war, German was still the language used
in these communities. Parochial schools are still preferred to
public schools.

Not only among the Russo-Germans but also in other
isolationist areas, education beyond elementary school is
frowned upon. Not every isolationist county ranks low in
school attendance, but of seventeen North Dakota counties
showing the lowest proportion of fourteen- and fifteen-year-
olds attending school, all but four are in the isolationist list.
Five of eight Minnesota counties ranking lowest in school
attendance, eight of fourteen in Wisconsin, five of eleven in
Nebraska, nine of fifteen in Iowa and three of eleven in
Kansas are among the counties showing more than a 20 per
cent Democratic drop in 1940.

The explanation is hardly the simple one, that isolationism
stems from lack of education. Rather it would seem that
resistance to education is a symptom of a cultural isolation
in which ethnic prejudices, once established, do not change
quickly.

A good example is Stearns County, which is roughly 90
per cent German-Catholic. When August Lindbergh, "Lucky
Lindy's" grandfather, settled near Melrose in 1861, Stearns
was at the outer edge of the frontier, beyond the reach even
of the railroads. Once August slipped at a sawmill in Sauk
Center and had an arm severed at the shoulder and four ribs
cut. It was three days before a doctor reached him.

Today, the bus will speed you from Minneapolis to St. Cloud, the Stearns County seat, in two hours. Off on the side roads, though, the farmers still follow many of the traditions and customs their grandfathers brought from Germany three generations ago.

Many native-born farmers speak German with greater ease than English. In some townships, as late as two years ago, prayers were still said in German. In the home, discipline is autocratic. Although about half of the farms are electrified, some farmers let REA wires run by their homes, refusing to use them. "We want to do things the old way," they explain.

Two years ago a study of educational attitudes in St. Martin's township was made by William Cofell under the direction of Douglas Marshall of the University of Minnesota. A questionnaire was circulated among the grade-school children. Asked what they disliked most about school, a number replied, "English, because it is so hard." What did they want to be when they grew up? Most of the children wrote "farmer," "priest," or "nun." Of thirty-eight questionnaires I saw, not a single child wanted to be a lawyer or doctor, or even a flyer or ballplayer. Their imaginations were limited to their local experience.

A valiant effort to lift this level of interests is being made at Melrose High School—with those children, that is, who get to the high school. "By the time the children reach us they are pretty well disciplined," observed the principal. "Our problem is to unfreeze them and to encourage them to speak up." So suspicious of education are most parents that the school has not been able to organize a Parent-Teacher Association. To get acquainted with the parents, teachers take turns riding the school bus. Also teams of teachers, one of whom can speak German, are sent out to the farms from time to time.

The parish priest at St. Martin's has also been trying to stimulate a greater interest in education. When Father Cyril

Ortmann first came to St. Martin's in 1940, he found that the Young Men's Society still had a provision in its constitution requiring all officers to have a command of German. He had the society drop the provision. An indirect assist to Father Cyril's efforts to lift the interest in education has been the high birth rate.

Since the pressure of population has exhausted all available land nearby, the young people have been drifting into Minneapolis and St. Paul. Here they have found their German accents and poor English a liability. In their letters and on visits back home they emphasize these handicaps, which has made many parents more open-minded to the advantages of education.

Father Cyril is unquestionably the most influential person in the community. I was advised to talk to him before trying to see any of the farmers. "They're suspicious of strangers and won't open up unless they know you've seen him first," I was told. During our talk, I kept asking Father Cyril what the attitude of his parishioners was on various issues. Invariably Father Cyril replied by giving his own opinion. In his mind, it was clear, he spoke for the parish.

As might be expected, Father Cyril was outraged over communism and government spending. He liked one Republican campaign slogan: "Get the reds out of the government and the government out of the red." Not that Father Cyril believes in *laissez faire*. He favors government intervention to help poor people and to see that farmers get "fair prices" for their crops. The Taft-Hartley Law he thought a "good thing," but he criticized Taft sharply. "He's against federal aid to parochial schools," explained Father Cyril, "and if a man will be unjust on one issue he will be unjust on others."

Father Cyril wanted Spain recognized as an ally (this was late in 1950), protesting, "Why aid Tito and not Franco?" He denounced "letting a man like Lattimore decide our China policy" and "this Korean mess." Father Cyril wasn't opposed to Truman's sending American troops into Korea—"we must take a stand against communism"—but he was against "all the blunders that went before and got us into Korea."

Making the rounds of neighboring farmers, I was struck by how closely their views paralleled those of the priest. The same question, "Why aid Tito and not Spain?" was raised several times by Mrs. Otto Kaschmitter, whose husband is one of the township's better educated farmers. On the kitchen table lay a copy of the *Congressional Record* and the *Catholic Messenger*. Mrs. Kaschmitter was distraught over the Korean War. She had one son of military age who worked on the farm. "If they take him we might as well retire," she complained. Bitter about communism, she felt no settlement with Russia was possible.

"Then, do you feel we ought to go to war?" I asked.

"I don't want war," she replied.

"But if you can't come to terms with Russia on any basis, isn't war inevitable?" I asked. "What other alternative is there?"

Her tone was one of hopeless frustration as she replied, "Our only hope is prayer."

Several other farmers I talked with were almost as upset over the Korean War. When I asked John Arceneau whether he knew anyone who voted Democratic in 1948 and Republican in 1950, he guffawed, "Me, I'm one!" and went on, "I'll never vote Democrat again! Not even if they run a Catholic for President."

"Why?"

"The war," he boomed back. "Democrats always bring wars. If we hadn't gotten into the First World War we wouldn't be in the mess we are in today."

The same view was expressed, more calmly, by another farmer, Matt Classon. An old Non-Partisan Leaguer, he voted for Lemke for President in 1936, "because Father Coughlin recommended him." Classon felt our entry into the First

World War "wasn't necessary." If we hadn't mixed in, he explained, "England and Germany would have had to come to terms. There wouldn't have been a second war and Russia wouldn't be where she is now."

Not only in Stearns but in other German-American counties I visited—like Plymouth in Iowa and Putnam in Ohio— I found this same tendency to see the Korean War as vindication of their earlier opposition to America's wars against Germany. Through the whole country the Korean "police action" generated a feeling of frustration. With many former isolationists, the frustration was etched more deeply by the feeling that "our real mistake was getting into the last war."

This *memory of opposition to the last war* seems the real mainspring behind present-day isolationism. The strategic concepts put forward by Herbert Hoover, Joseph Kennedy and Robert Taft are of incidental importance politically. What really binds the former isolationists is not a common view on foreign policy for the future, but a shared remembrance of opposition to American intervention in the last war. The strength of the Republican appeal to the former isolationist voters is essentially one of political revenge.

Even a cursory study of the dominant Republican propaganda line in Congress reveals a consistent effort to develop an emotional chain reaction between the frustrations of the cold war and the German wars. No opportunity is let slip to harp on the alleged mistakes of Teheran, Yalta and Potsdam or to blame the "rise of world Bolshevism" on the way the last war was conducted. This constant raking over of the past is almost literally a raking over of the ashes of isolationism in the hope that some embers of outraged memory can be provoked into flame again.

Buried in those isolationist ashes will be found Catholic feeling over the Spanish Civil War, as well as what persists of Coughlin's anti-Semitism. The isolationists were always strongly anti-Russian. They also favored a policy of concentrating our military effort against Japan rather than on beating Hitler first. More than likely, General MacArthur is an emotional symbol of that feeling.

The fact that with the war's end Germany has been changed from an enemy to a potential ally and Russia from friend to foe undoubtedly strengthens the feeling among isolationists that Russia was "the real enemy all along." Their sense of vindication has probably also been stiffened by the loss of China to Communist control.

The importance of Alger Hiss lies in his being so convenient a symbol of so many of the prejudices which some Republicans are seeking to link together. I believe Hiss was guilty of perjury. But, as Alistair Cooke points out in *A Generation on Trial,* the vehemence with which Hiss was pursued reflected less a sense of outrage over his guilt than a craving to see a "full-blooded New Dealer" on trial. Moreover, Hiss's presence at Yalta, even as a minor diplomatic aide, could be distorted to stir suspicions that "Communists in the State Department" had somehow contrived to have Roosevelt betray America's real interests.

That Hiss fell victim to this curious American passion for fighting the last war over again is not without irony. It was as associate counsel to Senator Nye in the Munitions Inquiry that Hiss first achieved prominence. Buoyed aloft by one isolationist crusade, against the bankers and profit system, he was dashed to ruin by the second isolationist crusade, whose target this time was the New Deal.

5. "Slap Vishinsky's Face"

In banking so heavily on the revival of isolationist sentiment the dominant Republicans are taking heavy political risks. They may solidify around the administration the many voters, Democratic and Republican, who dread a repetition of the tragic isolationism of the 1920's.

A second danger is that an abrupt change in the strategic

picture could quickly melt what is left of the so-called isolationist following. More than a fifth of the counties which broke most sharply against Roosevelt in 1940 are predominantly Catholic. Would their emotions favor a policy of withdrawal from Europe if it threatened to leave the Vatican at the mercy of the Soviets? If Germany were overrun by the Red Army would the German-Americans favor a policy of not "intervening in Europe's quarrels"?

One is tempted to conclude that isolationism can serve the Republicans for only one election—no more. With the help of Senator Joseph McCarthy, the Republicans may succeed in resurrecting the vengeful memories of those who opposed our getting into the last war. But for how long can one continue to fight the war that is past? There is no Treaty of Versailles to keep alive the spirit of pro-German revenge as after World War One. In the present strategic situation American foreign policy is bound to seek to make Germany an ally.

The fact is that the same turn of the strategic wheel which left Russia and the United States the only major military powers in the world has all but destroyed the ethnic base of isolationism in this country. A foreign policy based on the old isolationist ideology has not only become strategically impossible; it cannot even command the political support of the ethnic elements, which were most violently isolationist in the past.

If anything the former isolationists are more belligerent today than the country as a whole. In none of the German-American counties I visited did I find a single person who believed a settlement with Russia was possible. There was much criticism of the administration for being "too soft" with the Communists, with some persons feeling, "If there has to be a war, let's get it over with."

None of the ethnic resistances which obstructed our getting into war with Germany would be raised against war with Russia. On the contrary, they probably would obstruct the making of peace if a settlement with the Soviets ever became possible.

It is also questionable how much of a revival of isolationism actually was evidenced in the 1950 elections. Of the Congressional seats won by the Republicans, all but two were won by the Democrats in 1948, which would indicate the shift was largely of an off-year character. Senator Millard Tydings appears to have been hurt badly by McCarthy's charges of "whitewashing the Communists in the government." Yet, Tydings' lowest vote in Baltimore came in the Negro wards, which elsewhere in the country held strongly for the Democrats.

In no sense could Taft's re-election be considered a mandate on foreign policy. Resentment against labor was mainly responsible for Taft's victory, as is brought out fully in a later chapter. "Mr. Republican" deliberately played down issues of foreign policy. What he did say was so vague that persons listening to the same speech got diametrically opposite views of what Taft meant. At the Isaly's dairy in Youngstown, where Taft spoke, one worker thought Taft's criticism of administration "bungling" in the Far East meant we had no business meddling in the affairs of other nations. A second worker, of Yugoslav descent, thought Taft was ready to go to war with Russia.

Taft ran strongly in Ohio's German-American counties, but his most spectacular urban gains came in Jewish neighborhoods, where Roosevelt's memory still gleams untarnished and where Truman's foreign policy is generally supported.

A check of German-American counties through the country showed some resurgence of isolationist sentiment, but no evidence of a spontaneous nation-wide sweep as in 1940 and 1948. In several old-time isolationist counties, like Clinton, Illinois, the Democratic vote held up better than the Republican vote. In the German-American counties which I

visited, anger over Korea was more pronounced among tradi-
tionally Republican than Democratically inclined voters, and
among farmers who opposed the administration's farm program than among those who favored it.

My own net judgment was that the Korean fighting
brought only a partial resurgence of the old isolationism. A
more important factor behind the 1950 swing to the Republicans was the general mood of frustration which the Korean
War produced, and which was apparent wherever I went.

Take the mixed emotions of one elderly farm couple—
the Leon Hunters—near North Liberty in Knox County,
Ohio. The Hunters seemed glad for the chance to voice their
views. Mrs. Hunter gave me a piece of cake which she had
baked the day before for her knitting club and we talked for
some time. Silicosis had forced Hunter to leave a factory job
in Mansfield and take up farming. Strong for unions in the
past and always Democratic, he voted for Taft because he
felt "it isn't good for labor to have too much power" and
because "Truman and Acheson are too soft with the Communists."

"Why doesn't Truman get rid of those Communists in
the government?" Mrs. Hunter demanded. "With our boys
dying in Korea, he won't kick out the people who are fighting us—it makes me sick!"

Hunter was against all farm subsidies. "I co-operated one
year and had to make five trips to town to get thirty-eight
dollars in benefits," he said. "The farm program doesn't help
little farmers like me." (North Liberty is not good farming
country.)

Although the Hunters saw no chance of agreement with
Russia, they were reluctant to say that war is the only alternative. Nor were they content with the present nightmarish
twilight of neither war nor peace. "We ought to do something to show those Russians where they get off," said Hunter.
"When Malik and Vishinsky say those things about us in

the United Nations, someone ought to go up to them and slap their faces!"

As I got ready to leave, Hunter tried to sum up his feelings, "I guess what I've been trying to say is that it's time we got back to the American way of living."

Throughout the country there tosses this sense of frustration, compounded of a variety of emotions. The cold war has roused strong feelings of patriotism which are finding no satisfactory emotional outlet. The casualties in Korea cut all the more deeply because—as several persons protested—"we're not even fighting the real enemy." There has been a drop in confidence in Truman's personal abilities. The biting taxes and inflationary price rises which the Korean War brought has given nearly everyone a sense of economic grievance. I also found appreciable opposition to "giving all that stuff to foreign countries," particularly among lower income voters.

It may be that a new isolationism is taking form, reflecting, not ethnic factors but, a general disillusionment and weariness with the cold war. And yet some of the people who complained about aiding Europe went on to say, "We ought to build up our defenses and get ready to fight Russia alone—we'll have to anyway." Perhaps what the widespread feeling of frustration really signifies is that the strains of continued, indecisive stalemate are becoming less tolerable to the American people. Certainly, those strains are working to disrupt the Roosevelt coalition, as will be seen in our next chapters on the farmer and organized labor.

8

Battle for the Farm Vote

1. Why Truman Won the Farmer

More than fifty farmers had flown into Dexter, Iowa, on their own planes to hear the President deliver his first major speech of the 1948 campaign. The obvious prosperity of the audience contrasted sharply with Truman's shrill prophecy of the shape of things to come if the Republicans were to win. Already, he charged, the Republicans had "plunged a pitchfork into the back of the farmer" in refusing to erect adequate corn storage bins and the "gluttons of economic privilege" were waiting only until after November to remove price supports and "let the bottom drop out of farm prices." Had the farmers forgotten the last time the Republicans were in power, when hogs sold for three cents a hundredweight and corn was burned for fuel?

For the most part the audience was undemonstrative. When the President finished, though, one listener jerked his hat off excitedly and shouted, "Hi, Harry!" A neighbor nearby called over, "Hey, you're supposed to be a Republican." Waving his hat again, the excited man retorted, "You mean I was."

This little interchange was missed by the reporters accompanying the President, which was unfortunate for them. Had they caught the incident and its significance, they might have been spared those predictions that Truman hadn't a chance to win. For the excited man who was waving good-by to the Republican party was the Rev. L. C. McDonald, the Methodist pastor in Guthrie Center, the county seat of religiously Republican Guthrie County. "Iowa will go Democratic the year Hell goes Methodist," Senator J. P. Dolliver once remarked. Hell might not have changed its religion, but here was a Methodist minister going Democratic.

What lay behind the swing to Truman of Iowa and other farm states? Was it a basic, enduring political shift or a passing, freakish fancy?

While doing a post-mortem of Truman's victory I sampled Guthrie County. On the eve of the 1950 elections I revisited it, searching out the same farmers I had talked with two years earlier. Had their attitudes changed? How? Why?

No county in Iowa typifies the whole state. Guthrie, however, is something of a cultural and economic crossroads. The rich, fertile lands for which Iowa is famed are found mainly in the upper half of the state, which was settled principally by homesteading German and Scandinavian immigrants. In sharp contrast, Southern Iowa, which was settled chiefly by native Americans, most of them from New England, is badly eroded, with some of its counties below Mississippi in per capita income. Despite its poverty, Southern Iowa has been the most staunchly Republican part of the state, also the most zealously prohibitionist. Democratic in 1932, most Southern Iowa counties returned to the Republican fold in 1936.

In social make-up Guthrie, which is 98 per cent native born, is part of Southern Iowa. Economically, it fringes on the better lands and, while less prosperous than the richest Iowa counties, is better off than the Southern area.

Guthrie, moreover, is not isolationist country. As in other parts of the farm belt, Truman's biggest Iowa gains came in the same German-American counties which showed the heaviest Democratic fall-off in 1940. In Guthrie, though, Roosevelt's vote did not drop much in 1940; yet the county swung for Truman, the second time since the Civil War that it favored a Democratic President.

Guthrie, in short, seemed an ideal area to explore what else besides the German-American swing lay behind Truman's spectacular farm gains.

One of the biggest voting shifts occurred in the county seat. Little more than a slowdown on the Des Moines–Council Bluffs highway, Guthrie Center has one Main Street of stores, a movie which is open evenings, two grain elevators, a brick high school and a courthouse which is crumbling to pieces. In the rambling two-story, frame structure which serves as the town hotel, none of the rooms have private baths. In the room I occupied was tacked a placard, "Fire Escape." Beneath it hung a heavy manila rope. In case of fire you threw the rope out of the window and let yourself down to the ground.

What political changes have taken place in Guthrie cannot be laid to population shifts. Over the 1940-50 decade the county's population dropped from 17,210 to 15,156, while Guthrie Center remained almost stationary at 2,028. The new blood in the community can be said to be represented by Howard Randolph, who has built one of the most prosperous egg-gathering services in Western Iowa. Randolph is too much of a "live wire" for many Guthrians. He has been trying to make the town "wet," has fought the zoning restrictions and almost got himself elected mayor in a whirlwind, last hour, write-in campaign. What the townspeople seem to resent most, however, is that Randolph insists on remaining a bachelor.

It was hardly any surge of radicalism which caused Guthrie to vote for Truman. To the contrary, an almost instinctive conservatism was responsible. This may surprise people who think of the Republicans as the nation's conservative party. But to many Guthrians, Dewey—not Truman—seemed the dangerous radical.

The mood of the community was expressed perfectly by the

Rev. McDonald, as we sat in the church basement the week after the election. No previous minister in the church's existence had voted for a Democrat for President. Explaining his shift, McDonald argued, "We have a strong agricultural policy and have done very well under it. Why change when the Republicans were so speculative?"

Dewey's promise of a "great house cleaning" in Washington disturbed McDonald. "What would be swept out with the house cleaning?" the minister asked. "Price supports and other agricultural aids? If another depression comes what will the farmer do?"

This same fear of the Republicans as "too risky" was voiced by farmers outside of town whom I interviewed. "I talked about voting for Dewey all summer," Roy Burgett explained, "but when the time came I just couldn't do it. I remembered the depression and all the good things that had come to me under the Democrats."

With a wife and child Burgett had arrived in Iowa in 1932 from the Dakotas where he had been jobless and homeless. "I had exactly $2.25 in my pocket when I came here," Burgett recalled. "Now I have a 160-acre farm, all paid for, a new Plymouth car, a nice herd of cows and money in the bank." He had bought his farm in 1940 with the aid of a government loan, as had his brother in a nearby county, and had paid it off in four years. Concluding his narrative, he remarked, "That's what the government did for me."

Another farmer nearby, James Stringham, had refused to vote for Roosevelt "because of his extravagance." Stringham's family had always been Republican. He was a "dry." In 1948, though, he cast his ballot for Truman. The reason? Again, it was the memory of the depression.

Stringham had been a renter through the lean years. One harvest brought barely enough to cover his rent. Another season put him so deeply into debt that he was three years struggling out. In 1940 he bought a $20,000 farm, borrowing the down payment. In three and a half years he had the farm paid off.

"We know it took a war to bring those high prices," interjected his wife. "And we're not happy at the thought that it was a war which helped us. But we've worked hard to get this farm."

Stringham nodded his assent, "If we were to lose this farm we wouldn't try farming again. It's been too hard getting where we are now. We just weren't taking chances with Mr. Dewey."

In 1950 I found Stringham in his field operating a corn picker. Whom was he going to vote for as Senator, Al Loveland or Bourke Hickenlooper? "Loveland," he replied. "He's the farmer's man." Under questioning, Stringham explained he still considered himself a Republican and had no use for Truman personally. Either Eisenhower or Stassen would get his vote in 1952. What about Taft? Stringham squirmed, then grinned, "You've really got me there."

After a pause, he added, "No. Right now things are going good, but a depression is sure to come eventually, and the farmer will need a friend again."

2. *Fears in Balance*

FARM BELT TURNS REPUBLICAN read the headlines after the 1950 Congressional elections. To many editorial writers and columnists the Republican gains heralded a triumph of old-fashioned "rugged individualism," indicating the farmer had sickened of government handouts and controls. My talks with farmers in nine states leave little doubt that this interpretation misjudges what happened. The voting shift between 1948 and 1950 did not reflect any basic change in the farmer's political attitude. Mainly, the shift reflected a subtle, but significant change in the general economic climate.

Fear of another depression dominated the 1948 voting. The price of corn, which was about $2.15 a bushel when

Dewey was nominated in June, started slipping almost simultaneously with the adjournment of the Republican convention. By September it had dropped below parity. By early October it was under the government support price. By election time it had fallen to $1.20 a bushel. For the first time in ten years farm income in 1948 showed a decline.

Throughout the farm belt this drop in the price level was looked upon as a tumbling barometer, warning that an economic storm was approaching. Getting ready for the expected postwar collapse, farmers everywhere were paying off debts and buying machinery with cash, not on credit. There was no speculation in land, as after the First World War. In Marathon County, Wisconsin (Republican in 1944 but for Truman in 1948) an elderly farmer sold his farm the month before election and retired. The day after election he stamped into a hardware store in Wausau, exclaiming, "I never would have sold out if I thought Truman had a chance. I felt Dewey was sure to win and it would have been just awful for the farmers."

The outbreak of the Korean War altered the whole economic atmosphere. The black clouds of imminent depression were blown away. A new fear took its place: inflation. With it came a changed attitude toward government aid. While war threatened, the ordinary workings of supply and demand favored the farmer, ending the need for price supports at least temporarily. Along with this lessened sense of economic dependence on the government came a livelier tendency to question whether the costs of Government aid did not outweigh its benefits.

In Putnam County, in northwestern Ohio, Warren Bridenbaugh backed Truman in 1948 but swung for Taft two years later. "The Democrats are pushing too far," he explained. "The other day one of my war bonds came due. When I cashed it, I thought how much more I could have bought for the money back in 1940 than now. This inflation has got to be stopped."

Bridenbaugh has a special reason for wanting to safeguard the value of his war bonds. The farm he is operating belongs to his mother. When she dies Bridenbaugh will have to buy out his brother's interest. The greater the inflation, the more he will have to pay and the less his savings will be worth.

Inflation has been playing havoc with the whole farm inheritance picture. When the war ended considerable numbers of older farmers began to retire and to move into town, letting their sons take over operation of the farm. The sons, naturally, are anxious to acquire title, but the fathers are refusing to sell since "who knows what money will be worth a few years from now." In one such instance I ran into, it was obvious that father and son were embittered toward one another as a result.

Rising land values have been turning many a tenant's dream of becoming a farm owner into a nightmare. Ralph Brooks, who runs an agricultural training course for veterans in Columbus Grove, Ohio, told of one young farmer who had been ready to start in on his own three times only to find, each time, that costs had leaped and he needed more capital. In Marshall County, Iowa, a young farm tenant said flatly, "I'd like to see farm prices come down. If they stay up I'll never be able to buy a farm."

Farmers are supposed to favor cheap money, almost as a matter of tradition. This certainly was true during the 1930's. But in 1950 throughout the farm belt the prevailing sentiment was ranged against inflation. Many farmers no longer have a debtor's psychology. Their mortgage indebtedness has been cut more than half since the 1920's. An unusually high proportion of the farmers' assets are now in cash, which depreciates with inflation. In 1940 the Agricultural Balance Sheet showed only 7 per cent of all farm assets in bank deposits and U.S. Savings bonds. By 1950 these cash holdings accounted for a full 15 per cent of farm assets.

Moreover, a disastrous price slump still is expected. A poll of farmers taken after the Korean War by *Wallace's Farmer and Iowa Homestead* showed that 46 per cent feared "a slump might come anytime"; about one-third felt assured of "one good price year," while hardly one farmer in four thought it safe to go into debt. That these fears reflect mainly the memory of the depression is clear from the sharply different attitude of farmers under thirty-five and those older. Only one of four younger farmers saw a slump coming, against more than half of the older farmers.

This memory of the depression and dread of another economic debacle seems to be the strongest, single psychological force among farmers today. It is reflected in their farm operations. It may well be the strongest single factor, apart from inherited tradition, influencing their voting.

Since the end of the war, a new voting pattern has been taking shape in the farm belt. The old tradition was that farmers voted for Democrats in bad times and for Republicans in good times. The new key to the farmer's voting appears to be his attitude toward the role that government should play in economic life. In popular imagination the Democrats have become the party of government controls and government spending while the Republicans symbolize economy and opposition to government controls. When fears of depression are in ascendancy, the tendency to look to the government for help is stronger and with it comes a Democratic trend. When fears of inflation are uppermost, resentment against all forms of government spending grows and with it comes a Republican trend.

The balance of voting in the farm belt today can be said to reflect the balance between these two fears, of depression versus inflation.

It is a changing balance, shifting both with the times and with the emotions of individuals. I found that the attitude of farmers usually mirrored the vividness of their personal misfortunes during the depression. The swollen national debt is a worry common to all, but farmers who suffered most in the depression find it easier to shrug off.

As a young rancher near Mount Vernon, Oregon, put it, "I pay as much in taxes as my whole income during the depression, but I can afford it." When this rancher was graduated from high school, he remembers that only one boy in his whole class could afford a new suit. Beginning farming in 1935, he "came out of hock" in 1940. "The dollar isn't what it used to be," he conceded. "Maybe these inflated dollars are hurting us, but people are better off than they ever were."

The disposition to scrap all government programs was strongest among those who suffered least from depression or who felt they were in a position to ride out another collapse. "My farm is debt free and my machinery is all paid for," a twenty-four-year-old Ohio farmer told me. "A depression is bound to come. The way I see it the sooner it comes the better. Let things hit bottom and then they'll come back."

The shifting balance between the fears of depression and inflation is also important in determining the strength of isolationist feeling. The raging conflict among the one-time isolationists, as we have seen, is primarily a tug of war between the economic appeal of the Fair Deal against the emotions stirred by war. The approach of war not only sharpens ethnic grievances but it weakens the sense of economic dependence upon the government. Peace, in contrast, tends both to quiet ethnic emotions and to stir fears of another depression. The German-American swing back to the Democrats in 1948 was unquestionably strengthened by the threat of postwar collapse, while the partial resurgence of isolationism in 1950 was strengthened by fears of inflation.

After the 1950 election, in a number of German-American counties, farmers protested angrily to me, "Why can't we have good times without war?" To a fair number of farmers the Democrats have become emotionally linked with war while the Republicans are linked emotionally with hard times.

The Brannan Plan was a casualty of the fighting in Korea. Secretary of Agriculture Charles Brannan devised his plan to take care of unmanageable food surpluses. By the time his plan was broached to farmers, no surpluses threatened. He couldn't even get a hearing for his views.

Some farmers I talked with were prepared to scrap all farm subsidies "if nonfarm subsidies are also eliminated." Larger numbers are ready to strip the farm program of "nonessentials." But most farmers are still too troubled over the future to be willing to rely solely on supply and demand. There is a general desire for a minimum floor below which farm prices won't be permitted to drop. "Right now we don't need much government help," observed one Ohio farmer, "but the government ought to be ready to step in if it becomes necessary."

This teetering between the fears of depression and inflation has only begun to make itself felt politically. It may last only as long as the memory of the 1930's holds. It may also be eclipsed by issues which have developed since 1950, like that of corruption in government. As long as the cold war rages, however, our economy is likely to be shivering between war and inflation on one turn and peace and deflation on the other. Moreover, all the many frustrations of the cold war, from the casualties in Korea to higher taxes, would tend to ease with a relaxation in international tensions.

One point is worth bearing in mind. If farmers do swing from one party to the other, it should not be leaped upon rashly as evidence of a fundamental political revolution. Even while shifting parties, the farmer is likely to be voting for the same thing. His basic motive is apt to be the desire to preserve the gains of the Roosevelt-war years. When those gains are menaced by approaching depression, as in 1948, he sees safety in a "do something" government. When war and inflation threaten to devour those gains, the "safe" vote appears to be against a government which promises to do too much.

In this respect the farmer's attitude is not too different from that of the urban middle class which, as an earlier chapter showed, also favored Truman in 1948 as the "safe" candidate.

Truman's 1950 blunder was to campaign as if it were 1948. In asking for a Congress which would do his bidding, he misread the temper of the voters who were seeking a check against the government going too far. But those who hailed the 1950 elections as evidence of a revolt against government subsidies are repeating Truman's mistake in reverse English.

The farmer remains conservative politically, but conservatism means something quite different to him from what it means to the businessman. Business has identified conservatism with the absence of government controls. The farmer, desperately eager to preserve the gains of the last two decades against both inflation and depression, seems worried both over too little and too much government.

3. The Town Comes to the Farmer

Over the last dozen or more years Republican leaders have fallen into the habit of blaming Democratic victories in the farm states on what Raymond Moley once described as "the Gentle Rain of Checks." Santa Claus is their political enemy, so the Republicans have reasoned, complaining in effect that the voters are being bribed. If government bounties were all the Republicans were up against, their political problem would be simple. Actually, they have been on the wrong end of a long-brewing, political revolution.

A quiet sort of revolution, its force has been obscured by the practice of lumping all rural residents, townspeople as well as farmers, as part of the same farm vote. Separating these two voting elements, one discovers that the mainstay of Republican strength in the countryside has not been the farmer at all. The citadel of Republicanism has been the small town which serviced the farmer. The backbone of the Republican farm vote has been the courthouse ring rather than the "grass

roots" farmer, the man on Main Street rather than the man
with the hoe.

One of the more significant aspects of Truman's gains in
the Midwest was the rise of Democratic strength in the towns.
A number of Iowa towns went Democratic for the first time
since 1932. Like the Rev. McDonald of Guthrie Center, lifelong Republicans voted Democratic for the first time. This
cracking of the Republican allegiance of the rural towns may
reflect new forces of political realignment at work in the farm
belt. It also raises the question whether the reasons for the
Republican farm losses are not so basic that they will survive
even a Republican Presidential victory.

The table below is worth careful study. Prepared by John
Ellickson for *Wallace's Farmer and Iowa Homestead*, it shows
the differing Democratic percentages of the Presidential vote
in the larger Iowa cities, in towns under 10,000 population and
in townships inhabited entirely by farmers. Not only have the
farmers been more consistently Democratic, but the voting
relationship of town and country has been changing steadily.

Year	Dem. % State	Dem. % Farmers	Dem. % Towns	Dem. % Cities
1916	44	44	41	49
1920	25	24	25	29
1924	23	26	21	22
1928	38	43	31	37
1932	59	70	51	53
1936	56	61	48	56
1940	48	49	42	51
1944	48	47	43	52
1948	52	54	45	53

In both 1916 and 1920 there was little difference in voting
between townspeople and farmers. By 1928 a wide gap had
developed. Where the towns show a relatively small Democratic rise over 1920, the farmers almost doubled their Democratic percentage.

In part this reflected an ebbing of the isolationism of the First World War. The mainstay of the Iowa Democratic party has always been the German-Americans, particularly the Catholic Germans. So violent was their reaction against Wilson in 1920 that in some parts of Iowa the Democratic party all but disappeared. Candidates could not be got to run for Congress on the Democratic ticket. Although the size of the Iowa electorate has jumped 35 per cent since 1920, the all-time high Republican vote was recorded then, never to be equaled since. Of the six Iowa counties Al Smith carried all but one broke badly against Roosevelt in World War Two.

But Smith's gains in 1928 also reflected growing resentment against the long agricultural depression which began in 1920. By 1928 economic conditions were so bad that farm state delegates to the Republican convention pleaded with Republican leaders not to "drive farmers of the Republican states out of their party," by turning down a plank promising some farm aid. Their plea was ignored.

The relatively low vote given Smith in Iowa, 37 per cent, was widely interpreted as proof that the farmer's Republicanism was so strong that even bad times could not shake it. Had the G.O.P. leaders separated the vote of the farmer from that of the townspeople, they might not have been so smugly self-confident.

With the deepening depression, the gap between farmers and townspeople widened to where there was a 20 per cent spread in their balloting in 1932. Although seven of every ten farmers favored Roosevelt, the towns went Democratic by less than one per cent.

Since 1932 this gap has narrowed. One reason was the wartime break of German-American farmers. Far more significant, though, has been a revolutionary change in the relationship of the town and farmer.

In the original pattern of agricultural settlement, the farmer's relation to the town was not unlike that of the

Eskimo to the Hudson Bay trading post. During the home-steading era, of course, the whole farm belt was a kind of colonial empire for the industrial and financial East. The towns which dotted the railroad routes were the trading out-posts for the numerous agencies of business. Farmers went to town for the financing needed to tide them through the grow-ing season. After harvest they brought their crops into town to pay off debts and to trade for the things they needed. For the townspeople, many of whom were agents of railroads, banks and grain and feed companies, the chain of identification was not with the farmer but with business.

The town also provided the farmer with political leader-ship. Politics were monopolized by courthouse rings. Since there was no telling when a favor might be needed at the court-house, most farmers found it expedient to register as Republi-can. A virtual one-party system prevailed in most farm states with the G.O.P. as dominant in states like Iowa and Min-nesota as the Democrats in Georgia and Alabama.

The town-country relationship, in short, provided the original frame of farm politics. It probably is safe to say that each successive stage in the farmer's political awakening re-flected some shift in his status vis-à-vis the town. Certainly, all the agrarian political uprisings—from the Grange through the Populists and Non-Partisan Leaguers to the Progressives—were uprisings of the farmer against the town as well as of the Midwest against the financial East. The first attack of the new farmers' organizations was to take over the functions of the middlemen in the towns and to attempt to by-pass the urban financial agents in the small towns.

That the farmer's struggle for political parity was not won quickly is not surprising. Most of the conditions of farm life tended to keep the farmer in a status inferior to the town. He had to market his crops within the distance a team and wagon could cover from sunup to sundown. He had to look to the local banker for credit. Interest rates were high. Nor was credit always extended graciously.

Then, there always was a higher proportion of foreign born among the farmers than among the townspeople. With foreign accents and an inability to speak English undoubtedly went a sense of shame and other handicaps. The driving urge of farm life was to get off the farm, away from its loneliness and harsh living, to town. Even while he resented the town's overlordship, the farmer continued to look upward to the town as his superior in almost all things.

This sense of inferiority has vanished. If anything, the townspeople are beginning to look to the farm with envy. The major forces responsible are the farmer's vastly improved economic position, the automobile, better education and rural electrification.

As late as 1935 coal-oil lamps still flickered in nine of ten farms. Today electric lights gleam from eight of ten farms. Electrification is not only making many farm operations more efficient. Psychologically, it has meant a revolutionary lift in social prestige for the farmer, particularly for farm women. Some years ago a young farm wife had quite a time reconciling herself to the poetical but back-breaking oaken bucket. The farmer taking a wife today can carry his bride across the threshold into a kitchen as modern and fully equipped as any city kitchen.

Guthrie County, for example, doesn't rank high on the prosperity scale for Iowa. Yet, last year the 3,200 members of the Guthrie REA Co-operative had among them 3,800 radio sets, 1,200 electric cooking ranges, 600 electric water heaters, 2,700 electric refrigerators and 500 television sets. Yet when the Guthrie REA was set up in 1938, John McLuen, the manager, was worried that many farmers might not use the 45 kilowatt hours of electricity for which a minimum charge was assessed.

At the time, McLuen recalls, many local merchants were

hostile to the REA as another example of "government inter-
ference with business." Today, the merchants, who have seen
a profitable market for electrical appliances spring up where
none existed before, are among the most ardent supporters of
rural electrification.

In numerous other ways the townspeople have become more
conscious than ever before of their dependence upon the
farmer. Bank deposits in rural towns have increased ninefold
since the worst of the depression. Studying his accounts, the
local banker is likely to find many farmers with more ready
cash than the banker himself. More farmers are debt free now
than ever before. In 1932 thirty-eight of every thousand farms
were foreclosed; in 1950 only one in a thousand, an all-time
low. Where interest on farm mortgages took 11 per cent of the
farmer's income in 1932, it now takes hardly one per cent of
his income.

Possessing an automobile and truck, the farmer doesn't have
to take his crops to the nearest town unless he wants to. Much
of his marketing and buying is done through farmer co-ops.
The local merchant, seeing the farmer drive through town to
some nearby city, is likely to try harder to hold the farmer's
trade. The wife of one Guthrie farmer told me how vividly
she remembers one depression day when she vainly tried to
cash a check at three different stores in town. "Now those
merchants are eager to extend us credit," she observed, "but
we don't need it."

Good roads and the automobile have also enabled the farm
family to participate more actively in the civic life of the
town. The farmer no longer considers himself part of an
isolated crossroad hamlet. His community has expanded to
take in the town itself. In Guthrie Center, the Rev. McDonald
draws most of his church support from farmers, not townspeople. School buses bring farm children into the same con-
solidated schools which are attended by the town children.
Where once it was possible to spot farm children by their

clothes and backward manners, there now is no telling them apart from town children. Half of the members of the Guthrie Center high school football team are farm youngsters.

Among farmers, an ever-increasing proportion are college-educated. One Kansas educator has remarked, "A decade ago we were training farm boys to leave the farm. Now for the first time we are educating them to go back to the farm." There also has been a steady drift of retired farmers into town, with their sons and relatives left out on the farms.

All these changes are not credited to the Democratic party, of course, though the Democrats definitely are given credit for rural electrification. The fact that these changes have occurred largely under Democratic rule, however, has greatly weakened the traditional "rum, Romanism and rebellion" prejudices against voting Democratic. Perhaps most significant, the small town is no longer a mere outpost for business, which it was as late as the 1920's. As the farmer has come into his own, the town has come to the farmer.

Conflicts between town and country still persist, of course. Among the townspeople many still feel linked with business emotionally, economically and ideologically. But a greater proportion than ever before now identify their own welfare with higher farm income and government price supports. Not too many years ago the Main Street merchant or banker was likely to announce his political beliefs dogmatically, without regard to what the farmer thought. Now the merchant is more apt to ask the farmer, on whose business he depends, "What do you think?" Farmers who are serving as PMA* committeemen probably acquire a new importance locally because of their direct contact with Washington.

Since the full influences of the farmer's changed social status have not yet made themselves felt, one cannot fully appraise its political significance as yet. This much is already clear.

* The old Triple A committeemen are now known as PMA (Production, Marketing Administration) committeemen.

The town-farm relationship which supported the old era of Republican political dominance is gone, beyond restoration. If the Republicans are to recover their political hold in the rural countryside it will have to be in terms of the new town-country relationship. They cannot simply reassert the interests of business and expect farmers or even the rural townspeople to follow their lead unquestioningly.

Nor would neglect of the farmers' interests by any Republican administration be tolerated for long. Twelve years of farm depression, from 1920 to 1932, were required for the farm belt to forsake the Republican party. Since then the New Deal has demonstrated how much can be done through the government. A new farm depression could be expected to bring a quicker and sharper political swing than in the past.

The Republicans probably cannot hope to recover more than part of their rural political strength. Through much of the farm belt the voters today are in transition toward a new system of two-party politics. The tradition of voting Republican because it "is the thing to do" has been replaced by widespread ticket-splitting for "the man" and by deliberate calculation of which party favors the voters' interests.

This shift to two-party politics has not yet been made fully. It is stronger in some states than in others and in national than local politics. As late as 1940 the Iowa Democratic party lacked an effective organization in eighty of the state's ninety-nine counties. In some counties, the Democrats still do not run full slates of candidates for county offices.

If the Democrats put vigorously competing candidates into the local field, the resulting upheaval might be little short of sensational. In Guthrie the Democrats could not fill their county ticket in 1948. A local postmaster happened to ask the help of Jake More, the Democratic state committeeman, in getting shifted to an R.F.D. route. More promised his aid provided the postmaster found someone to run for state representative. A young schoolteacher, Mrs. John Crabb, was per-

suaded to make the race. To everyone's amazement, she swept
to victory with Truman, the first Democrat to be sent to the
legislature from Guthrie County in forty years! In 1950 Mrs.
Crabb was re-elected.

In national politics, however, Iowa, along with other farm
states, seems definitely committed to two-party warfare. One
of the more striking things about the farmer's voting since
Roosevelt has been its consistency. If allowance is made
for the wartime isolationist dip, the voting of the farm areas
shows surprisingly little change.

Outside the South, 106 counties, more than 40 per cent rural,
have remained Democratic since 1932. Another 96 counties,
more than 40 per cent rural, were Democratic in 1932 and
1936, broke during the war, but returned to the Democratic
column in 1948. Thus, there are about 200 rural counties outside of the South which can be considered as normally Democratic in Presidential elections.

By and large, in other words, the farm vote seems closely
divided. Neither the Republicans nor the Democrats have the
full confidence of the farmers. I rode on a bus with one young
Ohio farmer who voted for Truman in 1948 and for Taft in
1950. He was on his way to Madison, Wisconsin, to bring his
fiancée home for the Thanksgiving holidays. "I wish I knew
more about politics," he said. "I don't know what to believe.
Maybe the best course is to see that neither party gets too
strong. If I saw one party getting too much power, I'd vote
for the other in the next election."

Few farmers may be as consciously aware of their mistrust
of both parties as this young Ohio farmer. Subconsciously,
though, much of the farm belt seems to be trying to balance
one party against the other. The vote of many agricultural
counties in the last fourteen years shows that many farmers
have followed the practice of voting for a Democrat for President and for a Republican in Congress. The tendency for
Republican strength to perk in non-Presidential years is not

simply the result of a smaller vote, as Democrats like to believe. The Republican off-year gains also reflect a widespread desire to guard against the Democrats' going too far.

The voting behavior of the farm belt raises the question whether farmers really want to break the deadlock between Congress and the President which has prevailed in Washington since 1938. The desire to perpetuate the prevailing political stalemate is probably not a conscious one. Mainly, it would seem to stem from the deadlock in the farmers' own interests, between their fears of inflation versus deflation, their uncertainty over what the proper role of government should be and their only partial break from inherited Republican tradition and from the G.O.P. monopoly which still prevails in many counties.

This division in the interests of farmers is particularly noticeable when one talks to them about the farm program. The present program is anything but popular. However, even more strenuous criticisms are voiced of any alternative that is proposed. Those who cry "end all farm subsidies" do not speak for the bulk of farmers. But those who would substitute any specific new plan are also in the minority.

Most farmers want some kind of farm program but there is no consensus among them as to the form this program should take. The burden of proof would seem stacked against whoever proposes to change the status quo. In the absence of agreement over a new program the conflicting interests of farmers appear to cancel out into an uneasy acceptance of the prevailing program as something that hasn't hurt the farmer—yet.

As long as farmers remain so torn in their own emotions, they must be considered as a force for perpetuating the prevailing political deadlock in the country. They may swing from one party to another, but their fears seem too conflicting to permit them to join in any fundamental, enduring political realignment right now. The inflation and tax increases that came with the Korean War tilted the balance against the administration, but did not lessen the farmer's uncertainty over the future.

Yet, merely to prolong the present stalemate offers no solution for the farmer's problems. Economically, the present farm program fails to meet the nation's needs. Politically, it raises the grave question whether the interests of the farmer can be kept in balance with those of labor and other segments of the population.

9

The Dynamo Slows Down

1. History Fails to Repeat Itself

The same photographs of Franklin Roosevelt and Frank Murphy hung on the wall but it was hard to believe that it was the same place. When I first visited Chrysler Local Seven of the United Automobile Workers a few days after Roosevelt's third term victory, the scene was one of belligerent activity. Bulletin boards bristled with photographs of police clubbing strikers and of tear gas riotings. When the union's educational director heard that I was analyzing the election for the *Saturday Evening Post*, he stiffened suspiciously and seemed about to have me thrown out. Then, he began boasting freely of how class conscious the auto workers were and how ready they were to vote Roosevelt a fourth or a fifth term. He wore a lumber jacket. With his feet on his desk and a buzzer by his hand, he looked the very picture of newly arrived power.

Returning eight years later, after Truman's victory, the whole atmosphere of the local had changed. The strike photographs had come down from the bulletin boards and had been replaced by idyllic snapshots of the union's annual outings and sporting events. An honor roll listed fifty-nine union members who had been killed in the war. Nearby stood a cabinet filled with loving cups and other trophies won in city-wide UAW tournaments. The "class-conscious" educational director was gone—ousted in the UAW-wide fight against Communists

179

which Walter Reuther led. On their desks, the new officers had propped the slogan, "UAW Americanism for Us." They were wearing green jackets and green silk legion caps.

In 1940 the flavor of the local was one of street barricades and sitdown strikes; eight years later it was almost like a lodge hall.

Not only Chrysler Seven but the whole American labor movement has undergone a striking transformation in recent years. The change may not be as sharp as the contrast between my two visits to Chrysler Seven suggests. Still, the dynamic near-revolutionary surge, which doubled union membership from 1935 to 1938 and which brought such industrial giants as General Motors and U.S. Steel to the bargaining table, is now gone. The labor dynamo has slowed down.

Whether the labor movement has become a conservative force, as Frank Tannenbaum contends, depends on how one defines the word. Certainly a decade of full employment has altered organized labor's inner stresses and drive. As late as 1940 in houses near Chrysler Seven one could still see signs advertising "sleeping rooms for rent," mirroring the old half-boom, half-broke nature of auto employment. By 1948 these signs were all gone. The going wage in the auto industry was three times the depression low. Every fourth or fifth house was freshly painted. The grocery which handled food stamps in 1940 gleamed with fluorescent lighting. By 1948 almost half of Chrysler Seven's members owned their own homes.

With their new stake in the economic system, many workers had become wary of political radicalism. When Henry Wallace came campaigning into Detroit, Chrysler Seven was having its first strike in ten years. Wallace tried to join the picket line, but was jeered off. I was told of one elderly union member who had been indifferent to the campaign until several workers started sporting Wallace buttons. "Give me one of those Truman buttons," he demanded angrily of his shop steward.

Some union leaders, like Reuther, still talk of trade unionism as the revolutionary force of our times through which society is to be remade. But the inner mechanics of Reuther's own union today resemble more closely the momentum of a bureaucracy than the trampling of a new social movement. A few years ago strikes flared in the auto industry at the drop of an unkind word by a foreman. Much of that militancy reflected two struggles—the bitter factional rivalry for power within the UAW and the grudging refusal of employers to concede full union recognition.

Both these minor wars have been settled, not alone in autos but in all of the mass production industries. With their leadership stabilized, the unions have become a disciplining and stabilizing force upon their own membership. With union recognition no longer in dispute, the grievance machinery which has been set up in the various industries has acquired a status all its own, with an established body of precedents accepted as binding by both labor and management.

In the giant industries, custom—a new kind of common law —is becoming the final umpire in more and more of the disputes between workers and management.

Nor are Reuther's dynamic public utterances supported by such actions as his signing a contract with General Motors for five years. The five year contract was a hedge against expected depression. But, as one astute observer in Detroit remarked, "When Reuther agreed to stabilize working conditions and wages for so long a period, he removed the major incentive for militant political action from one immense segment of his union."

The threat of inflation has sparked the labor dynamo with a new fighting cause—to keep wages rising with living costs; apart from this though, the urgent sense of grievance, so evident even fifteen years ago, is gone. Last summer one union leader complained to me at being asked to draft the platform for a state CIO. "Ten or fifteen years ago I would have welcomed the assignment," he remarked. "There were so many things I was mad about. But what can I agitate for now? We don't have any really big issues left."

Still, despite the general well-being of its members and its seemingly formidable power, the whole trade union movement remains permeated by a basic sense of insecurity. The very statistics of labor's opulence—more than 15,000,000 union members, an annual income of $400,000,000 in dues alone, 55,000 full-time employees—suggest one troubling question: How much of its gains can labor hold in event of another depression?

As fear of economic collapse is the constant cloud in the farmer's sky, so that dread hovers like smoke over our factories. For workers as well as farmers, the memory of the depression is perhaps the most important single psychological factor influencing their political outlook.

The very fact that union leadership, once entrenched, changes so slowly, tightens the grip of the past and its memories. The average age of the CIO's executive board today is fifty-four years, only six years younger than the members of the Supreme Court. Always older, the A. F. of L.'s executive Board averages sixty-six years.

Most of the nation's top labor leaders are veterans of one or both of two grim ordeals—the depression and the losing battle for union recognition of the 1920's.

David Dubinsky, who heads the Ladies Garment Workers, lives in a Manhattan penthouse today, but during the depression he couldn't pay the rent on a four-room flat in the Bronx. Joseph Curran, then still a seaman, was sleeping on park benches. Walter Reuther was working a thirteen-hour shift at eighty-five cents an hour and going to school at night.

More important than any hangover of personal insecurity is what happened to the unions themselves. During World War One, with unionization enjoying unprecedented government protection, the American Federation of Labor doubled its membership. By 1920 its membership of 5,000,000 covered

12 per cent of the total working force. With the war's end the industrial truce was replaced by an open-shop offensive. Strike after strike was called, fought out, and broken. In three years the A. F. of L. lost nearly 2,000,000 members.

By 1933 labor's strength was down to the 1917 level in numbers of members and back to 1908 in the proportion of the nation's labor force wearing union buttons.

When the last war ended most labor leaders expected the bitter struggle of the 1920's to be repeated. This ghost of the past became the real generalissimo directing labor's postwar strategy. Collectively and individually, the unions maneuvered to position themselves in anticipation of an economic collapse and a new antilabor offensive.

The significance of the labor-industry conflict since the war's end lies, I believe, in the fact that history has *not* repeated itself. Although labor has suffered some setbacks, a rout of union power, like that which followed World War One, has been prevented.

Still, the acid test of labor's enduring strength is yet to come. Although even the most pessimistic labor leaders may feel confident that the grim twenties will not come alive again, none can be sure how much of the gains of the Roosevelt Revolution they may lose. Many labor leaders are painfully aware that much of their following was recruited under the patronage of a friendly government, rather than through labor's own strength. What if an unsympathetic administration comes to power? What if that coincides with a recession?

The still unexploded dynamite in the Taft-Hartley Law lies in those fears. Compared to earlier antiunion statutes, the Taft-Hartley Law is relatively mild. The real threat in the act lies in its union-busting potential during a period of unemployment, when labor's bargaining power is weak, and when a government hostile to labor might be in power.

For the present, the defense boom puts off the Great Test, which labor ultimately must face. Temporarily, at least, the inflation of the cold war strengthens unionism. The general wage ceiling means that pay increases can be obtained most readily through unions appearing before government boards. In terms of militancy, rising living costs are like a shot in the arm to trade unions, giving them a new "big issue" with which to agitate for their members.

Whatever labor gains through inflation, however, is likely to aggravate its inner sense of insecurity. After the boom is over then what? The higher wages, prices and other costs are forced, the more disastrous may be the possible recession in the future. Instead of falling out of the second or third floor, our economy might well fall from the sixth or seventh floor.

Labor's position, in this respect, is not too different from that of the farmer, business or other economic groups. All find themselves under increasing pressure, as a result of inflation and the general expansion of government activity, to protect their own interests through sustained political action. Labor, however, does face a peculiar political dilemma of its own. Politically, it has been most effective when its membership is lean and hungry. The very gains which labor is seeking to preserve undermine the zeal for political action among union members. Those gains also tend to divide unions from one another and to make it more difficult to harmonize labor's interests with those of other voting elements.

Several years ago when labor's high command proclaimed "labor is in politics to stay," they acted as if they had made a decision of revolutionary importance. Since then labor's political strategists have learned through painful experience that, far from settling anything, the decision to stay in politics has brought new hazards and headaches.

2. Pork Chops and Human Justice

The sirens screeched through the night as the limousine sped along the New Jersey highway to Passaic where a 1936 Roosevelt campaign rally was being held. It was the first time in his life that David Dubinsky had ever had a police escort.

Never the quiet meditative type, Dubinsky was bug-eyed with excitement. Turning to two union aides, he began reminiscing of the days when he first became interested in politics.

Meyer London was running for Congress on the Socialist ticket in New York City, and recalled Dubinsky, "I made speeches from a soapbox and was an election watcher. I slept for three nights with my wrist strapped to the ballot box so Tammany leaders wouldn't throw the box into the river. Now look at me! In a limousine! With a police escort!"

Sinking back into the luxuriously plushed seat, Dubinsky sighed, "I wonder whether I would do all that over again?"

Figuratively, that could be asked of the whole labor movement—and merely to raise the question is to suggest the answer. Every Presidential election spurs talk of organization of a labor party. But the simple truth is that, having enjoyed the confidences of Presidents and ridden behind motorcycle escorts, the nation's labor leaders are not going back to the old soapbox days. Organized labor has far too much at stake in the immediate operations of government to return to the impractical gestures of splinter party politics. It must make its influence felt through the regular party system.

At present, in fact, labor has little choice but to remain in the Democratic party. As long as the prevailing Republican drift is toward the formation of a nation-wide conservative coalition, labor's only practical alternative is to align with the so-called liberal Democratic wing—or, as some labor leaders have threatened, "to sit out the election," which would confess defeat in advance.

Moreover, it is questionable whether the leaders of labor could move the bulk of the workers out of the Democratic party today. The ties binding the laboring masses to the Democratic emblem—as earlier chapters have shown—are ethnic and religious as well as economic. The strength of the Democratic appeal reflects the many different ways through which Roosevelt touched and lifted the aspirations of the urban masses. Any attempt to lead them out of the Democratic fold would run against insurmountable psychological barriers.

For labor to remain in the Democratic party, however, brings its own frustrations, stemming mainly from two sources —the difficulty in harmonizing labor's interests with the rest of the Roosevelt coalition, and the fact that trade unions are organized primarily to protect their occupational interests and not for political action.

The decline in labor's political influence in recent years is partly the result of the clash between the narrow job interests of the individual unions and the general interests of all of labor.

When the New Deal coalition was formed, these general interests were uppermost in the minds of workers and labor leaders. The millions of unemployed or part-time workers had no occupational interest until they were put to work. The struggle for union recognition was a common struggle for all unions. The depression years had left so heavy an accumulation of grievances that both workers and leaders really felt themselves part of a "crusade for human justice," which Samuel Gompers once described as his ideal for the labor movement.

Prosperity, however, has thrust these general interests into the background. Meanwhile, the diverse occupational interests of the individual unions have come to the fore. The change can be seen in the different attitudes of unions toward political activity. By and large, the unions most energetic in national politics are those operating in national labor markets. For example, the occupational interests of unions like textiles which suffer from the competition of the unorganized South incline them to favor minimum wage and other legislation which will equalize labor conditions throughout the country. On the other hand, the job interests of craft unions, like the Teamsters and Building Trades, tend to make them more concerned with local labor markets—and local politics.

Are the A. F. of L. unions really so much less interested in political activity than the CIO as many people assume? Or do A. F. of L. unions concentrate on state and municipal politics, while the CIO's interests are primarily national?

Nor does the fact that some unions oppose government controls make them necessarily less politically-minded. When the Meat-Cutters Union objected to price ceilings on livestock it was not being indifferent to politics. On the contrary, its action represented a calculated political decision that government inaction would favor butchers more than government regulation.

Similarly, when John L. Lewis testified against all price and wage controls was it because he believes so unswervingly in *laissez faire*? Or did he feel that the uncontrolled workings of supply and demand would favor his miners?

When the New Deal began, few labor leaders were more eager for government intervention than Lewis. A rugged individualist of the Herbert Hoover economic school in his early years, Lewis lost his faith in the virtues of free competition during the 1920's, when he found his mine union being chopped to pieces by competition from unorganized mines in the South and from more efficient fuels, such as oil.

By 1929, beaten in the coalfields of West Virginia, threatened in Ohio, losing out in Pennsylvania and facing rebellion from his own miners in Illinois, Lewis was ready to abandon free enterprise. Through Senator Thomas Watson of Indiana he proposed a moratorium on the antitrust laws to allow coal producers to fix prices. In return they were to recognize the miners' right to organize. This formula later was worked into the NRA.

Since 1923 the number of bituminous miners has dropped from 640,000 to 350,000 and still is declining. While there were twice as many miners in the country as were needed, Lewis was desperate for government intervention. Now that he holds an effective corner on mine labor, he can proclaim his independence of government protection. Lacking such a corner on their labor, other unions still have to look to a friendly government.

Prosperity tends to weaken the political solidarity of union members as well. In Indianapolis, after the 1950 elections, I sampled a workers' precinct which was Democratic in 1948 but which had just swung Republican. One woman and her husband had bought a second house which they were renting out. The husband voted Democratic because it "was the worker's party" but the woman voted Republican because "rent control prevents us from raising our tenant's rent."

After World War One there was a similar ebbing of the emotional drive of trade unionism. The complaints of union organizers today echo the complaints of organizers in the 1920's—"workers are beginning to speculate on the stock market" or "workers have bought so many things on the installment plan that they don't like to go out on strike for fear of falling behind in their payments."

It would seem then that the limits between which labor's political pendulum can swing are set by the job interests of individual unions and workers on one side, and the general interests of the whole labor movement on the other. While occupational interests are ascendant, unions will differ considerably in political outlook and so will individual union members. In pursuit of their own job interests, some unions will ally themselves with whichever party happens to be in power locally. Some may even support a Republican for President. But any all-out effort to destroy trade unions or a serious threat of economic depression would solidify labor's ranks politically.

Must labor wait for another depression before its political militancy can be revived? Or can workers be educated to expand the concept of their job interest to embrace sustained political action? Although their objectives have never been stated in those terms, that, in essence, is what the CIO's

Political Action Committee and the A. F. of L.'s Labor League for Political Education are trying to do today. They are searching for some means of electrifying labor politically, without having to wait for the shock treatment of mass unemployment.

The substitute is being sought in terms of intensive organization and the expenditure of huge sums of money. Both the PAC and Labor's League for Political Education maintain full-time staff workers and registration lists of voters in many of the important cities. Never before has labor gone in for so much doorbell ringing and for so much machine politics. However, the failure to beat Senator Taft raises the question whether the immediate effects of all this effort may not be doing labor more harm than good politically.

3. Labor Re-elects Taft

Election day of 1950 brought Gregory Stebbins a warm, satisfied feeling. An organizer for the steelworkers, Stebbins led the anti-Taft offensive in the Seventeenth Ward of Columbus. With seventy helpers he canvassed every house in the ward, stuffing mailboxes with leaflets and exhorting people not to miss voting in "the political battle of the century." When crowded polling booths indicated a record turnout, Stebbins glowed. Going to bed before the ward returns were available, he felt serenely confident that the Seventeenth had turned in its usual heavy Democratic majority.

Because Stebbins left town early the next morning, it was several days before he could check the ward results. He was astounded. Probably three fourths of Ward Seventeen's families are union members, mainly railroaders and steelworkers. Not many of their frame houses would bring more than $10,000 even in today's inflated markets. Yet, a sizable majority voted for "labor's worst enemy," as Taft had been tarred.

Bewildered, Stebbins called in his union stewards, but none

could explain what had happened. Three weeks later when I saw him in the course of doing a postelection analysis of the Taft vote, Stebbins confessed, "I still can't understand it. We thought we needed only to get out the vote. Well, the vote came out but it went against us."

A good part of Taft's 430,000 majority can rightly be credited to his opponent, Joseph Ferguson, the state auditor. Shortly after "Jumping Joe" won the Democratic primary a canny Ohioan observed, "If the Democrats want to win, they should send Ferguson on a mission abroad." Ferguson's habit of slipping on grammatical banana peels repelled many voters. Others whom I interviewed couldn't recall his name. Even those kindly disposed felt that "Joe is a nice guy and okay for state auditor, but I wouldn't want him in Washington with war threatening."

But if Ferguson's dismal showing confirms the adage, "You can't beat somebody with nobody," the real significance of the election was that it proved to be a dramatic referendum on what Ohio voters thought of labor unions. Taft had been singled out as the prime target for what was intended as a mighty demonstration of labor's political power. It turned out to be a shattering demonstration of labor's political weaknesses.

Those weaknesses might be summed up:

1. An overly militant labor campaign provokes so much fear and opposition that it promotes an antilabor coalition.
2. Labor and the Democratic party are still uneasy, mutually suspicious allies.
3. Labor is unable to deliver its membership except in the direction toward which that membership is inclined— as for example, in voting for Roosevelt.
4. Even among union members there is a deep distrust of labor's becoming too big politically.

"We didn't want labor to go too far" and "we didn't want

labor running the country" were the most frequent reasons given me by voters in explaining their support of Taft. This feeling was expressed both by farmers, never overly sympathetic to labor, and by persons who believed in unions. "I used to work in a department store for $3.50 a week," a barber's wife told me. "When I think what stores pay now how I wish we had had unions when I was working. But labor shouldn't have too much power. We have only a little shop here. The union made us raise the price of haircuts to a dollar and a quarter and business fell off. We have to close at six on Saturday nights. We're poor people. It would mean so much if we could open an hour longer."

In three counties I visited it was commonly bruited about that the local Democratic chairman had voted for Taft— which, even if untrue, shows how intense was the friction between labor and the regular Democratic organizations. Many old-line Democrats took their cue from Governor Frank Lausche. With an eye to 1952, Lausche refused to endorse Ferguson and almost openly supported Taft. In some localities there were bitter quarrels between labor leaders and the regular party heads. In many places labor virtually took over the campaign. Whether this was because the unions had the campaign funds, or because the regular Democratic politicians were laying down on the job, the effect was the same. The more labor pushed to the forefront the more resentful became other Democratic elements.

A farmer in Holmes County explained how his neighbors felt, "If Ferguson won, labor would have taken all the credit and farmers wouldn't be represented."

The operator of a super market in Columbus Grove, a registered Democrat, observed, "I felt we had to vote for Taft to keep the Socialists from taking over the Democratic party."

At no time was there a real meeting of minds between labor leaders and the Democratic regulars. Unable to agree on a mutually acceptable candidate, they left the choice to a wide-open primary in which Ferguson won over five other contestants. Both the unions and the regular Democratic organizations felt let down. Thereafter no unified strategy guided the anti-Taft forces.

Not only was much of the normal Democratic vote alienated, along with the bulk of farmers and nearly all of the urban middle class; the unions could not deliver their own membership. An Akron beer-trucker, who voted for Ferguson, startled me by remarking, "Don't get the idea I'm too disappointed that Taft won." This trucker had been denouncing Taft as a "rich man." He said, "I've never had any use for rich men since the depression when I drove a big car for a millionaire at fifty cents an hour." He went on to explain, "Ferguson would have been a yes man for the labor party. I don't want a labor government here, like in England."

Many workers seized upon Taft's candidacy to voice a protest against their own union chiefs. In Toledo the rank-and-file hatred—the word is used advisedly—of Richard Gosser, the local auto-union boss, spilled over so violently that Thomas H. Burke, a CIO member of Congress, was defeated for re-election. An auto worker, a Navy veteran, explained, "He was Gosser's Congressman, not ours."

In a Youngstown dairy an employee was laid off. A delegation of fellow workers asked the union for help in reinstating the man. They were told, "Forget it. Our first job is to beat Bob Taft."

"Right there," two dairy workers told me, "we decided to vote for Taft."

In Cincinnati a cutter—he belonged to the Amalgamated Clothing Workers, the home union of PAC-head Jack Kroll —complained, "Sure we elect our union officers by secret ballot, but there's only one slate to vote on. That's like Russia." In 1948 this cutter opposed the Taft-Hartley Law. "I'm for it now," he said. "There have been fewer strikes. When other workers strike, business drops and we get laid off."

A machinist who belonged to a company union liked the Taft-Hartley ban on the closed shop. "It means if I quit my job I can go to work elsewhere," he said. A drop-forger in Toledo, remarked, "Under the Wagner Act the union bosses had the upper hand. If you said something they didn't like, they could kick you out. Now you are protected."

One union head confessed, "We couldn't convince the workers Taft-Hartley is a 'slave labor law.' They've been living with it for three years and nothing bad has happened to them."

Part way through the campaign, the labor chieftains tried to soft-pedal Taft-Hartley as an issue. But Taft kept hammering at it. Carrying the fight directly to the workers, he visited more than 300 plants. Efforts to turn these visits into anti-Taft demonstrations backfired repeatedly. In one factory, on the day Taft was scheduled to speak, a union official appeared and stuck a Ferguson button on every worker's overalls. I found that probably half of that plant's workers voted for Taft. When Taft came to Campbell Sheet and Tube in Youngstown, the local CIO chief ordered a walkout of the power unit. Before operations were resumed several thousand men had lost almost a full day's pay.

Their anger was written, hot and loud, into the vote of four precincts adjoining the mill, whose residents are mainly millworkers. Truman got 56 per cent of their vote in 1948. Taft got 63 per cent in 1950.

It wasn't difficult to find workers in these precincts who had voted for Truman two years ago and had swung to Taft. Their reasoning was summed up fairly well by one white-haired mill hand. "I didn't like the CIO shutting the mill," he told me as he stood by his open door. "And I don't like the war. We oughtn't to be fighting in a place like Korea, so far from home, losing all those boys and not on the real enemy. I've been a Democrat, but I'm ready to vote Republican. We need to clean house in Washington. There must be some

Communists in the Government or the newspapers wouldn't be printing all those charges."

Until recently, this millworker had been planning to retire. "With all this inflation," he complained, "I don't know what my pension will be worth a few years from now."

Down the street, Richard Bates, Jr., a gunner in the last war, got out the orders calling up his reserve unit. Quite philosophic about going back into the service—"by getting in now, I figure I'll get out earlier"—Bates did not blame Truman for the Korean War. A Truman voter in 1948 he voted for Taft because "I didn't like that kid stuff the union pulled, like shutting the mill. Then they beat up Skinny Greenwood next door for campaigning for Taft."

President Truman, along with some labor leaders, has tried to attribute Taft's victory to the enormous sums spent in his behalf. The impression left with me was that each side had all the money it needed and that if labor had had more money it might have suffered a worse defeat. The plain fact was that the campaign put on by labor divided its own membership while solidifying the opposition.

In Cleveland, the CIO alone marshaled a force of 800 election workers, the largest number it ever has had in a single city. Taft got more votes in Cleveland than in either his 1944 or 1938 campaigns, and came fairly close to carrying the city.

The essence of Taft's whole strategy was to gamble on being re-elected by labor. The Taft forces drummed insistently on the theme of "outside political carpetbaggers" coming into Ohio with "unlimited funds" to "tell Ohioans how to vote." They reprinted and circulated the more abusive attacks on Taft made by labor leaders. One, which became a virtual Republican battle slogan, was the boast of James Petrillo, the head of the musicians union, "There will be nothing we won't do to knock your [Taft's] silly head out of the U.S. Senate and keep it out."

The political weaknesses of labor which were demonstrated

in the Taft campaign have cropped up in other elections in which labor has been the prime issue. Akron, for example, once an open-shop citadel, became strongly prolabor during the depression. When the rubber workers struck in 1936 the newspapers were benevolently neutral; local merchants donated $25,000 of foodstuffs. That November, seven of every ten Akronites voted for Roosevelt. The next year, though, when the CIO tried to elect its man mayor, he got only 44 per cent of the vote. The Republicans bettered their vote over 1936 in every ward, indicating that the whole city, including many union members, shared the fear of labor going too far politically.

In Detroit, the CIO has made four vigorous tries at electing a mayor. In 1937, when the Negroes had not yet solidified in the Democratic party, the CIO candidate got only 37 per cent of the vote. In 1943, 1945 and 1949 the CIO candidates got much the same vote, 45, 44 and 40 per cent.

Six wards in the city varied only 1 to 3 per cent in all four elections, while another five wards showed a variation of less than 4 per cent over the last three elections. A good part of Detroit, in other words, has voted virtually the same way each time a labor candidate ran for mayor. Who the candidate was seems to have made little difference, or how much money was spent, or how effectively organized labor was.

This rigidity in voting indicates that most Detroiters have a fixed attitude on the place of labor in politics. The dominant sentiment is clearly to keep labor at arm's length. While this feeling is strongest among Republicans, of course, it holds for Democratic voters as well. This distrust of labor seems motivated less by a desire to destroy unions than to check what are popularly regarded as the "abuses" of union power, and to balance labor off against other segments of society.

Perhaps one can sum up the shift that has taken place in the public's attitude to labor in these terms. During the depression and in the first Roosevelt years the dominant mood in the nation favored giving labor a green light. Today the feelings in political ascendancy favor a yellow, "go slow" light.

At least for the time being labor's battle to repeal the Taft-Hartley Law has been lost. The law may be altered somewhat to become more satisfactory to labor but some regulation of unions will remain in force, if only because of two things:

First, as the growth of mighty concentrations of business forced government regulation, so the expansion of labor unions makes it unlikely that they can ever again be completely free of all government supervision. Few large-scale strikes nowadays are regarded as mere private disputes between workers and employers.

For some time to come labor leaders are likely to look upon every effort to restrain unions as an attempt to destroy them—and this motive will inspire some labor legislation. It probably will be some years before a balance is struck between the protection unions feel they need and the protection needed by the rest of society.

The second major reason why labor will have to accept some kind of restraint as its normal lot is the political one. We have already noted that at present labor's maximum political strength can be mustered only as a part of the Democratic coalition. The interests of labor and other pro-Roosevelt elements can not be harmonized except in terms of some regulation of unions.

The basic reason is that the inner dynamics of the Roosevelt coalition have shifted from those of *getting* to those of *keeping*. The dominant concern of most of the Roosevelt elements today is not to get more but to preserve the gains of the last twenty years. To preserve those gains—as will be shown more fully in the next chapter—each of the major elements in the coalition must be kept from pushing too far. lest the gains of other elements be imperiled.

This need of restraint is not one confronting labor alone. It is the common dilemma of the whole Roosevelt coalition. The mutual contradiction which wracks all the Democratic elements is that each wants a friendly government, according to its own lights, but how can a government, tugged by conflicting interests, remain friendly to all its supporters?

Thus far, the signs indicate that, in their struggle to preserve their gains, the Democratic elements are tearing themselves apart politically. Before leaping to the conclusion that the Roosevelt coalition is disintegrating, however, let us examine the peculiar equilibrium of conflicting interests which has kept the clashing, discordant Democratic elements together for so long.

10

A New Theory of Political Parties

1. The Democratic Sun

When Henry Wallace tossed his boomerang into the Presidential ring late in 1947, his followers claimed he would draw 10,000,000 votes. Although these estimates later were drastically reduced, with Wallace hacking from one side and the Dixiecrats from the other, the long predicted disintegration of the Democratic party seemed at hand.

The self-searching that followed Truman's surprising victory centered mainly on the failure of the pollsters to guess how the election would turn out. A more fruitful question would have been : How well do we understand the workings of the American party system? Why is it that our major parties always seem on the verge of flying apart, but rarely do? Why do third parties always look so formidable in May and so hollow in November?

Most writing about politics seeks to establish a pattern of continuity between the present and past. This is natural. When we gaze at clouds, our imaginations instinctively twist their formless fluff into some resemblance to things we live with. American political history readily lends itself to being pictured as a succession of struggles revolving around the same, recurring themes—the Hamiltonian versus Jeffersonian tradition, the "people versus plutocracy," capital pitted against labor, agrarians against the city, states rights against federal centralization.

But simply because politicians invoke the issues and slogans of the past does not mean that they are the heirs of these earlier political movements. Our study of isolationism showed that the same emotional yearning to avoid war with Germany was allied with agrarian socialists in the First World War and with conservative business during the second. Again, socialism is supposed to be a philosophy born of urban slums, yet before World War One Eugene Debs pulled his highest vote percentage in Oklahoma.

The fact is that at various times quite different groups find it convenient to invoke the same ideological concepts. Important as the ideas themselves are, what often happens is a revolt of certain voting elements, which grab whatever slogans happen to be available.

A second popularly held theory of the nature of our political parties is that they really are fundamentally the same. The platforms of the major parties often seem copied from one another. Liberal Democrats and liberal Republicans, it is pointed out, have more in common with one another than with conservative members of their own parties. Some scholars —notably Herbert Agar—have gone to considerable effort to prove that this similarity of our parties is perhaps the saving virtue of our political system. To win the Presidency each party must appeal to a cross section of the voters, to Midwesterners as well as Easterners, to employers as well as factory workers. Extreme differences must be conciliated, thus putting a premium upon the arts of compromise, which have helped hold the country together.

But if this necessity to appeal to diverse interests explains why the major parties resemble each other, it fails to explain the strong differences between them.

Let us see whether we can construct a somewhat different theory of the nature of American political parties—a theory which will explain both their likeness and difference, both their attachment to the past and the obvious break in continuity that occurs whenever one party loses its normal dominance to another.

Thumbing back through history, we find relatively few periods when the major parties were closely competitive, with elections alternating between one and the other. The usual pattern has been that of a dominant majority party, which stayed in office as long as its elements held together, and a minority party which gained power only when the majority coalition split.

Our political solar system, in short, has been characterized not by two equally competing suns, but by a sun and a moon. It is within the majority party that the issues of any particular period are fought out; while the minority party shines in reflected radiance of the heat thus generated.

The essential strength or weakness of an American political party is not to be measured simply by the votes it commands, but by the *timeliness* of the elements which compose the party's following. Thus, the rise of Jacksonian Democracy marked the coming-of-age of the western frontier and its alliance with the agrarian South against the commercial East. Within this Democratic party the issues of slavery were fought out. Not until the political heirs of Andrew Jackson split hopelessly was the emerging Republican party able to break through.

In the period following the Civil War, the Republican party served as the arena in which the decisive conflicts of that era were battled out—all the issues of westward expansion, of the nationalizing of business and the growth of manufacturing interests under the protection of the tariff, of the struggle to bring the trusts under some measure of public control which would balance the older ideals of agrarian democracy against the new interests of a rising industrialism.

With the restoration of the South as a political force in 1876, a twenty-year period did ensue in which Democrats and Republicans tugged almost evenly, and indecisively, with neither party winning the Presidency twice in succession and no President gaining a clear majority of the popular vote. Even through this period, however, the Republicans were the party moving forward into the future, while the Democrats instinctively pulled back toward the past.

The Southern Democrats could hardly avoid being a party of nostalgia—what could their program be but to yearn for a lost past? In the North, the Democratic appeal was aimed primarily at those who were alarmed over the Republicans pressing too far and too fast, at those who felt themselves being ground under the rising money power or who were shocked by the corruption which accompanied the quadrupling of the federal bureaucracy and the distribution of the public domain to enterprising and greedy exploitation.

After 1896, when Bryan failed in his crusade to hold back the hands of the clock, Republican dominance became unquestioned. It was broken only by the Bull Moose split, until the depression and the revolt of the city brought a new majority party into existence.

Today it is within the Democratic party that the issues of our times are being fought out, for better or worse. Civil rights, how to balance the interests of the newly emergent labor power against those of the rest of society, the yearning for security against another depression, the hunger for social status of the climbing urban masses—these are do-or-die problems for the elements in the Democratic coalition. They are not the issues which agitate most strongly the Republican voting elements. These latter elements remain rooted in business interests, which suffered comparatively less in the depression. Their struggle for social and economic standing was fought out in terms of the agrarian frontier that has now passed.

This lack of timeliness in its voting elements is the basic reason for the "negative" Republican attitude to so many major problems. The G.O.P. dilemma does not arise out of a lack of "leaders" so-called, or "ideas" so-labeled, but out of the fact that the Republicans remain what the Southern Democrats were after the Civil War—essentially a party of nostalgia. There is one instinctive Republican program, in whose favor all doubts are resolved—to turn the clock back to an earlier era.

That does not mean the White House is out of Republican reach. On the contrary, as the party of the past, the Republicans are ideally situated to attract all voters who feel the Democratic majority is pushing too far, or who would evade the vexatious issues which wrack the Democrats. The problem of the Republicans, which is treated more fully in the next chapter, is whether—once they have won the presidency because of the excesses of the Democratic majority—they can hold it. Can the Republicans come to grips with the problems of our times? Or by ignoring them, will they restore the vigor and unity of the Democratic majority?

For the minority party the immediate problem of political strategy always revolves around one question: Which element in the majority coalition can be split off most readily? The more heated the frictions within the majority sun, naturally, the more luminous are the chances of victory for the minority moon. But what many politicians overlook—and this is what makes American politics so baffling—is that the same frictions which give life to the minority party also serve as the great, unifying force within the majority party.

The dynamics of conflict which hold a political coalition together are indeed akin to those of the sun. Astronomers tell us that the sun is a seething mass of broken atoms, in violent movement and constantly threatening to whirl off into space, but held together by gravitational pull. The American political party is also a powerful magnet, which draws together, in constantly colliding coalition, a bewildering variety of conflicting elements. That these elements can continue in alliance seems to defy every law of logic. But, like the sun, this apparently unstable political mass has its own gravitational equilibrium.

In their ceaseless friction, the different elements give off both positive and negative charges of political electricity. They both repel and attract one another. The common binding attraction is the desire of each element to win dominance in the party. When any one element becomes disaffected, the power of antagonistic elements is automatically enhanced —and so is their attachment to the party. Precisely because the party elements are so hostile to one another, the bolt of one helps to unify the others.

No third party, in brief, is ever a complete liability. If it diverts votes, it also adds votes in counterattraction.

Here, I believe, lies the secret of why American political parties seem ever on the point of breaking up and yet almost never do. During the era of Republican supremacy, secession after secession rocked the G.O.P. ranks, without destroying the Republican coalition. The Populists in 1892 appeared certain to wreck the Republican party. Yet, when the Populists and Democrats fused in 1896 under Bryan, they only cleared the way for a decisive Republican triumph.

Political writers often list the dissidents within a party and, by subtracting the estimated strength of these wrangling antagonists, come up with prophecies of victory for the opposing party. The fatal error in such predictions is that it is virtually impossible for all the clashing elements within a party to fly apart simultaneously. That happens, in fact, only when the party has been shattered to its core. Then, both parties are reshuffled and a wholly new political solar system is created.

Each time one majority sun sets and a new sun rises, the drama of American politics is transformed. Figuratively and literally a new political era begins. For each new majority party brings its own orbit of conflict, its own peculiar rhythm of ethnic antagonisms, its own economic equilibrium, its own sectional balance—and its own version of the Welfare State.

After the Civil War the Republicans solidified their power through the tariff, the Homestead Act and generous land grants to the railroads. The Democratic party under Roosevelt found a substitute for the tariff and public lands in the public debt.

Each new majority party also brings forth its own opposition. Under our system of separation of powers, whoever loses the Presidency continues the battle for control of the government through Congress. It is not surprising that the anti-Roosevelt coalition in Congress took form in 1938, at the very next election after the formation of the Roosevelt coalition in 1936. The year 1938 opened with the Southern filibuster against the proposed antilynching law; 1938 also marked Roosevelt's unsuccessful purge of the more conservative Democratic Senators. It was the year in which John L. Lewis tried to capture control of the Democratic party in Pennsylvania and lost; and of the CIO's unsuccessful battle to win control of the Ohio Democratic party. It was also the year in which the old alliance of isolationism and economic liberalism was shattered, and, with it, both the Wisconsin Progressives and the Minnesota Farmer-Laborites.

By 1938, in short, the alignment of issues and forces which have held the nation in deadlock since had taken form.

With the creation of a new majority coalition, the continuity with the past is shattered. The same voting elements may be discernible in the new as in the old era; but they will be subject to different gravitational influences. They are likely, in fact, to move in exactly the opposite political direction. Witness the isolationists, who moved leftward economically in the Republican era and rightward economically in the Democratic era.

If this theory is valid, it follows that the *key to the political warfare of any particular period will be found in the conflict among the clashing elements in the majority party*. This conflict controls the movements of the minority party as well as of the third parties which may appear. The Moon and the lesser planets revolve around the majority Sun.

The special significance of third parties is that they shed such penetrating light on the inner torments of the majority party. As the majority ages and changes, some elements grow more insurgent than others. New tensions and agitations arise to disrupt and test the party's inner equilibrium. By tracing the vote of successive third parties one should be able to lay bare the hidden springs of conflict and reconciliation within the majority coalition—whether, in growing older, the majority party is slowly disintegrating or actually solidifying its power.

One should also be able to judge the likely effect upon the coalition as a whole of an attempt to split off any one of its elements. Would a Republican appeal for Southern support, for example, bring a G.O.P. Presidential victory? Or would it solidify the other Democratic elements and defeat the Republicans? What would be the effect of a Republican bid for other elements in the Democratic coalition, such as the old isolationists, or the farmer, or the urban middle class?

By putting this theory to the test of past elections, let us now see whether we can determine just what it is that enables the Democratic coalition to hang together in such wondrous friction.

2. Where Was Gideon's Army?

In his 1948 campaign Henry Wallace tried in every possible way to establish himself as the heir of the old Progressive movement. He adopted the same party label, sprinkled his speeches assiduously with biblical references to "Gideon's Army" and echoed the old La Follette slogan: "Return the Government to the people." To appeal to the Midwestern isolationists he wrapped himself in the banner of "Peace." Yet it was in the very area where the Progressive insurgency was strongest and where Wallace made his most strenuous bid, that

Truman picked up the additional votes which offset his losses in the cities and enabled him to win.

In Wisconsin Wallace got a mere 25,000 votes and only 27,000 in Minnesota. To the Midwestern Progressives Wallace sounded hollow and unreal, like a voice from another world— as indeed he was. It was the old Republican sun which gave warmth and life to the Progressive movement. It was the old Republican orbit of economic, ethnic and sectional conflict which the Progressives followed.

The years of the strongest Progressive surge, from 1900 to 1914, coincided with the coming-of-age of the offspring of the agrarian immigrants from Norway, Sweden and Germany. La Follette, himself, got his political start in heavily Norwegian Dane County. His emphasis on the direct primary reflected the struggle of the rising Scandinavian and German middle class for greater political recognition from the older, Yankee-stock Americans. Only by appealing over the heads of the party bosses directly to the voters could the upsurging minorities of that day make their numbers and power felt. Even the isolationism of the Progressives, as we have seen, took on the nature of a Scandinavian-German sectional alliance against the Yankee East.

Without realizing it, the Progressives of 1948 were controlled by a wholly new orbit of conflict. Wallace tried to revive the insurgency of the agrarian frontier, but almost all of his vote came from the cities, and primarily from the elements most sensitive to the issue of civil rights.

Of the thirty precincts in the whole country which Wallace carried, nearly all fit the description, laid down in an earlier chapter, of the new zone of protest developing along the urban frontier.

Wallace carried seven precincts in Tampa, Florida, around Ybor City, which are inhabited by "Latins" from Cuba, many of them cigar workers. All five precincts which Wallace carried in Los Angeles are declining Jewish neighborhoods, into which Negroes have begun to move; so are eight of the eighteen precincts in New York City which Wallace won. Of the other ten Wallace precincts in New York, eight are in slum-ridden East Harlem, whose population is a mixture of Negroes, Puerto Ricans and Italians, and where former Congressman Vito Marcantonio has a strong American Labor party machine. The other two are along Bronx Park East, where a workers' co-operative apartment house was built in 1927. Intended as a Communist heaven on this capitalist earth, the project has gone bankrupt twice and is now privately owned.

These two "Red" precincts, along with the eight Wallace precincts in East Harlem, continued to show an American Labor party majority in the 1950 election. The other Wallace precincts, however, gave the ALP only a small vote in 1950, indicating that their vote for Wallace was not Communist-inspired, but primarily a protest against Truman's stand on Palestine.

In the whole country probably three fourths of Wallace's vote came from Negroes and Jews. New York state, alone, gave Wallace almost half of his 1,150,000 votes and another 190,000 came from California. Although Truman's "shilly-shallying" on Palestine was the immediate cause of the large Jewish protest vote, several additional factors are involved.

During the war no other voting element in the nation formed so strong an emotional attachment to Roosevelt, who was, of course, the great antagonist of Hitler. After 1936, Roosevelt's pluralities in Jewish wards mounted steadily until, by 1944, in many cases they topped the 90 per cent mark. In several Brooklyn precincts in 1944 even the persons serving as Republican watchers voted for Roosevelt.

When Roosevelt died no group in the nation felt more homeless politically than the Jews. None broke as sharply in 1948. Truman held the majority of Jewish voters; but in some areas, like Pittsburgh's Squirrel Hill, predominantly

Jewish neighborhoods swung Republican. Elsewhere the break favored Wallace. Many Jews refused to vote at all.

The mental turmoil of Jewish voters in 1948 can be illustrated by one Brooklyn family which was solid for Roosevelt in 1940, except for one member, who opposed a third term on principle. In 1948 this family, enlarged by in-laws and come-of-agers, split eleven for Truman, eight for Wallace, one for Norman Thomas, while one stayed home. "I registered," she explained, "and must have changed my mind half a dozen times, but just finally gave up."

Failure to vote, it might be noted, is not always a sign of apathy. It can mean that voters are so emotionally torn that they can't bring themselves to cast a ballot for any candidate.

This movement of Jewish voters out of the Democratic party continued into 1950. Taft's heaviest gains were in Jewish precincts. Taft's record of friendliness to Jewish aspirations in Israel gained him the endorsement of several of Ohio's leading rabbis. But the break in voting followed economic lines. All through the Roosevelt years, Jewish voters, as a group, were more strongly Democratic than other voters at the same economic level. This trend has been readjusting itself.

In Cincinnati, for example, the predominantly Jewish neighborhood of Avondale was settled in a series of northward pushes, with better income groups pressing steadily toward the greener, near-suburban pastures. As a result, Avondale resembles a ladder, relatively poor at its foot and improving economically as one climbs to its northern tip, where $30,000 houses are common. In 1944 Roosevelt swept every Avondale precinct. Four years later Dewey carried the upper two thirds of the ward. Taft won not only these but the four northern-most precincts which Truman carried. When I went out into these precincts, with homes ranging from $6,500 to $10,000, I found the Taft shift mainly among small business and white collar elements—a lawyer, grocer, government employees—

not among factory workers. Homeowners were also more for Taft than were renters.

With Negroes, Wallace pulled strongest among those in the middle class. "We couldn't get the poorer Negroes to understand our arguments," confessed one Wallace worker in Harlem. She lived in Riverton Houses, where rentals run $20 a room and where the tenants are "all Negroes who have had a break in life." Although Dewey ran ahead of Wallace in Harlem generally, he ran behind Wallace in Riverton Houses; the project as a whole went safely for Truman.

The Riverton apartments are tastefully furnished. Book of the Month Club volumes grace the shelves. Many residents regularly enjoy one cocktail before dinner; others like to filter their smokes through cigarette holders. But if all the outward props of the contented middle class are theirs, these Negroes are even more painfully aware of their insecurity than less fortunate members of their race. "I've tried three times to get a job with a white newspaper," explained one Negro reporter. "The only job I can get is the one I have."

Ordinarily, the Republicans can expect to gain votes with an improvement in economic status. With Negroes, radicalism seems more pronounced in the middle class than among those with lower incomes.

If it had not been for the bolt of the Dixiecrats, Wallace undoubtedly would have cut in more heavily on the Negro vote. "After the Dixiecrats walked out of the Democratic convention," explained one Harlem editor, "there was no question how Negroes would vote. Negroes felt if they didn't support Truman no other politician would ever defy the Southerners again."

Wallace's popularity boomed briefly in Harlem when he "invaded" the South and became the target for ripe vegetables. But his shirt stains were forgotten when "for the first time in history," to quote the New York *Age*, "the President of the United States spoke in Harlem." More than 65,000

Negroes crowded around the foot of St. Nicholas Terrace on October 29, the anniversary of the civil rights report, to hear Truman speak. The previous "high" gesture of recognition of Negroes was Mrs. Roosevelt's visit to Harlem.

In New York, Maryland and Michigan, Wallace drew enough ordinarily Democratic votes so the Republicans carried these states. This cost Truman seventy-five electoral votes. Eisewhere Wallace helped elect Truman.

In Minnesota, in 1946, the Catholic hierarchy had denounced the Democratic-Farmer-Laborite party as a Communist front. In 1948 St. Thomas College alone sent fourteen of its faculty members to the state DFL convention in the spring. The Catholic delegates joined with other right-wing elements in wresting the party machinery from the fellow travelers. A clean break with the left-wingers probably would have been impossible except for the formation of the Wallace Progressive party. By compelling a showdown on Wallace versus Truman, the right-wingers forced the "Commies" out of the DFL.

With the "Reds" gone, the rest of the DFL following solidified. In St. Paul, a St. Thomas sociology teacher, Eugene McCarthy, ran for Congress and won. Strongly backed by the CIO, McCarthy and his wife, also a teacher, campaigned heavily in St. Paul's Catholic wards, stressing "the Pope's encyclicals assume a new liberal economic philosophy."

Truman's vote in St. Paul was about 10 per cent higher than Roosevelt's had been in 1944. Across the river in non-Catholic Minneapolis, Truman ran 6 per cent behind Roosevelt. The Dixiecrat bolt seems to have contributed to this heavier Catholic vote for Truman. Commented one young Italo-American in St. Paul, "The Dixiecrats reminded me of Al Smith."

Even where union heads were Communist sympathizers they couldn't swing their membership to Wallace. In East Pittsburgh the strongest local union was the United Electrical

Workers, then Communist-dominated. Its officers plugged for Wallace. They seem only to have provoked a record pro-Truman turnout among the heavily Catholic workers. In East Pittsburgh, Truman got nearly a fourth again as many votes as Roosevelt got in 1944!

Throughout the country Truman received a record Catholic vote, exceeding in some areas, even Al Smith's showing! This heavy Catholic turnout—perhaps the most astonishing single aspect of Truman's surprising victory—resulted largely from the return to the Democratic party of supporters of Father Coughlin.

That may startle persons who saw Truman's 1948 victory as a triumph of liberalism and as a new swing to the old native left. However, throughout the country one finds a remarkable parallel between Truman's gains and the vote given Coughlin's Union party in 1936. Of the thirty-nine counties, outside of North Dakota, where "Liberty Bell" Lemke polled more than 10 per cent of the vote, twenty-six were Republican in 1944. Seventeen switched to Truman in 1948. In the nine others the Republican margin fell.

A study of the few states where precinct returns are readily available shows that Lemke carried twenty-one precincts in Ohio and nine in Wisconsin. Six of the Wisconsin precincts and eleven of the Ohio precincts switched from Republican in 1944 to Truman in 1948. In all but one of the other precincts the Democratic vote rose, in many cases exceeding Roosevelt's best showing.

Perhaps the most vivid single illustration of the rhythm of ethnic emotions which vibrates through the Democratic majority can be seen in Boston. Since 1928 all the Democratic Presidential candidates have received a bit more or less than two thirds of the vote. Such statistical consistency gives the appearance of slight political change. Actually, the different Democratic elements have fluctuated furiously.

The table which follows lists the ten wards with the highest

Democratic percentage for each Presidential election since
1928. When Al Smith ran, the five top wards were predominantly Irish; then came the largely Italian wards (1 and
3). The two most heavily Jewish wards (12 and 14) do not
show up among the first Democratic ten in either 1928 or 1932.

Order of Boston Wards Most Heavily Democratic

1928	1932	1936	1940	1944	1948
2	2	14	14	14	2
6	6	3	2	12	6
7	7	1	6	2	7
10	1	2	12	6	1
8	8	6	7	9	8
1	10	7	8	7	15
3	3	8	9	8	10
15	15	12	1	11	3
11	11	15	15	10	9
13	13	11	11	15	13

With 1936, the Irish wards drop, as Lemke cuts in on
Roosevelt's vote, while the Italo-American and Jewish wards
move to the top. The outbreak of the war drops one Italo-
American ward out of the top ten and the other down to
eighth place. Meanwhile Roosevelt's vote in the Jewish wards
rises, becoming even stronger in 1944, when almost nine of
every ten voters in wards 12 and 14 favored Roosevelt.

In 1948 these two wards gave Wallace 10 per cent of their
vote, dropping out of the top Democratic ten. The two Italo-
American wards return to the list, while the highest wards are
once again, as in 1928, heavily Irish. The line-up for Truman
in fact, is almost identical with that for Al Smith, nine of the
ten highest wards being the same in both elections. Truman's
share of the total vote was 1 per cent higher than Smith's.

The pattern of attraction and counterattraction is unmis-
takable. As the Coughlinites forsook the Democratic party in
1936, the Jews came in. As Wallace pulled an appreciable
portion of the Jews out of the Democratic party, the Cough-

linites and Christian Fronters returned to the Democratic fold. Truman's heaviest gains came in the wards where Lemke pulled his highest vote.

In all these elections, it should be noted, the majority of Jews and Irish Catholics remained firmly anchored in the Democratic party. But something like 10 to 15 per cent of Boston's Jewish and Catholic vote fluctuated in mutual hostility.

In eleven Boston wards Truman set a new Democratic high. This Catholic outpouring was undoubtedly helped by the fact that referendum proposals to legalize birth control information and to crack down on trade unions were also on the ballot. But the heavy Catholic vote in other parts of the country indicates that local factors were not as important as might seem.

To sum up, if one traces through the third party bolts which have occurred thus far in the current era of Democratic supremacy, the thesis set forth earlier is confirmed—the disaffection of one element strengthens the attachment of other elements in the coalition. Although one cannot measure statistically each of the many antagonisms which run through the Democratic coalition, the broad pattern of reciprocal hostility can be discerned:

Isolationism clearly evokes the touchiest response among Irish and German Catholics. In the past, however, this was offset by the strong adherence to Democratic foreign policy of the Southerners, Jews, Polish-Americans and other ethnic elements outraged by Hitler. The war's end brought a fall-off in Democratic adherence among the Jews, but this was counteracted by a strengthening of Democratic allegiance among Catholics, particularly of Irish, German and Italian background. Although the strongest single factor behind this new Catholic voting solidarity seems to have been the end of the war and Roosevelt's death, it was certainly strengthened by Wallace's bolt and the removal of Communist influence from the Democratic party. Catholic unity also appears to have been bolstered by the Dixiecrat bolt, which also fortified the Negro attachment to the Democratic party.

To a remarkable extent, the conflicting Democratic elements have tended to neutralize one another. This fact largely explains why the Democratic coalition was not torn asunder by Roosevelt's death.

To round out our examination of this fascinating inner equilibrium of the Democrats, let us now consider the economic factors which unite and divide the Roosevelt coalition.

3. The Democratic Breaking Point

Deep in the Douglas fir country of Oregon is a small town which can serve as an intriguing political laboratory. Euphoniously named Sweet Home, its population numbered about 350 persons twenty years ago. The 1950 census recorded 3,620 inhabitants—an increase of almost 1,000 per cent, most of it over the last ten years.

This super-rapid growth makes Sweet Home a curiously significant study in political behavior. Here, if anywhere in the country, one can say politics had to start virtually from scratch. All but a few hundred inhabitants are newcomers. The states which contributed most heavily to the population rise—Oklahoma and the Dakotas—are about as far apart in political tradition as any states in the union. Sweet Home has also drawn from Brooklyn and has one refugee family from Europe. It is bits of America dumped quickly into one pot and brought to an immediate political boil.

Given these conditions one might expect a formless, erratic, political jumble. The striking thing about Sweet Home's politics is that they follow exactly the same pattern which prevails through the rest of the country. As a local lawyer expressed it, "Almost everyone on Main Street but the postmaster is Republican. Just about everyone else in town, all the working people, are Democrats."

This cleavage between the business community on Main

Street and the timber workers is social and economic as well as political. One group wears white collars and business suits, the other blue denim and hip boots. Possibly it is because no one knows when the fir trees will be exhausted and Sweet Home will become a ghost town, but Main Street's dominant interest appears to be to separate the workers from their earnings in as many ingenious ways as can be imagined. One evening I wandered through the town searching for evidence of any incentive to thrift. I could find none. In the cafes and beer parlors I did find plenty of pinball machines and punchboards for a nickel, a dime and a quarter a chance. Some cafes had a different punchboard at every counter seat.

Sweet Home furnishes dramatic evidence of the underlying class consciousness which permeates American politics today. Both its businessmen and workers must have brought a consciousness of class interest with them from wherever they came. Otherwise, they would hardly have moved into their respective political queues so quickly and instinctively, as if they felt it expected of them.

This same kind of class voting can be seen in every American city. Simply by looking at the homes along a street, or by noting the incomes and occupations of the people living there, one can determine with fair accuracy how any particularly urban area has voted in recent Presidential elections. There is no mistaking a heavily Democratic from a heavily Republican district. When one makes allowance for the voting shifts of different ethnic groups because of the war, the parallel between voting and economic status has remained remarkably constant—so much so that this division is coming to be accepted as normal by politicians in both parties.

Increasingly in recent years Republican campaigners have tended to stay out of Democratic income areas, concentrating on higher income neighborhoods. The Democrats, in turn, have ignored the silk-stocking districts, massing their sound trucks and doorbell ringers in working-class districts. The main emphasis on campaigning has been shifting from trying to change the minds of voters, to getting out the vote already favorably disposed to one's side.

Still, as we have seen, the Democrats have also developed a sizable middle-class following. Perhaps the political division in our cities can be described more accurately by mapping the progress of the climbing urban masses. The map of their migration out of the slums can be taken as the chart of Democratic voting strength. Heaviest in the poorest districts, the Democratic vote thins as one follows the map into middle-class precincts. Below this middle-class borderline the city is Democratic. Above it stretches "Republican country."

Before any basic party realignment can take place, this division of our larger cities into two such sharply marked off political areas would have to be changed. Some new issue would have to arise to cut across or erase this economic division. Without such a realignment, the Republicans may win the Presidency, but the old economic alignment will hover in the background ready to reassert itself under favorable conditions.

Is any such reshuffling of the urban vote in sight?

So far the answer is "no."

The ward returns in our major cities reveal no discernible break in the habit of voting according to economic status. If here and there Democratic ardor is plainly less intense than in 1936 or 1940, the basic line of class division remains.

In 1950, however, one issue did appear which cut into the Democratic strength at every income level—inflation. The anger against rising prices and higher taxes was as violent among low income voters as in the middle class.

In Chicago, Indianapolis and Columbus, Ohio, I went down the voting returns and picked a precinct, strongly for Truman in 1948 but which swung Republican in 1950. When I went out to look at these precincts, in each of the three cities I found myself in exactly the same kind of neighborhood—a moderate-to-low-income home-owning area, which had been built up right after World War One, close to railroad tracks and with hardly a house freshly painted. When I asked Democratic voters in these precincts why they had voted Republican, the most frequent reasons given me were rising prices and the increase in the withholding tax levied the month before election.

The residents of these neighborhoods were usually either elderly persons, retired or near retirement, and who therefore felt the pinch of higher prices immediately, or young married couples who had put all their savings into buying the homes they occupied. The cheap houses they purchased indicated how limited were their savings. The fact that these dwellings have been allowed to age without a coat of paint showed how close to the margin these families live. Rising living costs and the withholding tax had the effect of a wage cut, pushing them below the getting-along margin.

"I'm almost as bad off now as during the depression," exploded one snowy-haired patriarch in Columbus. Down the same street a young married woman, who had always voted Democratic told me, "My husband threatened to disown me if I voted for Taft. But I was so mad at the withholding tax I went to the polls determined to vote for him. When I got into the booth I just couldn't do it. I wouldn't vote for Ferguson either, so I came home without voting. But I'm ready to vote for a Republican for President."

With this anger over inflation went a resentment against all forms of government spending. In Indianapolis, a printer's wife, ordinarily Democratic, complained, "We're being taxed to death!" She then continued with a fierce denunciation of the Brannan Plan, and "socialized medicine" and of "giving all that stuff away abroad." Listening to her I wondered how many times in the past had she heard the same criticisms of "New Deal socialism," without paying any attention to it. As long as the New Deal was painless, the Republican attacks failed to register. Once the bite of taxes was felt, the Welfare State took on a new aspect.

This turn against the administration because of inflation was general throughout the country. It was evident among farmers, as noted earlier. It took place among the urban middle class as well.

The three West Boulevard precincts in Cleveland, where the Dewey-Truman vote broke evenly, all swung heavily for Taft. The housewife, who felt Truman was the "safe" candidate in 1948, voted for Taft because "the government is going too far." An elderly schoolteacher, who had been for Roosevelt and Truman, favored Taft, "even though I disagree with his foreign policy." Born in a Republican family, she switched to the Democrats during the depression when only part-time work was available. "I'm going to retire soon," she observed. "What will my pension be worth if this inflation keeps up?"

Inflation has clearly become the breaking point of the Roosevelt coalition. Yet, during the Roosevelt years it undoubtedly was a political asset to Democrats. Why should it be such a liability today?

The explanation, I believe, lies in the fact that the Democrats are no longer a have-not coalition. Much of the boldness which featured Roosevelt's earlier years can be credited to the fact that he was the leader of a coalition which started with nothing—and that was all it had to lose. The stalemate which has marked Truman's Presidency reflects the fact that the very successes of the New Deal bring the elements in the Roosevelt coalition into increasing conflict with one another.

There always were latent contradictions in the Democratic coalition, but it required recovery from the depression and subsequent prosperity to bring those contradictions to the surface. Not until 1937 were labor's gains sufficiently solidified for it to turn to organizing the South. The Southern organizing drive, in fact, was made necessary, if labor was to hold its gains in the North.

Similarly, in 1941 A. Philip Randolph could threaten to march 50,000 Negroes to Washington if Roosevelt did not create a Fair Employment Practices Commission to insure Negroes getting jobs in defense industries. In 1933 Randolph could not have organized a march on anything. The membership of his Brotherhood of Sleeping Car Porters was down to 658. At union headquarters the telephone had been disconnected and the electricity cut off for nonpayment of bills.

The slowed Democratic tempo in recent years usually is attributed to the fact that Truman lacks Roosevelt's qualities of leadership. Far more important, I believe, has been the fact that Truman has been unable to move far in any direction without threatening the gains of some powerful Democratic segment.

Even before the Korean War, the major Democratic elements were warily on guard against one another. These antagonisms have been sharpened acutely by the inflation which has come with rearmament. During the last war all sorts of idle resources could be brought into production, creating millions of new jobs and expanding the total national pie dramatically. Today, with the economy at virtual full employment, no such increases in national production are possible.

Pumping out more money under present conditions only cheapens the value of all the savings accumulated in the past. Which is another way of saying that *no new economic gains can be promised any group of Democrats today without threatening the gains of other Democrats.*

That is the political impasse to which the cold war has brought the Roosevelt coalition—none of its elements can press for much more in the way of social advance without hurting other elements in the Roosevelt coalition. During the recovery from the depression higher wages and higher farm prices meant bigger farm markets and more factory jobs. Today they increase the expenses of the farmer, thin the purchasing power of the worker's pay envelope and eat away the savings of both. It was no accident that the 1951 price control battle in Congress ended with farmer and labor representatives calling each other names.

All voting behavior is blurred by crosscurrents. Still, today's voting balance in the nation seems to hinge on the shifting fears of another depression against fears of inflation. Mirrored in this depression-inflation issue are so many other issues. Inflation brings stiffened opposition to all government spending: It lifts the political prestige of business, which is associated in the public mind with economy and opposition to government. It strengthens the feelings of isolationism and against large-scale aid to Europe. It probably saps even the party loyalty of Democratic officeholders, since most of them are on fixed salaries which do not rise as rapidly as prices.

The fear of approaching economic collapse, on the other hand, strengthens the pressures for government action. It lifts the political prestige of labor, while weakening the influence of business—since it is mainly to government that people look to solve the problems of large-scale unemployment.

In sum, depression and inflation both threaten to wipe out the gains of the Roosevelt-war years—but in different ways. Under conditions of inflation the danger comes from the government and from within the coalition itself, which naturally tends to disrupt it. When depression threatens, the danger comes from outside the coalition and helps unite it.

4. A Catholic in the White House?

One further matter must be considered in any examination of whether the Democratic coalition can hold together and that is the abrupt revival in recent years of the so-called "Catholic issue." Immediately after the 1948 election, some Catholic politicians felt that the time might be ripening for the nomination of another Catholic on the Democratic ticket, perhaps as Vice-President. That hope has probably been dashed by the storm of protest over Truman's appointment of Mark Clark as Ambassador to the Vatican.

If and when another Catholic bid for the White House comes it could prove a make it or break it test for the Democratic coalition. One major reason why the Republicans held their strength in the farm belt for so long was that in most Midwestern states the Democrats were so largely a Catholic party. Many Scandinavian farmers, for example, who were ready to quit the G.O.P., still would not cross over to the Democrats because of anti-Catholic feeling. Instead they found a halfway station in the Progressive and Farmer-Laborite parties.

The depression and the New Deal, as we saw, suppressed the anti-Catholic hostility of many voters beneath a stronger consciousness of economic interest. Some part of these voters probably would break against a Catholic candidate for either President or Vice-President.

How sharp this defection might be would depend on economic conditions at the time and, of course, on who the candidates were. Although Catholic voting strength is currently at its peak, in view of the maturing of the offspring of the Italians, Poles, Czechs and other former immigrant elements, still there is no Catholic political figure who remotely approaches Al Smith in his appeal to the urban masses. Almost all of the leading Catholic Democrats are products of machine politics, shrewd and dexterous in behind-the-scene manipulation, but lacking popular fire.

Quite apart from the possibility of another Catholic try at the Presidency, which seems unlikely today, the rising antagonism between Catholics and non-Catholics in recent years seems likely to increase in political importance in the future. The controversy over federal aid to parochial schools, which burst so explosively in the dispute between Cardinal Spellman and Mrs. Roosevelt, will probably grow more acute with time. The heavy sales of Paul Blanshard's books, whatever else may be involved, confirm the fact that, in the words of one Catholic editor, "Something has happened to Catholic and non-Catholic relations in this country."

To explore this "something" fully would take a book in itself, by a person of special competence. That "something," however, is partly the result of the forces discussed in this book. A few general observations on the political impact of the Roosevelt Revolution on American Catholicism may be worth noting:

1. It is well to bear in mind the central position of the Irish among American Catholics. The Church hierarchy is overwhelmingly Irish as are most Catholic political leaders. In the case of other one-time immigrant elements we have observed that as the immigrant generation dies off and their children and grandchildren rise to middle-class status, the group as a whole becomes more articulate and more militant in insisting upon its "place in the sun." That being so, the heightened militancy displayed by American Catholic leaders in recent years must be related at least partly to the expansion of the Irish middle and upper class—an expansion which was underway even before the New Deal.

2. For the Irish, the New Deal has had curiously mixed effects. At the start it was a tremendous patronage boon, the lion's share of judgeships and other federal posts going to Irish Catholics. But as the New Deal progressed, the Irish bosses have found themselves under ever heavier assault from the Italo-Americans, Polish-Americans, Jews, Negroes and other former minorities. This competition for increased recognition has been going on not only within the Democratic party but through the whole of society including the whole civil service—teachers, policemen, firemen and so on—which in many cities used to be dominated by Irish names. Over the years there is little question that the Irish have profited enormously from the Democratic party; but their current prospect is one of declining future importance.

3. For the Church, as well, the New Deal has brought a curiously mixed challenge. One tenet of Catholic philosophy is that it has its own "unique and distinctive"* attitude to all problems. The quickened pace of social change touched off by the depression and New Deal forced the Church leaders to become articulate on all sorts of questions which had lain dormant during the 1920's—like the expanding role of government, the sharpened class cleavage which the Roosevelt Revolution brought and the dramatic extension of trade unionism into the mass production industries where Catholic workers were so heavily concentrated.

A frame of reference for many of these problems had been laid down in the encyclicals of Pope Leo. These were couched necessarily in general terms, which had to be applied to concrete situations in this country. In the labor field, an Association of Catholic Trade Unionists (ACTU) was formed to compete with the philosophy of "materialistic socialism." A number of dioceses set up labor schools for union members.

4. The struggle of the Church to keep pace with the upsurge of the Catholic masses in this country inevitably brought a conservative-liberal tugging within the Church hierarchy, paralleling in many respects the similar conflict raging within the Democratic coalition. The larger part of the Catholics in this country still have low or moderate incomes, many being industrial workers. To them the New Deal came as an economic boon. However, particularly among the Irish and German Catholics, a sizable middle and upper income class has developed, many of whom have turned Republican.

5. Events abroad, as well, have operated to quicken the militancy of Catholic leaders. The fact that Soviet Russia has become the world's number one menace is unquestionably a powerful spiritual asset to the Church. The Church hierarchy has clearly interpreted the present world crisis as a challenge

* See the booklet explaining "What Is the Catholic Attitude?" distributed by the Knights of Columbus, with official Church approval.

to reaffirm the all-pervasive character of the moral doctrines of the Church and to establish Catholicism as the irreconcilable "we or they" antagonist of "atheistic communism"—a militancy which has disturbed many non-Catholic religious leaders.

Merged in with this distrust is the heritage of antagonism left over from the Spanish Civil War which, although it ended fifteen years ago, remains one of the more important political dividers in the country. Both Catholics and non-Catholics still are fighting to vindicate the positions they took in that struggle.

Usually when the members of any religious group feel themselves under attack, they tend to close ranks. The protests being stirred currently over such issues as aid to parochial schools, birth control and alleged Catholic censorship of films and textbooks can be expected to solidify the body of American Catholics. Whether this increased solidarity will be transferred to politics, however, is not so clear.

Since the war's end the role of the Catholics in the Democratic party has been a curiously militant, yet uneven one. In 1946 there was a significant break among Catholics against the Democratic candidates, partly over the issue of "Communist" influence within the party. Two years later, however, more Catholics voted for Truman than for any previous Democratic candidate. At times the election returns seem to point to a rapid fading of the traditional Democratic loyalty of the Irish Catholics, with many, particularly among the middle class, in transition toward Republicanism. At other times it seems as if the political solidarity of the Irish Catholics is being strengthened in a struggle to regain their old dominance in the Democratic party.

Probably many Irish Catholics are being pulled in both directions at the same time, which would not be unusual in a period of party realignment. Their situation, in fact, bears some resemblance to that of the Southern Democrats, who also give the conflicting impression of struggling simultaneously to drive themselves out of the Democratic party and to capture control of it.

Prior to the New Deal, for the bulk of Catholics as for Southerners, allegiance to the Democratic party was mainly a matter of inherited tradition. The transformation of the Democratic party, wrought by the Roosevelt Revolution, has altered the traditional place within the party which both the Southerners and Irish Catholics have held. Both are now in the throes of adjustment to that change.

Curiously, the two elements which will be under heaviest pressure to split off from the Democratic party in 1952 are the Southerners and the Irish and German Catholics. While the Southerners are most sensitive on economic and racial issues, the Catholics appear to be most sensitive to charges of "communism in government" and to a possible revival of isolationism. Should both the Southerners and Catholics bolt the Democratic ticket at the same time, a Republican victory is certain. The Democratic party could still win, however, if the Catholics and one-time isolationists vote Democratic to the same extent as in 1948—since the Negro vote can be expected to align against any candidate carrying the Southern banner and no third party is likely to pull anywhere as strongly as Wallace did.

In short, although it may not get into the headlines, the decisive political struggle in 1952 may well be between the forces embodied in the bolting South against the old isolationists. That, in turn, re-emphasizes the importance of the economic balance between the fears of depression and fears of inflation.

To sum up, whether the Southern bolt will defeat the national administration may depend on whether 1952 will be like 1948 or like 1950. Had the Presidency been at stake two years ago the Republicans would have won. If a relaxation of international tensions and fear of recession restore the mood of 1948, the Southern-Republican coalition could be defeated. All this has been stated without regard to the personalities of the candidates who will be nominated and therefore should not be considered a prophecy of what will happen in 1952. What I have tried to do has been to show the present precarious balance within the Democratic coalition and to project its major lines of conflict to where they are likely to converge this November.

The net conclusions arrived at, apart from the personalities of the candidates, are: (1) that the Roosevelt elements are sufficiently divided to elect a Republican President, but that (2) there still is no evidence that the Roosevelt coalition is disintegrating hopelessly and that a basic realignment of party strength is about to take place. Whoever wins the 1952 election, the political deadlock which grips the country will not be broken. At most the winner will find that he can take only half of the political purse.

The Democrats can win only by preserving the present stalemate. If the Republicans triumph, their victory, by itself, will settle nothing politically. What may develop after that, whether the Democratic majority can be broken for good or whether it will be restored, will depend on whether the Republicans can reorganize their own party after they have won.

11

The Republican Opportunity— and Dilemma

1. The Republican Moon

To most Republican leaders the problem confronting them seems to be the simple one of how to win a Presidential election. Actually, the problems of the Republican party will only begin after it wins. To stay in power the Republican party will have to transform itself. In the effort it could wreck itself.

Some Republicans will retort, "Just let us win and we'll be glad to do all the worrying that comes with victory." But the issue is not disposed of that easily. The major reason why the Republicans have found it so difficult to elect a President is because their Party has remained fundamentally unchanged, trapped by its own inner contradictions.

Having ruled American politics for so long in the past, the Republican leaders have never quite adjusted to their being the minority party in the nation. For a long time they consoled themselves with the thought that in Franklin Roosevelt they faced so devilishly clever a politician that no one could beat him. When Truman's victory shattered that alibi, many Republicans took refuge in a new excuse—that Dewey lost because so many Republicans did not vote.

Since the 1948 election was so close, it doesn't take much statistical ingenuity to show how an additional 100,000 Republican votes in selected states would have defeated Truman. The real question is: Did more Republicans than Democrats stay at home?

What evidence I have been able to collect indicates that more former Roosevelt supporters failed to vote than Republicans, which may well have spared Dewey from being buried under an overwhelming landslide.

Was it Republican strength or Democratic weakness, for example, which enabled Dewey to carry New York, Michigan, Pennsylvania, Connecticut, New Jersey and Maryland? Dewey got only 1,800 more votes in Maryland than in 1944, only 47,000 more in Connecticut, 67,000 more in Pennsylvania and not quite 20,000 more in New Jersey. In both New York and Michigan, Dewey got fewer votes than in 1944, carrying these states only because the Democratic fall-off was even heavier.

For Dewey to squeeze through in New York state by a mere 55,000 votes, Truman had to lose 520,000 former Roosevelt votes. In New York City every third or fourth Roosevelt voter appears either to have stayed home or cast a ballot for Wallace.

Dewey managed to come so close to victory, only because Wallace drew 1,150,000 votes, and another several hundred thousand former Roosevelt supporters did not vote.

In the few cities, like New Haven and Akron, where I have been able to check the figures, the Republicans voted a heavier proportion of their registration than did the Democrats. The heaviest single fall-off in Cleveland came in the Collinwood section, inhabited largely by railroad workers. While Dewey dropped 400 votes from 1944 in this area, Truman lost nine times as many. In 1940 every railroader I interviewed in Collinwood voted for Roosevelt. In 1948 more than half of the railroaders I talked with had not voted. Torn between their dislike of the Taft-Hartley Law and Truman's handling of the railroad strike, they stayed at home.

Figures can be thrown together showing that in several states Truman's margin of victory corresponded to the decline

in the Republican 1944 vote. But when the returns are examined county by county and ward by ward two significant
facts emerge:

First, appreciable numbers of persons who voted Republican
in 1944 swung to Truman, particularly among farmers and
among German-Americans, Italo-Americans and Irish-Americans who had opposed Roosevelt's foreign policy.

Second, in most counties where the Republican vote de-
clined there was also a rise in the Democratic strength. What
this indicates, in my judgment, is that many more voters were
on the verge of swinging Democratic but couldn't quite bring
themselves to do so and stayed home instead. Apathy and
laziness alone do not explain the Republican fall-off. Many
Republican voters were so divided in their interests and emotions that they preferred not to vote.

Dewey's failure to stir any enthusiasm unquestionably was
an important factor. But the relatively low turnout in 1948
was also evidence that among both Republicans and Democrats some groups of voters were beginning to realign. Among
the Roosevelt elements nonvoting was heaviest in areas inhabited by Jews and railroad workers. Both showed an
accelerated tendency to swing Republican in 1950.

Between 1948 and 1950 there is no question that the cohe-
siveness of the Republican voting elements was strengthened,
while that of the Democratic voters was weakened. In the
suburbs around Chicago, for example, Scott Lucas got only 31
per cent of the vote, the poorest Democratic showing since
the 1932 depression.

While doing my postelection study of Taft's re-election,
I made a special point of searching out voters who had favored
Truman in 1948 and had swung for Taft. Whenever I found
such a voter, I asked, "In voting for Taft were you voting
against Truman? Whom would you vote for in 1952?"

Roughly one third of these Truman-Taft voters stated
definitely that they had not been voting against Truman.
Perhaps one of four, however, was ready to support any

Republican in 1952. By far the sharpest turn against Truman was evident in the urban midde class—among shopkeepers, teachers, white-collar workers and little businessmen. The "we want a change" feeling was somewhat weaker among farmers and weakest among workers, although even among them Truman's prestige had sunk appreciably.

Which of the possible G.O.P. nominees had the strongest appeal to these one-time Truman supporters who were ready to vote for a Republican President?

General Eisenhower pulled strongest, with Taft second and Harold Stassen a lagging third. Dewey was generally considered out of the running. Mention of Governor Earl Warren of California usually brought a noncommittal, "Don't know him."

At this writing there would be little point in trying to guess whom the Republicans may nominate. The candidacies of Taft and Eisenhower are worth appraising, however, because even if neither gets the nomination, they still dramatize so well the conflicting strategies between which the Republicans must choose. However it may be resolved, their rivalry sums up the inner conflict which has torn the Republican party since 1938.

2. G.O.P. Dilemma

Although foreign policy appears to be the most important single issue of cleavage, the division between the supporters of General Eisenhower and Senator Taft runs much deeper. The sectional alignment of the Republican party is such that the so-called "isolationist" wing coincides fairly well with the party's conservative, Midwestern representation. In contrast, the internationalist "Republican wing—which includes Senators" like Wayne Morse of Oregon, Irving Ives of New York, Henry Cabot Lodge of Massachusetts and James Duff of Pennsylvania—coincides by and large with the liberal, urbanized wing of the party.

Significantly, this alignment represents an exact geographical reversal of the division in the 1920's, when the progressive Republicans hailed from the Midwest, while the Old Guard citadels were in the industrialized East. This change is not surprising when we recall the political reshuffling which accompanied the rise of the Democratic party to majority status.

In the industrial centers the revolt of the city shifted the balance of political power from employers to labor, from the descendants of the "old" Americans to the offspring of the former minority groups. To survive politically, the Eastern Republicans have had to adjust to the issues and conflicts of that change. In the Midwest as well, the Republicans were spun around in abrupt reversal, as the economic liberals among the Progressives drifted into the Democratic coalition and the isolationists were drawn into alliance with the anti-New Deal conservatives.

To maintain their strength locally, the Midwestern Republicans have had to emphasize issues which would preserve the anti-Roosevelt alliance of economic conservatives and one-time isolationists which lay behind the Republican gains in the 1938 Congressional elections. In contrast, the Eastern Republicans have been more sensitively attuned to the big-city elements which have formed the backbone of Democratic Presidential strength.

The basic Republican struggle, in other words, has mirrored faithfully the same President-Congress battle which divides the Democrats. Liberal Republicans, in order to disrupt the Democratic Presidential coalition, strive to demonstrate that they, not the Democrats, are the truly liberal party. The Midwestern Republicans, on the other hand, have pursued the sharply conflicting objective of strengthening the anti-New Deal coalition in Congress to the point where it can elect its own President.

Invariably, the delegates to Republican conventions find

themselves confronted with the same tormenting choice—of either adopting a "me too but better" position, similar to that espoused by the Democratic President, or of embracing the record of the conservative coalition in Congress and making that the voice of Republicanism.

For fourteen years the G.O.P. has been trying to wriggle off the horns of this dilemma, without success. Fearful of being tied too closely to the record of the dominant Republicans in Congress, the conventions have gone outside of Washington for their Presidential nominees. To preserve party harmony, however, these candidates have carefully refrained from repudiating the Republican record in Congress. As a consequence, the Republican candidates have not been able to campaign as either forthright liberals or forthright conservatives. They have given the impression, in the words of the New York *Herald-Tribune*, of wavering between a "flickering liberalism" and a "timid conservatism."

This dilemma has not been primarily one of the personality of the G.O.P. candidates. In his lectures on the Republican party at Princeton University, Governor Dewey contended that the party should be judged by the accomplishments of Republican state administrations. Republican governors, like Driscoll of New Jersey and Warren of California, have advanced measures of a New Deal character with considerable political success. In the day-by-day national arena, however, it is the Republicans in Congress, led by the Bob Tafts and Joe Martins, who define what are Republican principles.

The simple truth, of course, is that there is no automatic formula for determining who speaks for the Republican party. The question arises at every Presidential convention and, in the past at least, has never been brought to clear-cut resolution.

In 1948 Truman shrewdly capitalized on this Republican contradiction by calling a special session of Congress and demanding, in effect, that the Republicans put into law the platform which had been drawn up at the Republican convention. When Congress failed to act, Truman swept the country by making the Republican record in Congress the issue.

Dewey's defeat has been cited as an argument against "me tooism" and in favor of an all-out, no-issue-barred offensive against the New Deal. Since it was the Republican performance in Congress on which Truman capitalized, other Republicans have contended that Dewey's loss proves the necessity of truly "liberalizing, humanizing and modernizing" the Grand Old Party. Probably, the net significance of the Dewey debacle is that it demonstrates the political liabilities of being neither fish nor fowl.

Two footnotes to the "me too" debate are worth noting. First, while the Republicans lost in 1940, 1944 and 1948 with "liberal" candidates, the worst rout they suffered came in 1936, when Alf Landon and John D. M. Hamilton (now with Taft) waged an all-out crusade against "New Deal socialism." Second, although Willkie is generally considered to have been an internationalist, the fact is that the isolationist vote broke dramatically against Roosevelt anyway. The German-Americans and Coughlinites swung for Willkie even though he did not make the war his chief campaign issue. How campaigns are run is important, but the American people have become quite adept at voting for candidates regardless of what Willkie once so accurately dismissed as "just campaign oratory."

The constant Republican dilemma, to sum up, is the necessity of choosing between embracing or repudiating the conservative coalition in Congress. This will be the real choice before the Republicans in Chicago in 1952, regardless of what names are brought before the convention. It is in terms of this choice, and the President-Congress deadlock that stirs behind it, that the Taft and Eisenhower candidacies should be judged.

3. The Senator and the General

The prime difference between the two men in terms of the prevailing political deadlock in the country is that Eisenhower symbolizes the hope of lifting the nation above the divisions of party warfare, while Taft's candidacy implies an intensification of the prevailing party conflict.

The tantalizing appeal of the Eisenhower candidacy is that of a clean sheet of paper, free of all the bitter, repetitive partisan scrawlings of the past. That is his strength—and weakness—for it stirs uncertainty as to what may come to be written on that sheet of paper later.

In contrast Taft's strength lies in his having written out his position clearly for all to see. It is also his weakness in that he has perhaps written too much. If Taft's record on so many public issues has earned him staunch supporters, it has made him equally staunch enemies.

Pre-eminently, Taft is the candidate of the dominant Republicans in Congress. Deliberately or instinctively, he has handled himself in such a way as to have made himself a virtual embodiment of the major anti-New Deal trends. True, Taft's legislative record shows a liberal approach on some issues. But his political strength stems from the fact that he has become the symbol of outspoken opposition to almost everything the New Deal and Fair Deal are supposed to represent. Since the war's end Taft has been the Republican record in Congress. For a time he bowed to Senator Arthur Vandenberg's leadership on foreign affairs, but with Vandenberg's illness and death and the 1950 Congressional elections, Taft became the G.O.P.'s chief Congressional strategist on both foreign and domestic issues.

Taft's candidacy would represent the first frontal assault on the Democratic coalition since it was formed in 1936. The nature of his political appeal and the forces behind him are such that he would be assailing the Democratic coalition at almost every one of its wavering points. His record on labor legislation would appeal for the vote of those Democrats who distrust labor and favor union regulation. Taft has stumped the South in an open bid for the support of those States Righters who can "disentangle themselves from the Truman Democratic party." His insistence that the major issue of 1952 is "liberty versus socialism" is calculated to rouse the many farmers and urban middle class, who are sorely troubled over government spending.

On foreign policy, no matter how Taft explains the changes in his views, his principal appeal still is for the support of those anti-Roosevelt "isolationists" who feel that our entry into the last war was a mistake. I do not mean to challenge the sincerity of Taft's latter-day conversion to intervention in Europe's affairs. I do doubt that his change of heart will convince any but those who want to be convinced. Rarely do the words of a candidate erase the emotions and prejudices he has come to symbolize over the years.

Taft's candidacy, in short, would confront the various, divided elements in the Democratic coalition with a decision of one kind as an alternative to Truman's middle-ground position. That, of course, is the intention of his backers who have reasoned that such an all-issue assault is "the only kind of campaign which will elect a Republican to office." But is it?

By sharpening issue after issue, Taft would compel those who are divided in their feelings toward the Truman administration to take one side or the other, on foreign policy, labor regulation, civil rights, farm relief, government spending and so on. But which side would the voters take?

Forced to choose between Taft's all-too-positive position on so many issues, many Democratic waverers might prefer to cling, however halfheartedly, to Truman's known but limited liabilities. While most Democratic voters might agree with Taft on some one or two issues, few would agree with him on all issues. By hammering so furiously at the Democratic coalition, on so many different fronts, Taft could as readily solidify as split it.

Moreover, it would be a mistake to think of Taft as a strictly conservative candidate. To many quite conservative Democrats, concerned mainly with holding onto what they have, Taft may seem risky and even radical. We should not forget the many farmers, like those in Guthrie, Iowa, who were frightened at the prospect of a *laissez-faire* Republican in the White House during hard economic times.

The key question likely to determine Taft's fate, if he wins the nomination is: Will the more conservative Democratic voters see him as a threat or as an aid to the preservation of the gains they have accumulated during the last twenty years?

In his re-election fight two years ago, Taft profited from the fact that the general mood of voters favored a check on the administration. The same cautions against "going too far" could turn against Taft if fears of another depression were strong around election time.

If the effect of Taft's candidacy is to sharpen all issues for all men, the effect of Eisenhower's candidacy is to blur these cleavages. This is a highly valuable asset in times like the present, when the American people are torn by such evenly tugging fears that every choice of decision that is offered seems frightening. Being above the party battle, Eisenhower kindles new hope for all who have wearied of the attrition of indecision and yet who see no way out through either of the two parties.

Eisenhower might be termed a substitute for a reshuffling of both parties. At present neither party seems capable of commanding the trust of an effective majority of the country. Although party allegiances have weakened sufficiently to rob the established majority of vigor and unity, the forces of realignment do not seem to have progressed sufficiently for a new majority to emerge. So tangled are the lines of partisan cross-conflict, that it appears easier and quicker to achieve national unity by rallying around a personal leader than by waiting for the parties to reshuffle themselves.

To many Southerners, the glamour and prestige of Eisenhower's personality seems the much-sought justification for breaking from their traditional Democratic allegiance, while they might still falter before someone known as "Mr. Republican." Outside the South, Eisenhower answers the need of those Republicans who want to defeat the Democrats domestically, while going along with the administration's foreign policy. He is also the promise of something different to those voters in the North who have grown restive in the Democratic party but remain wary of the Republicans.

Still, the impression should not be left that Eisenhower's personality is so irresistible that he could be elected without any real contest. For reasons explained earlier, I believe that the nomination of Eisenhower would bring a Southern bolt from the Democratic convention. Such a bolt—as our analysis of the internal balance of the Democratic coalition has shown —would cause a counter realignment of some degree in the North. Moreover, my own talks with voters around the country indicate that considerable fears exist as to just where Eisenhower stands on issues of crucial importance.

Usually I found, that when a farmer or worker said, "I don't believe in a military man for President," what really troubled him was uncertainty as to what Eisenhower would do if elected. Rarely has the mood of the American public been dominated so much by fear as today. To leave those fears unquieted would be a risky course for the most popular candidate.

The election of Eisenhower would mean, of course, a continuation of the general outlines of the administration's foreign policy, with probably a much-needed change in its administrators. As to what an Eisenhower victory would mean politically, however, no one can even guess today. His victory would not solve the Republican dilemma. Eisenhower's popularity could be expected to help re-elect the more conservative Republicans now in Congress, probably strengthening their influence on Capitol Hill. Unless this so-called "isolationist" Republican wing reverses itself, Eisenhower, in order to carry through his program, would have to seek Democratic support. In short, he would have to find some means for either reorganizing the Republican party or, what would be more in keeping with his political character, of transcending the customary party alignments.

In effect, Eisenhower would have to turn himself into a one-man battlefield to which all the conflicting forces which have been deadlocked since 1938 would transfer their struggle. Through his person, all the unresolved issues of the last fourteen years would maneuver for decision.

Possessing considerable ability and diplomatic skill, Eisenhower might be able to lift many of these postponed problems out of the rut of attrition. His would be the enormous advantage of political youth, uncluttered by the deals and deadlocks of the past. By taking a new approach to old problems, Eisenhower conceivably could succeed in bringing them to solution and in restoring an atmosphere of at least partial reconciliation along the Potomac.

That is the glitter of his candidacy. The dross is that the odds will be stacked against him. For one thing, the problems which will confront the next President, particularly on the economic front, will be immensely more difficult than those which have been beyond Truman's capacity to resolve. Then, too, time will be working against Eisenhower.

Whatever he hopes to accomplish would have to be done in his first term as President. Not that he couldn't run for re-election, but that his political influence would be sorely weakened during his second term. All the forces opposed to what he was trying to do would dig in and outwait him. With a third term prohibited by the constitution, after his first term the balance of power in Washington could be expected to shift to Congress, where the forces of deadlock would be most strongly represented.

During his first term Eisenhower might command an influence as great as Roosevelt's in his first term. With Eisenhower's second term, the struggle over who was to succeed him would start anew. The hand of the past would reach up and claim its due.

The drama of an Eisenhower administration would be that of a struggle for a new unity against the old forces of deadlock, of how many of the old dividing entanglements could be cleared away during the spring and summer of Eisenhower's prestige before the bitter winter of attrition closed in once more.

No one can say in advance how much Eisenhower might accomplish and how much change he would bring. But the intensity of today's deadlock justifies the conclusion that many of the conflicts traced in this book would still be raging after his Presidency.

One further point, this appraisal of the Taft-Eisenhower candidacies has not touched on one important factor because it applies about equally to any Republican candidate—how strong the feeling of "turn the rascals out" may be among the voters. With the disclosures of the Kefauver Crime Committee and the RFC and Internal Revenue Bureau scandals, merging with the many frustrations of the cold war, resentment against the administration may be strong enough to elect anyone on the Republican ticket, even the proverbial "Chinaman," whom Henry L. Mencken thought could beat Roosevelt in 1936.

It is true that the Republicans were able to ride out the scandals of both Teapot Dome and the Grant administration. But in neither of these earlier instances had the Republicans been in office over such a prolonged stretch as the Democrats today.

Only once before in American history has any political

party won the Presidency six successive times. The Republicans held power unbroken from 1860 until Grover Cleveland's election in 1884. The feeling that the Democrats have been in office too long probably has been mounting with every successive Presidential election since 1936. The effect of the sheer erosion of time should not be underestimated.

But if their hour of victory appears to be striking, there could hardly be a more hazardous time for the Republicans to return to power.

4. Are the Republicans Really Conservative?

Should the Republicans win the Presidency in 1952 the next administration would become a running test of their ability to survive politically in this country. Having won the Presidency, at long last, the Republicans would have to prove that they really are the conservative party they claim to be—conservative enough to preserve the gains of the Roosevelt-Truman years and most of Truman's foreign policy.

While out of office a party can easily enough oppose all things for all men. Taft, for example, could talk in one breath of reducing the size of the military establishment and in the next, could bid for the support of General MacArthur, who, at the time, wanted to intensify the Korean fighting. Can one follow a policy of determined opposition to Soviet expansion, and still oppose the controls necessary to mobilize the resources required for the cold war?

Again, how much of the structure of New Deal laws could be pulled down without driving the voters affected into rebellion?

There would be nothing new, of course, in a President being elected on one program and then proceeding to reverse himself completely, once in office. In 1932 Franklin Roosevelt, declared, "I regard reduction in federal spending as one of the most important issues of the campaign." It is not improbable that any Republican elected President on the issue of "socialism" might set new heights for government intervention in a period short of war.

One of two tests—threatened war or threatened depression —seems certain to confront any Republican elected President in 1952. Each test would challenge the traditional Republican attitude toward the role of government. A worsened foreign situation would tend to force a degree of military and economic mobilization, which could not be carried through successfully without stringent controls. Should the danger of war ease, economic recession would threaten.

Were the economy to start plunging downward after 1952, the Republicans, assuming they are in the White House, would be no more to blame than Hoover was for the 1929 crash. But any Republican who undertook to hold to a policy of stern deflation would certainly suffer Hoover's political fate. Even Hoover was forced into trying to hold up farm prices through the Federal Farm Board and into saving the banks and railroads through the RFC. The pressures for vigorous intervention in event of another economic collapse would be far heavier these days.

The position of a victorious Republican President would not be much different from that of Winston Churchill in England. With the Laborites turned out of office, the Conservatives revoked the nationalization of the steel industry but were afraid to change the status of the other industries which had been socialized. In the United States the problem is not direct government ownership or even the degree of government regulation, but inflation. Our whole structure of prices, wages, profits, taxes and savings rests on the uneasy stilts of government spending and supports. Whether any administration will dare undertake a drastic deflation is questionable.

I do not intend to infer that our economic situation is hopeless. Competent management of our economic affairs would make a highly significant difference. My point here is that the economic situation likely to confront a Republican President will hardly be one which can be squared with a "let things alone" philosophy of government.

Any Republican who wins in 1952 cannot help but credit his victory to a turn of popular feeling against "too much government." Yet, the pressures of world crisis would compel the Republicans to devise their own program of positive governmental action or expose themselves as being incapable of doing more than shouting "no." However eagerly they yearn to return to the past, the policies and practices which were good enough for Harding and Coolidge cannot be invoked by the Republicans in 1952.

In 1920 the Republicans discredited Wilson's foreign policy and killed the League of Nations. They brought forward no alternative. Their "solution," in effect, was to have no foreign policy. The Republicans may succeed again in discrediting Democratic foreign policy. But if they do, this time, they will have to produce an alternative foreign policy. Perhaps, it is too much to expect any opposition party to do much more than criticize "the mistakes of the past." Once in power, though, the Republicans would have to meet the crises of the future.

Here we come to perhaps the most basic of all the Republican contradictions—the G.O.P.'s fondness for a weak President. Calvin Coolidge probably represents the Republican Presidential ideal. Coolidge's philosophy is neatly capsuled in a favorite aphorism he liked to repeat to Herbert Hoover, "If you see ten troubles coming down the road you can be sure that nine will run into the ditch before they reach you and you will have to battle with only one."

The difficulty in this philosophy, as Hoover adds, was that by the time the tenth trouble reached Coolidge it had "acquired such momentum that it spelled disaster."

The traditional Republican affection for weak Presidents stems from the fear that a strong executive might set himself up as a tribune of the people and curb the economic freedom of business. But the big question American business leaders must answer is: *Can you have a government that is weak at home and still will be strong abroad?*

For purposes of domestic profit making, the business community may prefer to have Congress dominant in Washington, but can that "scuffle of local interests," as Herbert Agar described Congress, be entrusted with the formulation of foreign policy? Can the problems of peace and war be met by a weak Presidency?

How the Republicans will resolve this dilemma, if they win, is anyone's speculation. The resulting ordeal would shake the G.O.P. to its deepest psychological roots. If the Republican party is not to fail utterly it would have to redefine its position on what the proper role of government should be in these tense times. In doing so it could not hold to the *laissez-faire* views which now parade as orthodox Republican doctrine.

To solidify itself permanently in American life the New Deal needs at least one Republican victory. As long as the Republicans remain out of office it is possible for politicians on both sides to stir deceptive fears that the whole New Deal is at stake. Once in office the Republicans will automatically endorse much of the New Deal, through the simple device of leaving things untouched. Extreme right-wing Republicans, who talk as if they would repeal every law passed in the last twenty years, would find they had to accept much of the New Deal under Republican administrators. The more ardent Roosevelt followers would find that most of what is loosely called the Welfare State was here to stay.

In that less heated atmosphere it might become possible to take a calmer look at the problem of how much government this country needs to survive in the sort of age in which we live.

Perhaps I am being too optimistic in envisioning so conciliatory an outcome of a Republican victory. The result may be to sharpen rather than narrow our political differences. Still, in any case—regardless of what policies the Republicans may pursue or if the Democrats win again—there certainly is pressing need for a calm, nonpartisan examination of what the role of government should be in these times.

That is what I would like to attempt in the next and final chapter. Has our present government grown so powerful that it jeopardizes the liberties of the American people? Or must it be strengthened even more if we are to survive? Can we adjust our enormously expanded government to our traditional system of checks and balances and to our two-party structure? Can we break the political stalemate which now binds us and regain the ability to achieve decision?

12

The National State

1. The Real Crisis in Government

Returning to the United States late in 1946 after eleven months in war-rubbled Europe, I remarked to friends, "Some poet ought to write an Ode to a Stable Government. It really is a thing of beauty and a joy forever."

In Germany I had seen the utter helplessness of people who had no government. They were voiceless, with no value to their exertions beyond sheer physical existence. Behind the Iron Curtain in Rumania and Hungary I had seen what happened when a government is turned into a shotgun and its citizenry into so many clay pigeons. There the Soviet puppet leaders were using every instrument of government, from systematic inflation to the secret police, to hunt down and destroy all who might oppose their rule.

In France the crisis of government took still another form. Here the government was not foreign-controlled, but it was sufficiently infiltrated so that no Frenchman could really call it his own. The whole country trembled with the fearful frustration of a family living in a house with an unwelcome boarder, who can neither be ousted nor put up with.

What I saw in Europe left me wondering how many of us appreciate what stability in government really means. It is like the air one breathes. When one has it, one takes it for granted. Let the critical supply of governmental stability be cut off, though, and all living becomes a frantic choking for breath.

Happily, today, the American government is the most stable in the world. Yet, unable to agree among ourselves how much government we should have, we sometimes appear bent upon tearing our government apart or of weakening it to the point where it cannot function effectively.

This conflict over the proper limits of government has intensified steadily until it has become the sharpest single political divider in the country. So furious has grown the exchange of abuse between the two rival coalitions, confronting one another over this issue, that they hardly seem part of the same nation.

Currently the balance in this struggle over the so-called Welfare State is held by a sizable segment of the voting population, which still is uncertain whether more or less government is needed. The election returns indicate that these wavering elements are most heavily concentrated among farmers and the urban middle class, although a good number of moderate income workers are also included. As their attitude toward government fluctuates with their changing fears, the political balance in the nation swings indecisively from side to side. One might say that these wavering elements, having climbed with the New Deal out of the depths of the depression and the slums, are now guarding their gains by marking time politically.

At first thought, this may appear like a healthy situation, in which the political moderates hold the extremists of both sides at bay. But at least two grave risks are involved.

First, the balance of power role being exerted by the moderates is a blind process. If the farmers, urban middle class and other independent voters have resisted being pulled finally into either the "more government" or "less government" camp, it is not because they are seeking deliberately to force a compromise. Mainly, it is because their own interests, emotions and fears are so divided that they haven't known which way to turn. Their balancing role is evidence, not of an orderly direction of traffic, but of a traffic jam, so thoroughly besnarled that little can get through.

The second—and far more serious—danger is that our raging political debate is not focused on the real crisis of government which threatens us.

The prevailing political stalemate reflects mainly the animosities and loyalties which grew out of the New Deal. But the cold war has transformed these old issues, and has raised new and perilous problems, which neither the Roosevelt nor anti-Roosevelt coalition seems prepared to meet.

As one simple illustration of how the struggle with Russia overshadows the older issues, consider the question of reducing federal expenditures. During most of 1951 some members of Congress contended that five or six billion dollars could easily be slashed out of the budget, while President Truman maintained as stoutly that the budget already had been cut to the minimum. While this controversy was going on, something like $12 billions were being added to the government's expenses by the failure to act in time to halt inflation. Rising prices added that much more to the cost of defense.

Figured on a dollar and cents basis, in other words, twice as much economy could have been realized by taking effective measures to halt inflation as could have been accomplished by pruning expenditures. On the reverse side of the political picture, what new social gains could Truman promise which would offset the losses inflicted on so many people by the upward spiral of prices which followed the Korean War?

With a fifth of our national income going into defense and still larger expenditures looming, one might think it obvious that you cannot have either a "free economy" or "free lunch." Yet the struggle for both, far from slackening, has actually sharpened.

Nor is this surprising. The cold war, in a crude sort of way, has transformed the American economy into a gigantic agency for the redistribution of our national income. So huge are the costs of rearmament and so slim the idle resources which can be brought into added production, that almost every spending action of the government involves taking something from one citizen and giving it to another. In the circumstances, control of the government becomes a more glittering prize than ever. Whoever sits at the levers of power in Washington can decide which groups shall bear the heaviest costs of rearmament and which groups shall escape lightly.

Through all of 1951 our raging political conflict reflected this struggle of our major economic segments to shift the burdens of the cold war to someone else. This struggle has been no less intense because it has been waged largely behind the scenes—through tricky stratagems like rigging the tax bill to favor this or that interest; by exempting one group from controls while clamping down on others; by protecting this or that interest through technical formulas for guaranteeing higher profits, higher prices, or higher wages. The net effect, as this is written, has been to plunge the purchasing value of the dollar to a new low, to lift taxes to a record high for a period short of all-out war, and to leave virtually no one satisfied.

The failure to curb inflation after the outbreak of the Korean War was not the result of uncontrollable economic pressures. During much of the period when prices were rising most rapidly, the government actually was showing a surplus. It was primarily a political failure, to which farmers, labor, business, the President and Congress all contributed.

This inability to distribute the burdens of rearmament equitably and without gutting the economy is the real governmental crisis tearing the country today. It cannot be overcome either by weakening the government, as anti-New Dealers have been agitating, or by advancing additional schemes of social improvement as Truman has been doing. The real need is to strengthen government—not to protect either business-as-usual or social-gains-as-usual, but to discipline both to the national interest.

The New Deal issues are not dead by any means. The conflict between the advocates and opponents of the Welfare States still is highly important. But the overriding issue is the new necessity for what might be termed a "national state"—for a government strong enough to define and enforce the national interest in a world in which atomic war constantly threatens. With this issue of the "national state," neither of our rival political coalitions has come to grips.

Politically, the cold war hits us at a strange time. For a full generation the political struggle in the nation has been fought with roughly the same alignment of forces, over roughly similar issues. Fierce partisan passions have been aroused. The political thinking of millions of Americans has virtually frozen. Yet, abruptly—while the bulk of voters are still marshaled emotionally for battle in terms of the hatreds and allegiances of the Roosevelt Revolution—a wholly new crisis has arisen: a crisis for which *neither* coalition has an adequate philosophy of government. Both the New Deal and anti-New Deal coalitions, in short, are prisoners of the past. The longer the cold war endures, the heavier will grow the pressures on both coalitions to realign their thinking and followings in terms of the necessities of the struggle with Russia. Perhaps that is how the political crisis which wracks the United States today should be pictured—as a struggle of the American people to break free of the emotional attachments of the past, in order to come to grips with the harsh realities of the present.

2. Test of Survival

At best, the period of political transition which lies ahead is bound to be perilous. Our political institutions will be subjected to their most crucial testing since the pre-Civil War period. Nor is it by any means assured that our structure of government will survive the ordeal.

For one thing, the heritage of conflict left by the New Deal still is too intense, in memory and in the interests at stake, to pass off quickly or easily. Then, too, our political institutions are constructed to slow up rather than speed change.

Our system of checks and balances, for example, served the nation well in the past. But is it doing so today? No previous President-Congress conflict in our history has raged as long as the feud which began in Roosevelt's second term and has continued to the present. One reason why this conflict has defied reconciliation is the fact that the constitutional separation of powers—in curious fashion—parallels the bedrock voting cleavage in the country.

In Congress rural voters are heavily overrepresented; while the urban vote is favored in the election of the President. A heavy plurality in a large city will often swing a state's entire electoral vote. Since the pro-New Deal elements are concentrated largely in the cities, it has been relatively easy for them to hold the Presidency. In contrast, the elements seeking to restrain and reverse the New Deal—the more conservative Southerners, one-time isolationists, Midwestern Republicans— have been rooted largely in agricultural constituencies. Thus it has been relatively easy for them to hold control of Congress.

The time-honored rhythm in American government is for strong Presidents to be followed by periods of Congressional ascendancy. Since 1938, however, both Presidential and Congressional leadership have been frustrated, as each opposing coalition has entrenched itself in a different branch of the government. As long as rural-urban differences remain so marked in the nation's voting, can we get a unified government?

Or, consider our political parties. The fact that both major parties are coalitions of diverse interests operates to blur the ideological differences between them. In the past this emphasis on moderation and opportunism worked as a unifying force. Historians like to point out that our parties did abandon their compromising function *once*—and the result was Civil War.

But the Civil War was not the only time our political parties failed the nation. The killing of the League of Nations was almost as tragic a failure of the American party system. It should not be forgotten that the League actually had the approval of a majority in the Senate but was defeated by a highly partisan minority, which blocked the two-thirds approval necessary for ratification. What happened, of course, was that the foreign policy interests of the nation as a whole were sacrificed to the exigencies of domestic politics.

The fault lay largely in the very nature of our parties and our governmental structure, which are organized to subordinate foreign to domestic issues. This preoccupation with affairs at home benefited us greatly in our earlier years, when we were a struggling Republic with a continent of our own to settle and when broad oceans and the British Navy stood between us and potential enemies. But it has become a source of crucial peril, now that we are the only major power left in the world aside from the Soviet Union.

Harsh indeed is the dilemma we face. Foreign policy has become *the* issue of national survival. Yet, politically, we are organized to make the needs of foreign policy secondary to even relatively minor domestic pressures. It is a dilemma, moreover, which is likely to grow sharper in the future.

Isolationism in the old sense, as we noted earlier, has been reduced to little more than the vengeful memory of opposition to the last war. But if the United States is now committed irrevocably to a course of international co-operation, that, in itself, settles nothing. As the last five years have shown, international co-operation sets off its own chain reaction of problems. Foreign policy is no longer merely a matter of proclaiming American intentions in high-sounding doctrines. The words have to be reinforced with grubby interventions in messy lands, with unproductive defense expenditures and aid to our allies. Actions must be taken which, as in the current limited mobilization, conflict sharply with numerous domestic impulses and interests.

This conflict between the general requirements of American foreign policy and separate domestic interests is likely to be a permanent one, from now on out. Situations will arise repeatedly in which the ultimate test of our ability to make good on our commitments abroad will hinge upon our ability to discipline individual domestic pressures.

That is perhaps the basic challenge posed by the cold war— this new necessity to define consciously what the American national interest is. In the past we tended to trust to luck or to the law of averages. The traditional pattern of American behavior has been a wide swing in one direction followed by an equally wide counterswing in the opposite direction. Economically, we have gone from boom to bust and back up again. In national defense we have alternated between fits of penury and extravagance, between mobilizing all out at one moment and demobilizing with equal speed at another.

To counter the threat of Soviet power, however, clearly requires a *continuity* and *steadiness* of American policy beyond anything we have demonstrated in the past. Our present peril, in fact, can be traced largely to the reckless haste with which we tore down our military power at the end of the last war, before peace was made sure. Even when the current defense program has been surmounted, we still will not dare demobilize to anything like normal peacetime levels.

Similarly, in virtually every phase of national life, the American pendulum will have to be adjusted to a shortened beat. Not that the old rhythm was all bad. It contributed to lifting American living standards to the highest level in world history, and to giving the American people more freedom than any nation has ever known. But the wide cyclical swings of the past required *time* for the good and bad to average out, and time is the one thing we have less of than ever before.

Bernard M. Baruch expressed it succinctly in an article in the *Saturday Evening Post* three years ago in which he wrote:

Time! The mainspring of American behaviour has been our having more of it than other nations. Our isolation, individualism, form of government, attitude towards war, all ticked in rhythm. War was apart from peace; America apart from the world; each American apart from his government, which held only the authority jealously yielded to it by the people.

The collapse of European power, the atomic bomb and other ocean-shrinking weapons, along with the necessity to prevent war, have eliminated the buffer of time which cushioned this detachment. We now must develop a new sense of inter-relationship between war and peace, between home and abroad, between each of us and "those bureaucrats in Washington."

This new "inter-relationship" will necessarily curb some of the free play that American citizens have long enjoyed. Above all, it means that we must think through what is our national interest and elevate it above the many, separate domestic interests.

What if we fail?

The answer is that we *are* failing—which is one fundamental reason why we are locked in political stalemate. The alternative to agreement on what is the national interest is to let the conflicting forces in the nation battle themselves out, in the hope that the workings of time will reconcile them.

But what if time is not working in our favor? There is also a crucial difference between "buying time," in the conscious belief that this is the wisest policy, and letting time take its own course because irresolution and disunity leave us no other choice. It is one thing to embark on a policy of buying time as a thought-through program, knowing what we want to do in the time that is being bought at such onerous cost. It is a far different matter to drift toward possible disaster, because we cannot agree among ourselves on how to unlock the enormous power that is America's.

Our inability to achieve decision, as has been stressed

earlier, cannot be laid to Truman's personal limitations. The American public likes to blame and credit Presidents for everything bad or good that happens during their terms of office. For our own self-interest, we should recognize that Truman is less cause than effect. He has been not a motor but a transmission belt. No shaper of history, he has been a remarkably sensitive instrument through which the tensions and conflicts of our times have registered.

Truman's indecisiveness reflects primarily the almost insuperable difficulties in reconciling the forces in deadlock. He has been a minority President, both literally and figuratively. Spectacular as was his 1948 victory, he still fell short of a majority of the total popular vote in the country. In Congress he has been able to command approval only for those proposals which do not alienate either of the warring Democratic wings.

It might have been thought that feelings of patriotism stirred by the danger of war would have restored unity to the Roosevelt coalition. Actually, its disunity has been intensified. That is understandable if one appreciates that fundamentally what divides the Democratic elements is their common struggle to preserve their gains of the last twenty years. This struggle naturally sharpens as mounting costs of defense and foreign aid leave less to divide at home and make demands for more, on the part of any one Democratic element, a threat to the gains of the other elements in the coalition.

To sum up, the political problem confronting the United States is twofold. First, we no longer have an effective majority in the nation. Second, the resulting governmental deadlock is being intensified by the fact that our political parties and institutions are geared to subordinate, if not sacrifice, the needs of foreign policy to domestic politics. Instead of unifying the nation politically to meet the perils of the cold war, our party system seems to be twisting the tensions of our

conflict with Russia in such a way as to widen the prevailing
divisions in the country.

If the shackles of political stalemate are to be broken, it
follows that a double realignment is necessary. Not only
must the varied voting elements in the country be reshuffled,
so that one major party emerges with a workable majority.
Simultaneously, both parties must be reorganized to become
truly national in the interests they represent. While sectional
and minority interests can never be eliminated from American politics, our major parties must become more national
in their scope and sensitivity than ever before.

3. The Politics of Twilight

But can we have truly national parties in these United
States? The Republicans have always been a sectional alignment, with virtually no representation in the South. The
Democrats, although spread physically through all parts of
the country, have really been two different parties under the
same emblem. How different became clear when the New
Deal thrust the Southern and the big-city Democrats onto the
same national stage.

Considering the failure of so many past efforts to form
national parties, it may appear foolhardy to predict such a
development now. Yet, it is my own feeling that the New
Deal has prepared the way for just such a nation-wide political realignment.

Wherever we have probed into the forces unloosed by the
Roosevelt Revolution we have found evidence of powerful
new pressures tending to nationalize American politics. For
example, in every city—regardless of the part of the country
in which it is located—the voting for President follows the
same general economic lines. If this has divided the poor from
the well-to-do, it has also made us more nearly one nation
politically than ever before.

One of the stronger pressures propelling the South toward

two-party politics, as we have seen, is this tendency for people of similar economic status all over the country to vote alike. In the Northern and Western cities, the consciousness of economic class has suppressed much of the racial, religious and ethnic tension, which was so strong a feature of American life as late as the 1920's.

In European countries, national parties generally have a class basis. That does not mean that national parties in this country must also be class parties in the European sense. A wholly different type of national party, distinctively American, is more likely. The class feelings stirred by the Roosevelt Revolution have been serving as a crucible in which older sectional and cultural antagonisms are being melted down; but, at the same time, the coalition nature of American politics continues to compel divergent elements to search for means of harmonizing their interests.

In an earlier chapter I made the point that the whole United States today seems caught up in a nation-wide adventure in social unification. Moreover, the militancy of the emerging urban masses has been directed, not at remaining apart from American society, but at quicker assimilation. This is enormously important. In Europe any number of ethnic elements have persisted in maintaining their separate "national" identities over several centuries. One major reason why the United States has done so much better than Europe with its minority problem is that the drive of our minorities has always been toward assimilation.

And as the urban masses have climbed, they have carried on their backs their own packs of conservatism. Twenty years ago the American disciples of Karl Marx were predicting the end of the American middle class. But the so-called "revolt of the masses" in this country has actually strengthened our middle class institutions. In large part the "March of the Masses" has really been a march of the heavy pre-World War

One birth rates. With the leveling off of these birth rates, the pace of the march has slowed.

At present the American middle class is divided politically. The prime cause of this division is the fact that the newer middle class elements are the products of a different historical era and that their climb out of poverty has left them with an "underdog" heritage. We shall have to wait on the future to see whether my faith is justified; but still it is my own belief that this new middle class is likely to prove the means through which a dramatic reintegration of American life will be accomplished. Through this new middle class two eras in American history—two cultural halves—are meeting and clashing, eventually to be reconciled.

The coincidence of the emergence of the former immigrant elements with the arrival of the Negro in the Northern cities could also prove one of the happier social accidents in American history. There has grown up in the Northern cities a new generation which, because it suffered the abuses of discrimination, is at least sensitive to the problems of racial and religious tolerance. One result is that the American people were probably never more *consciously* tolerant than they are today.

Of course, racial, religious and ethnic prejudices still burn fiercely in every part of the United States. Whether they can ever be eliminated entirely is doubtful. The important thing is that there never were more people at work forging a discipline of tolerance to restrain those prejudices. I dare say that there are few Americans who, in recent years, have not been on the verge of exploding, "Why that ————," only to check themselves and think, "All ———— are not like that."

The emergence of the civil rights agitation provides yet another example of how strangely the rhythms of American social conflict harmonize with the rhythms of world conflict. Nationalistic feelings are stirring the brown, yellow and black peoples everywhere in the world. Race has become a major weapon in our world-flung competition with the Soviet Union. Forty years ago we could not have shown much accomplishment in dealing with our racial problems. But the same two World Wars, which did so much to awaken the masses abroad, also awakened our own masses. Those wars brought the Negroes out of the South and the immigrants out of their slums into a position where they have been able at least to make an earnest beginning toward solving our racial problems.

Not only socially, but also in economic and governmental relations the Roosevelt Revolution has released powerful nationalizing forces. If our government has become an object of distrust to some Americans, who fear its use as an instrument of social change, then by the same token the government and people have been brought into more intimate contact with one another than at any previous time. True, our whole economy has become dependent upon government to an unhappy degree. One consolation is that this dependence could provide a base of political support for measures to maintain the economy at a sustained level of high employment. A repetition of the depression of the 1930's would not only be a domestic disaster. Strategically, it could wipe out whatever good has come from the Marshall Plan, and perhaps even nullify the North Atlantic Defense Pact.

Indeed, our present danger may lie in *too much* government intervention. Our politicians may be so frightened of recession that they will not have either the wisdom or courage to know when to leave things alone. There never was less need for government inflation, for example, than in the period immediately after the end of the last war. A huge backlog of wartime earnings was left to be spent. A tremendous unfilled demand clamored for anything that could be produced. Despite that, the administration and Congress joined in a series of measures which pumped out still more money into the economy.

In the years before the New Deal the solution usually proposed for any problem was "get the government to do it." With each passing year, though, it becomes clearer that the mere act of government intervention is no solution. Inefficient doctoring can be worse than letting nature take its course. All that government intervention really does is to set up the same problems in another arena—and on a larger scale.

It leaves the same old evils of corruption, inefficiency and greed to be wrestled with. The logrolling which made the writing of tariff schedules so scandalous in the old Republican era is being repeated currently in tricky statistical formulas for increasing the level of price supports or other government subsidies. Economic security has been the stated objective of government intervention. Yet inflationary spending creates ever fresh insecurities, by robbing savings of their value and making the whole economy uncertainly dependent on continued government tinkering. Are we any closer today to having a dollar of stable value than in the 1920's or 1930's?

Nor has the triumph of Big Government over the old *laissez-faire* philosophy altered the need to forge those restraining disciplines which Woodrow Wilson once described as the essence of all government. If anything the need for these restraining disciplines is more acute today than ever. Behind the "let things alone" philosophy was the belief that if each man were left to pursue his own advantage, the good and bad would average out into a natural balance which would benefit society as a whole. Having turned our backs upon the idea of an automatic balance of competitive forces, we now must find that balance through political means.

The expansion of government to its present scale has politicalized virtually all economic life. The wages being paid most workers today are political wages, reflecting political pressures rather than anything that might be considered the normal workings of supply and demand. The prices farmers receive are political prices. The profits business is earning are political profits. The savings people hold have become political savings, since their real value is subject to abrupt depreciation by political decisions.

In sum, both the good and bad features of the Roosevelt Revolution have operated to nationalize politics, and the cold war is intensifying this tendency.

How quickly a nation-wide political realignment will come is likely to hinge upon what happens in the South. Some kind of Southern bolt seems certain in 1952. Whether it will lead to the end of the one-party South will depend on the outcome of the election—on whether it is close enough to be thrown into the House of Representatives, or whether the Democrats can win without the vote of the South or on what the Republicans do with their victory if they win; also upon who gains control of the Democratic party after it is defeated.

Inevitably, there has been talk of a possible Republican-Southern "understanding" similar to that which gave Rutherford Hayes the Presidency in 1876 in exchange for leaving the South alone to handle the Negro in its own way. No sectional truce like that of 1876 can last long today, if only because the northerly and westerly migration of the Negro has made him a national rather than a sectional problem. Also it is difficult to see how any separatist political movement can persist against the nationalizing trends of the times.

Still, the mills of political realignment in the United States have always ground slowly. Most of the changes described in this book—and no American voter has escaped their influences—have taken place since 1938, when the Roosevelt and anti-Roosevelt coalitions first became formally deadlocked. Yet, far from having lifted, the political deadlock may be even more deeply rooted today than when it began. Barring a possible sweep by some dramatic personality who is above both parties, like General Eisenhower, it seems doubtful whether either the Democrats or Republicans can obtain a more decisive victory than Winston Churchill won in Britain last year.

Eventually the sands of stalemate must run out and an effective majority will be re-created in the country. For perhaps the next decade, however, American politics may remain the politics of twilight, with the Democratic sun on the wane, but with no new majority sun able to rise into clear ascendancy. Millions of voters are likely to continue to be tugged simultaneously in conflicting directions—by divided emotions and shifting fears, by their memories of the past and necessities of the present, by the crumbling of traditional party loyalties accompanied by a mistrust of both parties. To make this transition period all the more agonizing, it seems likely to be a period of continued attrition with Russia abroad.

Wise and courageous leadership can perhaps find the domestic balance which will release our government from deadlock and restore our capacity for decision. If not, the question that will be asked of us insistently in the years to come will be: For how much longer can we continue to pay the price of irresolution? Rich and powerful as this great nation is, there are limits even to America's capacity to evade decision.

Election Returns: 1916-1948

States carried by:

■ Democrats   □ Republicans

La Follette Progressives   Dixiecrats

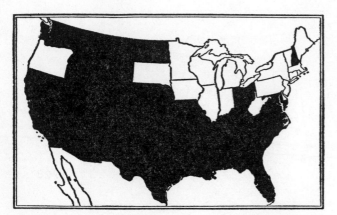

1916

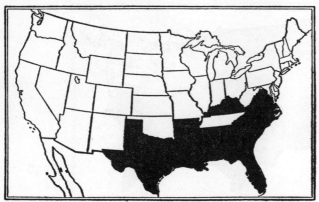

1920

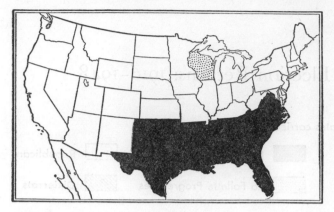

1924

1928

1932

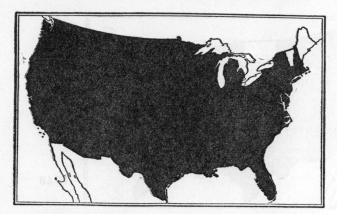

1936

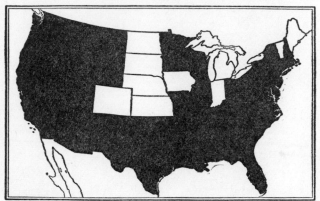

1940

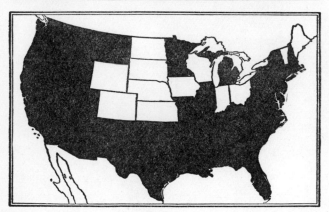

1944

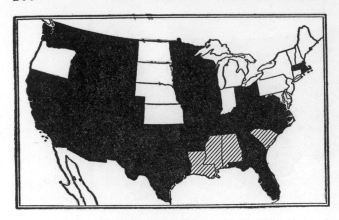

1948

Acknowledgments

Since this book has been in the thinking for more than ten years, it would be impossible to list all the persons who have contributed to the final product. I am indebted particularly to the John Simon Guggenheim Foundation for the fellowship which made it possible to complete this work; also to the editors of the *Saturday Evening Post*—Wesley Winans Stout, now no longer with the *Post*, and Martin Sommers and Ben Hibbs—who first started me off on my postelection surveys and who have encouraged me to continue them since.

Yeoman aid in editing the manuscript was furnished by John Fischer of Harper & Brothers and by Walter B. Everett of the American Press Institute of Columbia University.

Numerous other persons read and criticized parts of the text. Earlier drafts of the chapter on the South were gone over by Hodding Carter and Virginius Dabney, both of whom are among the best balanced writers specializing in the ever-changing yet elusively the same South; also by George S. Mitchell of the Southern Regional Council, which is doing such excellent work improving race relations below the Mason-Dixon line, and by Solomon Barkin, research director for the (CIO) United Textile Workers of America.

Barkin was also most helpful with comments on the chapter dealing with organized labor, which was also read by John Herling, who edits *John Herling's Labor News-Letter*, and by Morris Weisz of the Department of Labor. The farm chapter was read in draft by Donald R. Murphy, the able editor of *Wallace's Farmer and Iowa Homestead*; by M. L. Wilson, who fathered the Domestic Allotment Plan out of which Roosevelt's agricultural program evolved; and by these specialists in the Department of Agriculture: Carl C. Taylor, Margaret Hagood and Douglas Ensminger, all wise in the ways of rural life; and by Franklin Thackrey of the Bureau of Agricultural Economics. Arthur F. Raper, also with the Department, made some suggestions which proved valuable on my trip through the South.

An earlier chapter on the progress made by Negroes over the last fourteen years was read by Julius A. Thomas, Director of Industrial Relations for the National Urban League. Jack Alexander of the *Saturday Evening Post* and William Harrison of the Washington *Star* also went over parts of the book.

Needless to say none of these persons are responsible for the text as it finally appears, although all contributed to whatever merit it may have.

Some research work was done for me by an invaluable aide of the wartime Washington years, Mrs. Mary Mickey Simon, until she moved to suburban distances; and by Mrs. Hannah Fried Desser.

The county election returns used in my study are drawn primarily from the two volumes entitled, *The Presidential Vote* and *They Voted for Roosevelt*, compiled by Edgar Eugene Robinson of Stanford University. Between them these two books contain the Presidential vote for every county in the United States from 1896 through 1944. For my own study I plotted these results onto maps, county by county, in every state, enabling one to determine fairly quickly which groups of counties tended to move together in their voting.

The ward and precinct returns for various cities were gathered mainly on personal visits to these cities or by mail from local election clerks or election commissioners and the secretaries of state. Since the returns of several score cities were collected, the names of all of the election officials who were so co-operative cannot be listed here. A few, of whom I made repeated requests which were graciously filled, were Harry Chapman, Deputy Registrar of Voters for Los Angeles County, Harry T. O'Connell in St. Paul; Tom Terrell in Cleveland; Louis A. Urban in Detroit; Walter Gaedke in Milwaukee; David Wilson in New Haven and I. A. Fink in Duluth.

Many of the communities whose votes were collected and analyzed are not mentioned in the book, but that does not mean that the returns were not used. On the contrary, only by checking and cross-checking my findings in numerous areas was I able to write with certainty of the places mentioned.

The table on page 34 showing the declining Republican strength in the twelve largest cities during the 1920's was taken from Samuel J. Eldersveld's revealing article in the *American Political Science Review* of December, 1949, on "Influence of Metropolitan Party Pluralities on Presidential Elections." The number of young persons coming of voting age between 1936 and 1944 is an unpublished figure made available to me by the U.S. Bureau of the Census; the estimate of new voters during the 1920-28 period is less exact, being a projection of the age break-down shown in the 1920 census. Census Bureau officials were helpful in other ways, too numerous to be itemized. Dr. Joseph R. Houchens supplied me with valuable census data on the changing status of the Negro; Dr. Henry S. Shryock Jr. and Dr. Paul Glick on population and family changes, and Frank Wilson on many general problems.

I have used Paul F. Cressey's tabulations to show the physical spread of Italo-Americans through Chicago during the 1920-30 decade. The estimate that fair employment practices laws now cover about one fourth of the population was made by Morroe Berger in the May, 1951, *Annals* of the American Academy of Political and Social Science.

The Republican National Committee, through Floyd Mc-Caffree and C. J. North of its Research Division, was extremely helpful in making available copies of their own excellent statistical analyses of recent elections. No similar studies have been done by the Democratic National Committee, which did put at my disposal what it had, as did the CIO's Political Action Committee. Calvin F. Schmid of the University of Washington, in Seattle, was most generous in giving me photostats of tables he had prepared showing the percentage of the vote in Minnesota, by counties, for the most significant elections from that of William Jennings Bryan on. These tables greatly facilitated my work in analyzing the voting streams which formed the basis of the Farmer-Laborite party.

Every study of voting behavior that I could find was gone over in the course of my own project. While all these studies cannot be listed here the writings of the following were particularly stimulating: Louis Bean, Harold F. Gosnell, Edward Litchfield and Donald S. Hecock on Detroit; James K. Pollock on Michigan; H. F. Alderfer on Pennsylvania; C. H. Titus on California; V. O. Key on Southern Politics; William F. Ogburn; Cortez A. M. Ewing; Stuart Rice; Arthur N. Holcombe and E. E. Schatt-schneider.

The N.Y. Public Library was most helpful in arranging for the loan of various university theses; the staff of the Schomburg Collection were always co-operative in digging up the answers to questions dealing with the Negro.

My debt is particularly heavy to the many newspapermen who make politics their beat in the cities and states I visited. Invariably I made these reporters my port of call and, almost without exception, they were generous with their time and information. To mention a few: Morty Freedman of the St. Petersburg (Florida) *Times*; David Cameron of the Providence *Journal-Bulletin*; Charles B. Cleveland of the Chicago *Daily News*; Jack Meddoff of the Buffalo *News*; Alvin Silverman of the Cleveland *Plain Dealer*; Cliff Millen of the Des Moines *Register-Tribune*; Richard Neuberger of Portland, Oregon; Mike Halloran of the Minneapolis *Star-Journal*; Otis Sullivant of the *Daily Oklahoman* in Oklahoma City; Morris Rubin of the *Progressive* in Wisconsin; Brady Black, who heads the Columbus bureau of the Cincinnati *Enquirer*; Ralph McGill of the Atlanta *Constitution*; Calvin Kytle; Dawson Duncan of the Dallas *News*; and Clingan Jackson of the Youngstown (Ohio) *Vindicator*, who performed the additional service of vouching for me with over-suspicious local police. So tense were the feelings stirred by the Taft race in 1950 that when I started ringing doorbells in a workers' district in Youngstown, a policeman stopped me, thinking I might be a "spy for the CIO." It was the only time in all my postelection surveys that anything like that happened.

Finally, it has become the custom among writers to conclude their acknowledgments by tossing a kind word to their wives. The usual tribute runs "who was a source of encouragement at all times." In the case of my own wife, Helen Sopot Lubell, the truthful tribute would be, "Whom I bedeviled at all times." I impressed my wife to type parts of the book, to calculate innumerable percentages, to draw maps, to do library research and, often, at the end of a two-child day, to serve as an audience for my thinking aloud. That our household has survived it all is the measure of what I really owe her.

Index